NEW DIMENSIONS IN MUSIC

SOUND, BEAT, AND FEELING

TEACHER'S GUIDE

ROBERT A. CHOATE
BARBARA KAPLAN
JAMES STANDIFER

NEW DIMENSIONS IN MUSIC

SOUND, BEAT, AND FEELING

TEACHER'S GUIDE

AMERICAN BOOK COMPANY

ROBERT A. CHOATE, Formerly Dean, School of Fine and Applied Arts
Boston University, Boston, Massachusetts

BARBARA KAPLAN
Auburn University, Auburn, Alabama

JAMES STANDIFER, Chairperson, Department of Music Education
The University of Michigan, Ann Arbor, Michigan

AMERICAN BOOK COMPANY

New York Cincinnati Atlanta Dallas San Francisco

ISBN: 0–278–44845–3

1 3 5 7 9 11 13 15 16 14 12 10 8 6 4 2

Contents

NEW
DIMENSIONS
IN
MUSIC

SOUND, BEAT, AND FEELING

TEACHER'S GUIDE

Introduction

The general objective of New Dimensions in Music *is the aesthetic education of children in and through music.*

Within the context of general education, the particular concern of aesthetic education is the cultivation of attitudes, learnings, and skills in the arts through instruction of wide scope and quality.

As throughout history, the arts today are used by people as personal dynamic forms of symbolic expression and communication. They offer pleasure and refreshment, as well as color, and infuse with meaning our celebrations, worship, daily routines, and festive occasions.

In these times of rapid social and cultural change, compelling convictions are rising that the enhancement of the quality of life is vital to our national well-being, that the place of the arts is in the center of society, not at the periphery, and that the schools must bear a heavy responsibility in developing the full richness of our nation's cultural life.

Many community leaders, citizens, and educators are turning to the arts with informed awareness of their uniqueness in affording a balanced education for children and of their necessity in building the good community.

As never before in education, recognition has come that, when taught in meaningful ways, the arts can contribute significantly towards building personal identity; expanding the ability to imagine and create, and developing understanding and perception of the worlds of color, sound, thought, emotions, and social relationships.

In music, aesthetic education will develop the innate musical capacities and potentials of students through many kinds of interrelated experiences.

Principles evolving from this objective which are inherent in the instructional design of this text and which have implications for the school administrator and the teacher of music are:

The aesthetic component in music should receive prime emphasis in all music experiences.

As music is an aural art, students will learn to listen perceptively to hear sounds and their organization.

Students will experience music of many periods, styles, and cultures, learning to value exemplars. Sound performance skills in music will be developed.

The development of creativity in thought and in many kinds of expressions in music will underlie all learnings and experiences in music.

Study of the humanities will give students insights and understanding of life styles, thoughts, and aspirations of people of various ages and times which are revealed in their arts.

Works of art will be enjoyed as direct experiences. However, exploration and understanding of the constituent elements of various arts can develop students' visual and aural perceptions in the arts and in their environment.

Music instruction will develop the ability to "learn how to learn" through discovery and problem solving processes. Behavioral objectives in music and defined concepts about music will give focus and direction for the teacher. Evaluation of learnings will be made by students and teachers.

As many influences in the students' total environment greatly affect their music learnings, aesthetic education should involve the total program of the school, the home, and the resources of the community.

In the student text, music literature and experiences have been designed to attain the objectives of aesthetic education. In this guide, suggestions are given for directing and guiding students' education in music toward achievement of these goals. Full realization has been given to both the demands and the challenges confronting the music teacher in today's schools.

The music experiences presented in this text will necessitate adequate time for instruction, quality equipment, and preparation for teaching. It is believed the results can be rewarding for students and teachers.

Music in education should be more than mere amusement or a purely recreational activity. As one of the humanities, music is a fundamental aesthetic language which every child has a right to learn and enjoy. When taught in ways that have meaning, music offers many personal values and enriching new dimensions in the lives of young people in our schools.

ORGANIZATION AND USES OF *SOUND, BEAT, AND FEELING*

The worlds of music are vast, complex, exciting, and challenging. *Sound, Beat, and Feeling* involves junior high school students in the music of their time and provides interesting resources and strategies for developing knowledge of music of other times and other cultures. Opportunities are ample for furthering experiences in other arts.

The opening unit, "Sound, Beat, and Feeling," provides exploratory experiences in various kinds of music, poetry, and painting. These activities reveal the wide range of expression possible through unique uses of characteristic materials of each medium.

Unit 2, "Music and You," involves students in the creative and expressive roles of musicians—the composer, the performer, the listener. Intensive exploration of the musical elements of rhythm, color, line, texture, and design is made in Units 3 and 4.

"Minicourses" for basic instruction in guitar and piano are given in Unit 5, "Playing Instruments." Selected music and art from the many "Ethnic Worlds" afford points of departure for humanistic studies. (Unit 6)

Unit 7, "Temporal Worlds," presents an exciting panorama of significant developments in music and other arts from the Middle Ages to the present, supplemented with enrichment materials in the *Teacher's Guide.*

Unit 8 includes a wide variety of materials for the Chorus.

USE OF STUDENT TEXT. Many factors affect the decisions and choices which the teacher must make in selecting music literature and specific experiences for the class. After examining the text thoroughly, the teacher must ask, "What can students learn in music with the greatest satisfaction and benefit to them in the time allotted and with the resources available to me?"

Music experiences provided in this text include singing, listening, playing instruments, and many types of creative activities. Suggestions are made for extensions in the humanities and related arts.

The organized units in *Sound, Beat, and Feeling* are based on these premises: (1) adequate time and instructional resources are available to the teacher; (2) the serious, but enjoyable, study of music can contribute in many ways to students' intellectual and emotional development; and (3) although music, when heard or performed, comprises many constituent elements, the concentrated study of each element leads to deeper, more functional knowledges and personal satisfactions.

It is desirable then, that the concepts presented in those units be studied consecutively, although spaced over several class periods. Variety in the music class will be afforded by using songs already learned, reviewing listening lessons, or by including activities and songs from other units in the text.

The wealth of literature and sources in the text will serve the purposes of the teacher who wishes to use the text more flexibly to meet curricular demands of correlation with other subjects, newer scheduling practices, or innovative instructional methods.

THE TEACHING-LEARNING PROCESS. In this text, the underlying approach to learning is that of stimulating personal intellectual involvement and critical thinking on the part of students. This procedure involves *questioning* by the teacher rather than *telling.* Through consequent answers and discussion by students with the teacher as guide, insights, concepts, and deepened understandings are developed. Intrinsic involvement and interest in the activity or performance in progress, self-motivation, and refined aesthetic sensitivities usually result from utilization of these strategies of *discovery* or *problem solving.*

The student book contains many questions which can serve initially to stimulate thought and inquiry. The *question-answer-discussion* process should be concise and pertinent. It should relate to and enhance performance of the music, further aural perception, or clarify problems in creative activity. Verbalization should be as minimal as is feasible in the music period. Aesthetic experiences in music are attained through listening, creating, and performing music.

RECORDINGS. Recordings for *New Dimensions in Music* have been designed as an integral part of the instructional program. The sounds of young voices, instruments, vocal and instrumental ensembles, a variety of accompaniments, authentic recordings of music of other cultures, and electronic and experimental music are very important in developing dimensions in music for teenage students.

All songs in the book and all listening lessons are recorded. Songs which include foreign language texts are sung in that language. Ethnic music is recorded with native instruments. For teaching convenience, all songs are separated by locked grooves. Records for the listening program, however, have two types of bands: (1) locked grooves to separate individual compositions or specific examples for listening, and (2) standard five-second bands which separate movements of an orchestral work or arias of an opera. The recordings are available from American Book Company.

USE OF THE TEACHER'S GUIDE

To assist the teacher in planning for maximum learnings, the following materials are included in this guide:

1. *Annotations on each page of the student text.* These are categorized under "Learnings and Skills" —possible behavioral learnings, concepts or skills which may be outcomes of use of the page content; "Student Involvement" which are suggestions for procedures, motivation or interest; and "Related Activities."

2. *Behavioral Objectives for Music Learnings* for each major unit in the student text.

3. The *Table of the Elements of Music* on pages 264 and 265. These concepts about music summarize the basic musical content of Units 3 and 4. The concepts also serve as bases for comparative studies of music of other cultures.

4. The *Comparative Style Chart* on pages 194–195. A valuable source for the study of historical periods in music is Unit 7, "Temporal Worlds" which gives perspective to this study.

5. *Suggested Procedures* for music experiences presented in this text include: Singing, Listening, Music Reading, Humanities and Related Arts, Creative Activities, and Experimental Projects in Composition.

6. *Suggested Enrichment.* As aesthetic education must be concerned with the total environment of students, brief indications are given about the total school program, relations with the home, and utilization of community resources.

SUGGESTED PROCEDURES

During adolescent years, growth of students is rapid and constantly changing. Approaches to students of different ages will naturally vary. The teacher will select activities and experiences appropriate for students' physical development, their behavioral characteristics, interests, and unique needs. When possible, attention should be given to the individualization of instruction. The following are suggestions which may be of value:

Maintain the highest expectations for students. Most children can perform well in music. Find their strengths and reinforce them constantly.

Have simple, clear routines, yet provide an open, warm classroom atmosphere.

Let students assume responsibilities whenever possible as assistants, class officers, conductors, accompanists, monitors, section leaders, chairpersons of research or composition projects, equipment and bulletin board managers.

Let the class help establish rules and procedures. Maintain a balance between *teacher-structured* and *student-structured* situations.

In a music class, plan for variety of music—varying moods, rhythms, different tempos, and types of compositions. Include varied activities within a period—listening, singing, playing instruments, and creative projects. Plan for interest.

Praise individuals and the group whenever possible and deserved.

Provide opportunities for students to explore a variety of sensory experiences and express themselves in some creative manner.

SINGING. In most schools, singing is the important experience in the general music class. Since the voice is the most personal expressive instrument for making music, every effort should be made to develop it. Attitudes in the home or of peer groups may not be conducive to singing. Yet most students can be motivated to participate enthusiastically if songs of interest are used, if they learn to use their voices properly, and if they feel a sense of satisfaction from the musical performances of the class.

Some suggestions are:

At the beginning of the term develop successful singing experiences as quickly as possible. Teach music by rote, by the use of recordings which accompany the text, or by playing parts on the piano. Use songs which have appeal for the students and which let them feel the delight that singing affords. When a positive emotional tone is set and an adequate repertoire of music is learned, the way is open to many kinds of active learnings in music which are far superior to the dull, passive non-interest of many classes.

Let students make settings of poems or write words and music for songs of their own, using various types of accompaniments.

When feasible, ask students to teach songs of ethnic origin or ones learned in community groups which are suitable for classroom use. Artists, folk singers, or other musicians may visit and add to students' repertoire.

Performances for other classes, assemblies, and parent or community programs can develop enthusiasm and stimulate the class. Unit 8 contains songs suitable for such programs. Other songs in the text are also suitable for public performance. Performance gives the incentive to perfect choral techniques.

LISTENING PROGRAM. Development of the abilities to hear and produce sounds accurately are prime objectives in music instruction. Perception of the qualities and quantities of sound, its movement, and its organization into patterns, structures, and form underlie all music activities. The teacher must nurture the capacities of students to focus or concentrate on sounds which are heard–to discriminate, to develop tonal memory, and to produce sounds accurately. Patience and resourcefulness will be required of the teachers; literature and teaching processes must be adapted to students' backgrounds, interests, and previous achievements.

Call Charts. Throughout the text there will be recorded music for listening with which *Call Charts* will be used to direct attention toward specific music events. The teacher calls out the *call number*. Students are to concentrate on what is happening in the music at that point. Some of the "happenings" in the music are listed to the right of the call number. With repeated listenings, students will become increasingly familiar with the given musical characteristics and begin to discover more subtle ones. The teacher is to use the call chart material as a means of "priming the mental pump" of students' minds from which other and new discoveries will flow.

After students have been introduced to the call chart technique, the teacher should step aside and permit the students to present the charts–making additional versions (in class and on their own), including other events discovered. Call charts should be constructed when composition themes do not already have them.

Recorded compositions of many periods and styles are included in this text. Most listening lessons are integrated with units of study and are planned to extend and reinforce concepts. Compositions using sound sources and uses of the elements in untraditional ways have been included. Contemporary music, electronic and experimental works, and ethnic music will extend students' concepts of rhythm, melody, timbre, texture, and form. Repeated hearings and direction in listening will assist in evoking deepened responses.

The following are guidelines for developing the listening experience:

In some instances, suggestions for focus in listening or background information may be given about a composition, but it would be desirable from a discovery point of view for the teacher to play the composition without comment. After the students listen, they should be allowed to respond freely as to *what* they heard. Such responses should be from *musical* viewpoints, not the story the music brought to mind. Initially, the teacher may ask questions such as: "What kind of music was this? a march? humorous? quite serious? Were there melodies? What instruments were predominant? Did you recognize the rhythm set? What mood did you sense or feel?"

The teacher should not comment on responses, continuing to encourage student reactions.

A second hearing will dispel or confirm their first reactions. Pertinent information may then be presented. On another day, the teacher should help the class analyze the work more thoroughly, drawing out principal themes, the form, characteristic rhythm patterns, or use of instruments.

The importance of such a procedure to the students lies in their repeated exposure to the music and their consequent attention to and focus on the sounds heard.

After several listening lessons, assist students in formulating criteria for listening. Such criteria might be: (a) the rhythm set (and changes) in a composition; (b) obvious themes and their repetition; (c) possible construction of form; (d) characteristic rhythm patterns; (e) mood or feeling expressed; (f) other qualities or use of predominant elements such as color, tempos, contrasts, and dynamics. With experience, they will learn to listen attentively and be able to discuss works heard in a progressively sophisticated manner.

When a major composition is studied, the principal themes should be placed on the chalkboard. Students may learn to sing and play them.

The time span for listening should be carefully controlled. If a work is quite lengthy, the entire composition should be played, and then sections of it should be studied over several periods. To enable students to become thoroughly familiar with the composition, it should be played several times.

Instruments In The Classroom. Instruments allow further experimentation and acquaintance with many kinds of sounds. They may be used for extending experiences in singing and listening and developing concepts related to the constituent elements. Creating simple accompaniments, ostinatos, and counter melodies; improvising and making sound effects for dramatization are highly motivational activities. Percussion instruments are invaluable for composition projects in sound shapes, sound stories, sound pictures and for film accompaniments in multimedia ventures. Resonator bells and recorders are suggested in the text for use in many ways.

Instruments desirable for the classroom are: piano, melody instruments–resonator or song bells, recorders or song flutes–and a variety of percussion instruments–tone blocks, drums of various sizes, bongos, rattlers and shakers, castenets, tambourines, finger cymbals, cymbals, claves, gongs, maracas, guiros, and coconut shells. Students who play band and orchestral instruments should be asked to demonstrate instruments and play as often as possible.

Experiments and projects in composition with percussion and other instruments will be found in the section on *Composition* in this introduction.

If a piano is available, it should be used by students for basic keyboard experiences, such as learning to play simple chords, accompanying songs, improvising on the black keys, and for exploring new sounds as suggested in Unit 5. Students who are studying piano should be encouraged to play for the class; they may also assist in teaching others in basic keyboard experiences.

Melody instruments such as the recorder, song flutes, and resonator bells may be used to play various harmony parts as students sing. After proficiency is attained, groups of these instruments may be used to perform rounds, songs with descants, or music in several parts as instrumental compositions.

Transposition For Orchestral Instruments. In the event that students play certain instruments with the class, transposition of parts must be made. The trumpet and clarinet sound one whole step lower than the notation on the staff. Therefore, music for these instruments must be written a step higher if performing with the piano, recorder, bells, or non-transposing orchestral instruments, such as the violin or flute.

Music Reading. Music reading is a desirable skill which should be neither neglected nor overemphasized. Objectively viewed, the notation of music is simply a written symbolic system for pitches, their duration, and other symbols which indicate the expressive intent of the composer.

When so considered, the desirability becomes evident for the *functional* use of this communications system as a means for interpreting the composer's musical intent and for students' skill and satisfaction in learning many kinds of music. As a retrieval system, the imperative to read music "at first sight" becomes of less concern as music for the vocal students may be decoded in numerous ways—through assistance by teachers or other musicians, by rote, or through use of recordings.

Learning to interpret notation is an intellectual process which involves abstract thinking and the ability to deal with rather complex symbols. Therefore, goals in music reading should be considered in relation to the backgrounds, abilities, and interest spans of the children. The reading program should be integrated with other music experiences.

Suggested procedures for music reading might be:

Analyze the meter and rhythmic structure of the composition, and proceed to clap, tap, or chant the melodic rhythm of the music. Discover like and unlike patterns or phrases, and isolate difficult or problem patterns for practice.

Analyze the melodic structure, with attention to contour, type of tonal progression, and phrases. Establish the tonality and meter and try to sing the song with words. If a crutch is needed, use syllables or numbers on those sections that the students could not sing. Playing those difficult sections on bells or piano as the students sing letter names is an alternate approach. The recordings may be used as a means of checking the ear. If the background of the class is weak, use the recordings first. Choose simple sections of the song for reading and teach the remainder by ear.

Part singing may be approached easily through descants, rounds, and canons and through brief passages moving in parallel thirds. Wide skips in vocal lines and many contemporary compositions may of necessity be taught by ear.

Singing by note should not preclude rote singing. Many songs may be taught by a combination of approaches. Music reading objectives should not take precedence over the prime objective of aesthetic response nor limit the breadth of music experiences of students.

THE HUMANITIES AND RELATED ARTS IN THE JUNIOR HIGH SCHOOL

THE HUMANITIES. The humanities are those studies of people as human beings—the expressions of their thoughts, feelings, needs, dreams, and their aspirations.

In evolving curriculums of many schools, the humanities are receiving increased emphasis because of their focus on individuals and their needs today. Such studies will enable students to develop a sense of direction, personal identity, and a pattern of values. They will afford insights about themselves, their relation to other human beings, and the universe. In contrast to traditional historical and data-oriented studies, the new humanities will include a broad range of issues and problems derived from anthropology and sociology, from the physical and natural sciences, languages and literature, the fine arts, and from the study of non-western cultures.

The humanities will center around personal experiences of students, nurture their creativity and critical thinking by extending class activities through independent study, special projects, travel, and by exploring community problems and resources.

Each faculty will develop its objectives and concepts in the humanities and means for implementing the program. Many possibilities exist. From the viewpoint of the arts, the following are broad suggestions of ways the sources in this text may be focused to afford a humanistic emphasis:

Develop understanding of the many kinds of symbolic languages man employs. Throughout history, people have developed many kinds of languages which express their feelings and ideas, and serve to communicate them. Verbal language is a basic communicative skill for all people. In this text, languages of several countries are used to bring this fact to the attention of students.

The languages of mathematics and the sciences are others. The non-verbal expressions of signs, symbols, facial and bodily expressions, mime, dance, painting, sculpture, and music are also languages which denote in equally expressive ways the wide range of human being's unique ability to symbolize their meanings or feelings. Development of a functional understanding of non-verbal communication is an essential factor in the study of the humanities.

Develop an awareness of the ways the arts are used in our society and by other cultures. "How do we use music?" (in games and dances; in worship; in singing about animals and pets, work, transportation, food, and nature; for holidays, celebrations, and special days; in expressing feelings of sorrow, humor, joy, and wonder about nature; and playing or listening for pleasure in leisure time) "How do young people of other countries use music?" (in similar ways) "Why does their music sound different?" (Each country develops its own kinds of music, depending on the climate, geographic conditions, its musical traditions, and different kinds of instruments.) "What basic elements, musical forms, kinds of music, and media characterize our music? How and why are these different from the music of other countries?"

"How do we use color, texture, design, and organization in our country?" (in clothing, homes, schools, public buildings, houses of worship, in decoration, city design and planning, etc.) "How do people in other countries use these elements?" (in the same manner, but in varying forms because of different economic, cultural, geographic, or climatic conditions)

Develop understanding of the functions of the arts in societies. Through art experiences with a minimum of verbalization, let students discover how literature, poetry, painting, music, and architecture serve to transmit or represent in symbolic forms the beliefs, religious or social customs, and traditions of both primitive and modern societies. The oral tradition in literature, poetry, and music may be investigated. In the developing world culture, folk as well as fine arts must be recognized.

Investigation of the institutions of various peoples —the family, religion, education, government, and economic structure generally reveal sources and functions of the arts.

By proper study, understanding and respect are acquired for the multitudinous folk and art expressions—the value systems—of other cultures. As people of different countries need to find areas for understanding in a world of instant communication, the arts may afford one avenue by which such understandings may be developed.

Investigate the social roles and contributions of

artists in our society. "What contributions do the symphony orchestras, opera, ballet, theatre, television productions, and individual artists make to the quality of our society?" "Who should support them?" (For example, in many countries, the government supports these performing arts.) "Should our government similarly subsidize artists and groups?" The roles of the city planner and designers may also be studied.

Lead the student to participate actively in various art media. This participation may be through: creating poetry, dance forms, dramatic productions, and stories; composing and performing music; engaging in various art activities; enjoying music; viewing art objects; and seeing plays and ballet performances.

THE RELATED ARTS. Through exploring various art forms, students can learn to compare and relate constituent elements in the arts and the sensitive ways in which artists and composers have used them in many combinations to create works of art. Through these comparisons and relations, students can develop awareness of the prevalence of rhythm and movement, line, color, design, space, and form in nature, in the arts, and in their everyday life. When seen in the context of another art form, the student's understanding and insights of a single element may be expanded greatly.

For example, line in art has many characteristics. It may be thick, thin, straight, curved, sharp, light, dark, broken, horizontal, vertical, diagonal. With line, the artist can achieve different kinds of movement, establish contrasts, and develop unity. In music, line, or melody, in the potentials of its *aural* expression may be used similarly. The use of rhythm, dynamics, and form may contribute to its expressive qualities.

Any work of art should be experienced directly as a single, unique expression. Let students react first to the expressive meaning of a painting, a poem, or other art work; then proceed to let them discern the elements and their uses by the artist or poet; finally, focus on the specific element or elements of the study through questioning and discussion. The discreteness or uniqueness of the element as used in the particular medium (painting, architecture, poetry) should be maintained.

In this text, several major styles of painting are included. These are: *objective paintings* in which the artist portrays people and objects with little alteration of their colors or forms although they may be naturalistic, idealistic, or dramatized to an extent; *abstract paintings* in which the essentials or fundamentals of a subject, rather than surface appearances, are portrayed. Depending upon the degree of abstraction involved, the object may or may not be recognizable; *non-objective works* which have no subject matter but depend on pure form and design for their effects; *abstract-expressionist paintings* which may be abstract or non-objective as far as subject is concerned, but in which the emphasis is on sensation, feeling, and highly emotionalized content. Not all works will fall into these categories, but they do suggest general classifications of paintings included. Such categories may be helpful in discerning the meaning of a painting.

Many available films on elements in the arts may be used to great advantage in enriching students' experiences and concepts of the elements in various arts.

Multimedia projects employing the work of students–films, music for the sound track, poetry or commentary can be stimulating and valuable to the class as a whole or to those working in groups. Cooperation with the art specialist and other teachers can generally be secured if needed.

USES OF PAINTING AND OTHER ARTS IN THE CLASSROOM

1. Review the section "The Humanities and Related Arts in the Junior High School" for general suggestions and procedures.

2. As an unusually wide variety of arts are included in this text, students should be encouraged to develop criteria and a more precise vocabulary to assist them in understanding and discussing works of art and making personal judgments about them. Specific questions and procedures which may assist in this process are:

What meaning or feelings does the artist express or communicate? Is the subject matter literal or symbolic? What does the work convey about the age in which it was completed?

How have elements of art (lines, colors, textures, values, perspective, and volume) been used by the artist to achieve his effects? How have shapes, forms, and patterns been organized to develop the structure of the work?

What is the medium used in the painting? (oil, watercolor, fresco, tempera, etc.) What are the materials employed by the sculptor? The architect? Are these appropriate for the function or uses of the work?

After careful study of the painting, have the students make a judgment concerning the appeal of the work to them.

3. Other aids for the teacher in this guide are:

About the artist: concise comments included in the overprint near the art work as it appears in the student text;

About the art: comments about selected paintings in the text. These brief paragraphs contain background material which may be of help in formulating questions or directing discussion about the significance of the paintings and/or the techniques and aesthetic values of the artists.

ABOUT THE ART. facing page 1.
Morris Louis, *Third Element*. The art critic Clement Greenberg wrote the following concerning the artist's "stripe" paintings: "The configurations. . .are not meant as images and do not act as images; they are far too abstract. They are there to organize the picture field into eloquence. . .Louis is not interested in stripes as such, but in verticality and color. . .And yet the color, the verticality. . .are not there for their own sakes. They are there for the sake of feeling, and as vehicles of feeling. And if these paintings fail as vehicles and expressions of feeling, they fail entirely."

page 17. Javier Cabada, *Portrait of Beethoven*. The heavy brush strokes and use of strong color contrasts by Cabada combine to form this dramatic portrait of Beethoven. Close examination of the painting and the total effect gained from viewing it from a distance afford insights into the craft and technique of painting, particularly when contrasted with paintings by Sheeler or Dali.

page 28. Marc Chagall, *The Birthday*. Chagall's childhood memories of Russian villages, folklore, fairy tales, fantasies, and the naive definition of objects—usually tender and nostalgic—characterize many of his works. Images are distributed on the surface, defining objects which touch off a chain of reflections which form a poetic rather than a realistic composition. The floating figures and well-defined objects both inside and outside the room are intended as emblematic suggestions which can be recomposed in the viewer's imagination.

page 29. Salvador Dali, *The Persistence of Memory*. Visual representations of fantasies, dreams, and visions came to a climax in Surrealism—a major painting style of the twentieth century. Objects are derived from the depths of the unconscious, and symbolism theoretically does not exist in them. Yet in Dali's *Persistence of Memory* the portrayal of objects leads us to the conclusion that time is defeated and the artist achieves immortality. Obvious symbols are the dead tree, the watches, and the jellyfish-like monster on the beach. One watch is attacked by scavenger ants without success. The organization, brilliant use of color, and portrayal of details are evidence of Dali's superb command of artistic resources.

page 29. Giorgio de Chirico, *The Mystery and Melancholy of a Street*. Chirico's dream world may derive from moods evoked by a childhood in Greece and Italy. In the painting, the incongruities of the empty furniture van or the girl with the hoop in the cold moonlight of the deserted square with its endlessly diminishing arcades are inexplicable. The strong lines, contrasting masses of color, and ominous recognizable objects create a strangely sinister scene.

page 29. Henri Rousseau, *The Sleeping Gypsy*. The genius of the "primitive" Rousseau is evident in the fantasy and dreamlike character of this masterpiece. The images prevalent in earlier works–exotic foliage, people, and animals–are replaced by the relative simplicity of the woman in a picturesque costume asleep in a moonlit wilderness; a great mythical lion is near her. A pitcher, mandolin, the line of hills on the horizon, a sprinkling of stars and the moon are rather stark components of this beautifully executed fantasy. Brown tones and horizontal masses are broken by the colorful patterns of the gypsy's robe, the mandolin, moon, and stars. This is a climactic work of Rousseau.

page 32. Charles Sheeler, *Continuity*. The industrial landscapes of Sheeler are composed of the precise, cube-like shapes of factory architecture. His subjects are viewed from unusual camera-like angles–steep upward or downward views and close-ups, with careful selection of details and unusual lighting. The paintings emphasize the formal, almost dehumanizing qualities of the machine world. This cubist-realist approach in his use of form gives Sheeler's paintings an exciting aura of modernity.

page 64. Frank Lloyd Wright, *Falling Water Terrace*. As in all Wright's buildings, the structure is intimately related to its site. The two levels of natural rock below are paralleled by two concrete porches jutting out into the open space above them. The vertical volumes of the fireplace balance the horizontal planes of the porches. The rock of the river bank is related in color and texture to that of the chimney. The natural and manufactured rhythms and colors form an expressive, dramatic combination.

page 92. Wassily Kandinsky, *Yellow Painting*. The principal works of Kandinsky are nonobjective. The pictorial content bears no reference to recognizable objects and the painting with its lines, shapes, and colors is its own referent. Titles were rarely given except of a general nature.

In *Yellow Painting* the multishaped objects and the infinite variety of colors on the yellow background excite and stimulate the viewer's imagination. The eye shifts quickly from one vivid group or section to another. As did many artists of his day, Kandinsky possessed a strong sensitivity to relations and interactions between the visual arts and the tonal colors and power of music.

page 93. Jackson Pollock, *Autumn Rhythm*. The artist executed this work by pouring, spattering, dripping, and dribbling his colors on the canvas rather than applying them with the brush. There is no reference to an object or to nature. The resultant texture exists as color, as line, as a sensuously rich surface with energetic rhythms. Variously called abstract expressionism or action painting, Pollock's style has a unique twentieth-century individuality, vitality, and inner momentum.

page 93. Alberto Giacometti, *Woman with Her Throat Cut*. The sculptures of Giacometti are essentially surrealistic in origin–imaginative, mysterious, and usually grotesquely elongated.

page 192. Joseph Pickett, *Manchester Valley*. Joseph Pickett was born in New Hope, Pennsylvania, in 1848. He taught himself to paint and recorded on canvas exactly what he saw. His "primitive" style captured the changing seasons, the various events of the day, and the countryside around him. His obvious enthusiasm for nature is most evident in his use of bright and fresh colors.

page 193. Unit 7, *Temporal Worlds*. This unit includes paintings, sculpture, and architecture of the twentieth century, the Middle Ages, the Renaissance, and of the Baroque, Classical, and Romantic epochs.

The reproductions contained in sections of the unit are exemplars in each medium. These may be studied as suggested previously although research projects and more intensive investigation would greatly enhance students' understanding of the works presented in the text as well as other art and artists representative of the period.

MUSIC OF OTHER CULTURES. This text includes music and art of other cultures. A functional knowledge of other musical languages can open the way to new concepts and a new standard of values for students. Concepts of other timbres, colors, rhythm, melody, and form prevalent in our music will be greatly expanded by performing and hearing music of other peoples.

An understanding of the social, cultural, and physical conditions of the country of origin will illuminate these musical experiences.

In an age of global mass civilization, a recognition of foreign cultures reveals its values and can strengthen a feeling of kinship in a meaningful manner.

CREATIVE EXPERIENCES IN MUSIC LEARNING

Exploration, experimentation, and composing in music afford excitement, enjoyment, and intrinsic learnings for students. Experiences of this nature demand imagination and resourcefulness in thinking. They are also important and vital components in the process of learning—in music as well as in other subjects. When students are confronted with projects or problems which require personal manipulation and use of the elements of music and which must be solved through the use of their minds, self-derived concepts, insights, and enthusiasm generally result.

In *New Dimensions in Music,* two general types of experiences which present such opportunities are suggested: creative activities related to song literature and the listening program, and experimental projects in composition, some of which are presented with suggested procedures in the students' texts. Other general approaches are also suggested in this guide in annotations on pages.

CREATIVE ACTIVITIES RELATED TO SONG LITERATURE AND THE LISTENING PROGRAM. Experiences in this category include creating and performing the following: new words to melodies; introductions, accompaniments, and codas to songs; ostinatos; chants and solo-response songs, and instrumental settings to accompany poetry. In listening lessons, students are encouraged to respond with appropriate movement and to accompany the composition with instruments when feasible.

Experimental Projects in Composition. In the students' texts, numerous projects are given which will allow for experimentation with compositional techniques by the students. These projects are designed to assist them in further development of their conceptual comprehension of the nature of music and of its constituent elements.

These experimental projects are not an alternative to singing, playing, and listening activities, but are planned to be complementary to them. Whether spaced throughout the year or used quite regularly, their use by the teacher adds an interesting dimension in the music class.

The use of experimental composition projects in music teaching is based on several premises:

> *When students are placed in the same relationship to the raw materials of music as the mature composer is, aural perception and comprehension of the nature, structure, and expressive qualities of music are developed to a heightened degree.*

In the music class, students sing, play, and listen to music composed by others. These are enjoyable experiences and an important part of their cultural heritage. From one viewpoint, these are *re-creative* activities. By experimenting and using the basic materials, an aesthetic, non-discursive means of expression is learned. Children learn to communicate through speech before learning to write, read, or study rules of grammar. Similarly, most youngsters have developed the ability to hear and perform music. Through using the elements of the languages of music functionally, they learn to hear more perceptively and gain insights into the nature of the art in ways that have meaning for them.

> *Music study should afford opportunities for students to hear and perform contemporary compositions as well as traditional literature.*

Music today reveals much experimentation and flux in a wide diversity of forms, styles, and sound sources. Any and all sounds become potential music material. Music of other cultures is an affective force in the uniqueness and richness of its timbres, rhythms, melodic organization and forms. Electronic, environmental, and non-tonal sounds, are in the sound vocabulary of students, and are included in the school music program. In compositional experiments, new sound sources may be used easily. Students will devise notation to meet needs not afforded traditionally. Through such study, students develop expanded proficiencies in hearing and notation, and bring new perspectives and interest to traditional music.

> *The vitalizing and informing process of creation, rather than the musical product, will be the critical factor in experimentation.*

The compositions of the students will be appraised by student-derived rather than adult musical judgments. The appeal is to their ingenuity as well as to their resourcefulness in developing understandings as to what music is, how it is made, and what can be expressed. As these insights are realized, their expressions evolve from the naive, sensory impressions of young children to surprisingly fresh, imaginative, but more disciplined experiments of teenagers. The challenge is to the teacher to believe in students' potentials and to develop inductive processes, the open environment, and organizational procedures which are prerequisites for such accomplishments by students.

General suggestions for conducting the projects are:

Through class discussion, help develop understanding of the word composer and the factors and musical process involved in composing. One approach may be to elicit by questions the following factors in composition: there must be a composer to select and arrange the elements of sound; some way to write down musical ideas (notation); performers to play, sing, or control sounds; someone to conduct the performers; and, of course, an audience, or listeners.

Determine the sound sources for a particular project which are most appropriate for the teacher and the class. These sources may be:

1. *vocal sounds* (other than the normal singing voice) which may be used to imitate sounds in nature, cars, planes, etc.; tongue-clicking, whistling, whispering, hissing, or guttural sounds
2. *body percussions* such as clapping, finger snapping, knee patting, and use of the feet

3. *object and environmental sounds* such as those made by a pencil, ruler, comb, paper, table knives, forks, spoons, wind, planes, automobiles, etc., or objects in the classroom.

4. *percussion instruments* which include as wide a variety as possible, tympani and a large gong, if available;

5. *orchestral instruments and piano*

The first experiment may be made by the entire class. Then let the class work in groups of three, four, or five students who will share ideas about ways to make an effective composition. In initial projects, no attempt should be made to notate the work. Later, works may be written by individuals or several students who will devise notation, rehearse a group of four or five players, and perform for the class with the composer or another student as conductor. It is important that all students accept responsibility for concentration and cooperation in group work.

Conducting by students is vital in the procedure. In initial *sound pieces,* after learning *attack* and *release* signs, simple up-and-down motions of the right hand and arm will be adequate for control and for indicating dynamic levels. The left hand may be used for giving cues for entrance of instruments. When specific rhythm sets are involved later, traditional patterns for conducting may be used.

After practice, tape the composition. The tape recording gives a perspective on the work, allows repetition of the composition for evaluation, and develops critical listening habits.

Let the students evaluate and criticize. The teacher should merely direct the discussion. Develop criteria for such evaluation with the students after discerning the level of competency of *free* reactions. Questions are helpful in this process. Ask: "What makes a composition interesting to you?" (strong rhythms, variety, kinds of sounds used, tempos, contrasts in dynamic levels and meter, fine melody, interesting harmony, texture, etc.) Evaluation of specific compositions and questions may be related to the elements previously indicated, to the mood, feeling of tension, release, climax, and to the ways in which the composition might be made more interesting or effective. In evaluation, develop a vocabulary of musical terms such as dynamics, tempo, rhythm, forte, piano, crescendo, diminuendo, timbre (tone color), motive, phrase, section, and form. Focus reactions on the musical elements and their uses, rather than on non-musical ideas.

When possible and desirable, let the pupils listen to recordings which may illustrate or exemplify problems being met by students in their work.

How to make a longer composition from a four-measure rhythm pattern or melodic phrase will arise as a problem after the self-generating "stories" of the initial projects. Ask the students to study songs they know in order to discern how a song is developed. Although many possibilities exist, lead them to discover: a pattern or phrase may be repeated; it may be repeated with variations; a second pattern or phrase may be developed and then repeated (AB form); or the first section may be repeated again (ABA form). Further possibilities are: rondo form (ABA-CAD, etc.); variations on the original pattern or phrase; or continuous development. Variety is gained through use of different instruments or different combinations of instruments, dynamic levels, and a variety in choice of tempos. One of the great values in the project is the constant reference by the teacher to vocal or instrumental compositions —how problems are met by mature composers or in music we know.

When possible, let the more capable students assist others. In some instances, students from junior high may be permitted to be assistants in lower grades.

Some projects may seem formidable or may not be successful. Proceed to others. Such experimentation requires patience, resourcefulness, tact, and time. Learning with the students and nurturing projects of this nature, will help the teacher develop routines and procedures which will facilitate instruction through class, group, and individual projects. The genuine interest, student involvement, and growth in music understanding are significant outcomes when used with other music experience. As the term *experimental projects* implies, no explicit methodology or techniques are involved in compositional experiences. A spirit of inquiry and inductive thinking by students are necessary. The teacher serves as guide, director, and resource individual.

EXPERIMENTAL PROJECTS IN COMPOSITION

In *Sound, Beat, and Feeling,* numerous experimental projects in composition are presented. Specific objectives, concepts, and further suggestions for student involvement are presented on the following pages in the text:

page 35: "Prelude," Sound Exploration I," "Sound Exploration II"
page 36: "Randu's Holiday"
page 90: "Music Project"
page 92: "Seeing Sounds"
page 93: "Soundscene"
page 70: "Composition with Rhythms"
page 71: "A Sound Story"
page 88: Composing With Tape: Simple and Multiple Sounds, Sound Settings for Words, Non-representational Film Score
page 89: "Chameleon," "Comics," "World of Words," "Your 2500th Birthday"
page 124: Composition of Variations
page 125: Basic resources, "Follow the Leader," "Improvisation,""Imagination,""New Tonal Sources," "Exploring Textures," "The Morning Paper," "Jazz Improvisation"
page 173: Composing with African Rhythms
page 188: Settings for Japanese Haiku

BEHAVIORAL OBJECTIVES FOR MUSIC LEARNINGS

In *Sound, Beat, and Feeling,* specific learning objectives underlie the experiences in music and other subject areas presented. These objectives are given for each unit in the text. They are stated in the last section of this guide.

The objectives for music learning in most instances indicate what overt, observable student behaviors might be expected as evidence of the student's "knowing," "appreciating," or "understanding." The unit objectives include those based on possible knowledge about music, a wide variety of skills, and the development of attitudes where such an objective is appropriate.

In planning instruction, careful study of these objectives will afford focus and direction for the teacher. Students' responses will be more positive when goals of instruction are communicated to them. These listings of objectives may also serve in assessing students' progress and in evaluating their attainments, attitudes, and development of skills in music.

CONCEPTS IN MUSIC INSTRUCTION

Concepts in music are formed as a result of experiences in music which have a real meaning for the individual student and which remain as a part of his or her intellectual understanding of the constituent elements, their interactions, possible uses of instruments or other sound sources, or other factors inherent in music instruction. Concepts are developed through a cycle of perceiving and forming an understanding, thinking or reflecting on this perception, trying out or *acting* on the perception, and through so doing, determining its validity.

In learning, no person can give a concept to someone else. Each person makes his or her own concepts and thinks only with those self-produced concepts. Concepts have been derived from sense-perceived data—not from verbally memorized information. In this text, the emphasis on student learning is that of *seeing, doing,* and *thinking,* in order that students may arrive at their self-derived perceptions and concepts relative to music.

Behavioral objectives and statements of concepts which can afford functional or self-attained knowledge of music through experience by the individual student are presented. When used properly, these objectives and statements give direction to teaching and guiding activities and involvement in music learning.

The teaching-learning process then follows: (1) after creating interest and motivation, present the experience (singing, playing or creative activity which afford focus on the concept to be learned); (2) through questioning and discussion, let students briefly verbalize the concept; and (3) immediately reinforce the learning or concept through additional experiences or experimentation. When the concept is seen in a new context against another art form, further insight may be afforded. Concepts about music should not be forced, but should be a natural outcome in music teaching. Extreme verbalization should not replace emphasis on enthusiastic participation and aesthetic response to music. In *Sound, Beat, and Feeling,* concepts presented in the text are found in the "Table of the Elements of Music" on pages 264 and 265.

MUSIC IN THE TOTAL SCHOOL PROGRAM

An effective music program can and should contribute not only to the personal enrichment of children, but to the cultural and social environment of the entire school. If the full potentials of aesthetic education are to be realized, administrative support and cooperation of music consultants, colleagues, and community leaders are necessary. Realistic objectives and curriculum content in music instruction should be established, adequate instruction time and equipment provided, and ways and means explored for extending opportunities for increased involvement of students in music.

Objectives in music and curriculum content should be designed for each school, using criteria which meet the concerns and individual needs of youth. Planning should begin at the cultural level of each community, with identification of the unique artistic contributions as well as the aesthetic needs of all ethnic and socioeconomic groups involved. Extrinsic goals related to students' social and group adjustment, self-esteem, emotional release, and the development of avocational uses of music are important for many schools.

If music education is to be effective, regularly allotted instruction time and high-quality equipment must be provided. A record player, tape recorder, records, books, and a piano are basic, and band and orchestral instruments should be available for interested students. The school library should include books on music and composers, as well as adequate source information about ethnic groups and other cultures. School or area instructional centers should include films, filmstrips, video tapes, and other resource materials for music instruction.

In the curriculum, relationships with other areas—social studies, language arts, art, science, and physical education—should be encouraged, but not at the expense of a concentrated study of music. Curricular developments in the humanities will recognize the infinite resources in music and other arts.

The vocal teacher can cooperate in many ways with the instrumental teacher to further instruction for talented students.

Extensions of the music program may include: visits to individual classes of musicians from the community; assemblies and music programs; and formation of all-city groups as well as bands and orchestras in each school. Many schools sponsor solo and ensemble festivals. Special classes after school, on Saturday, and during summer months offer opportunities for intensive study.

Excursions or field trips to art centers, concerts, and interschool visitation or exchange programs may develop pride in the cultural heritage of ethnic groups and the experience of live performances. Classes may perform for other students in the school, parent organizations, or in special events such as a "Winterfest," or "Spring Arts Festival" which involve the total school. Such events provide motivation and satisfactions which come through music performance. These projects may also help bridge the gap between the school and the community.

TEACHER-HOME RELATIONS IN MUSIC

That the home is a powerful educational agent is axiomatic. Children learn their language, their attitudes, and most of their values in the home. The home may be used optimally as a valuable enriching force by wisely using many aspects of the mass media, cooperating in reinforcing school instruction, encouraging music activities, and participating in or using the cultural resources of the community. In turn, the teacher may inform parents of the aims and activities of the music program and supply information concerning students' general progress.

Communication with the home may be made through parent conferences, group meetings of parents, newsletters of class activities, samples of student work sent home, and short notes about student progress. Parents should be encouraged to attend school functions and parent visitations—open house, PTA, room teas, and class programs or performances.

Exceptional musical talent should be brought to the attention of parents and with their cooperation, plans made for sound development of the student's abilities.

COMMUNITY RESOURCES AND MUSIC EDUCATION

The home and the school are major influences and molding factors in the growth and development of children. The community is also an affective force. In this context, the community includes friends, neighbors, cultural organizations, the church, libraries, and groups and clubs to which youth belong. The attitudes and activities of students are strongly influenced by their peers, leaders in organizations, and the cultural opportunities provided by the community.

In what ways should the school music program be related to the community? If music instruction is to be *real* rather than just school music, several possibilities become apparent. In school, music should include songs and instruction on recreational instruments which children can enjoy at home, with their friends, and in recreation programs. A deeper or more educative function is the development of understandings in music which will generate their further involvement as participants or consumers in programs of cultural agencies in the community.

The school should also utilize both its immediate community resources and the broader potentials by inviting local artists, ethnic groups, and organizations to perform at the school. Concerts by high school, college or university groups, by ensembles of the Young Audience or Young Artists programs, and by local agencies are possibilities. In many cities, symphony concerts, ballet, opera, and soloists are sponsored in cooperation with the local or state arts councils or by parent-school organizations.

Many community or settlement schools offer excellent opportunities for private and group instrumental study in afternoon, Saturday, and summer programs. Where such schools do not exist, numerous projects are organized by parent-school councils to present concerts and to afford activities in the creative arts both during the school year and in the summer. Private teachers, private music schools, and preparatory departments of colleges and conservatories are other resources for talented students.

Community and church-sponsored activities—choirs, instrumental groups, and recreational programs—also offer opportunities for excellent music training and the possibility of performing with trained musicians.

Most communities have many cultural resources which can give breadth and interest to the school music program and develop students' skills, attitudes, and understandings far beyond that which schools generally can offer. Time and effort are required. With the wealth of musical support and resources at their command, schools can mold these resources into a total enrichment program of music education and enjoyment.

UNIT 1 Sound, Beat, and Feeling

Learning Objectives

The student should be able to:

1. Identify musical events as they occur in the music.
2. Discuss these events.
3. Distinguish patterns relating to pitch.
4. Distinguish various musical timbres.
5. Distinguish between beat and background.
6. Identify tempo and beat.
7. Recognize rhythmic patterns.
8. Distinguish between steady and flexible rhythms.
9. Play simple accompaniments.
10. Identify "effective surprises" in music.
11. Indicate the occurrence of tension and release in music.
12. Evaluate the impact of sound and silence.
13. Demonstrate his understanding of musical terms.
14. Distinguish between unique aspects of music and aspects of music which relate to other arts.
15. Identify musical experiences in terms of personal satisfaction.

Learnings and Skills

Sound, Beat, and Feeling is designed to provide for the student a kaleidoscopic experience of pitch, timbre, pattern, pulse, tempo, dynamics, and mood. Some students have had a rich experience with all kinds of music during elementary years; others have experienced music only through commercial media. The music of this unit has been selected primarily for its ear appeal—to provide a basic aural experience for those who have had little opportunity to know music in all its aspects, and to give more fortunate students materials which are interesting both aurally and intellectually. Both types of students should expand learnings and skills through developing their ability to:

Distinguish aurally between major and minor sound patterns.

Identify a tonal center (keytone, home tone, "do," "1")

Relate *tonal center* to key *signature*.

Possibilities derived from music in this unit are:	C Major	E Major	A Minor
	G Major		
	D Major		
	A Major		

Distinguish between duple, triple, and quadruple meters.

Relate the feeling of duple, triple and quadruple to the concept of a meter signature.

Possibilities in this unit are:

2	3	4	4	C	₵
4	4	4	2		

Hear and perform dynamic changes in music.

Demonstrate ability to follow a score.

Find contrasts in texture while listening and/or performing.

Compare characteristics of musical compositions.

Identify irregularities such as the triplet, the fermata, and syncopations.

Perform and hear distinctions in staccato and legato style.

Distinguish between principles of repetition, contrast, and alteration.

Determine the correct beat for the beginning of a composition.

Student Involvement

One key to student involvement is *activity*. Have students do things which keep them engrossed in the music by:

singing
playing a percussion part
playing a piano accompaniment.
playing chords on Autoharp or guitar
conducting

These performance-related activities are not the only type recommended. If the students are listening, be sure that they have something to listen for throughout the composition.

Use the call charts and make more of your own.

Encourage students to add other information to the call charts.

Use the discovery chart idea (see Unit VII manual (p. 35), "V'adoro Pupille," for an explanation) to determine beat or timbre while listening.

Determine and chart simple sectional forms (AB, ABA).

Even greater musical activities come from creating musical effects.

Suggest that students improvise or alter melodic lines of compositions in text, evaluating the effectiveness of the change.

Collect environmental sounds on a tape recorder and organize them in class according to general compositional principles, using alterations of speed and amplification.

Choose a key and "compose" a 20–30 note sequence beginning and ending on tonic. Play and make alterations as desired.

Choose a meter signature from those used in the unit and write 8–12 measures of rhythmic patterns (no two measures alike). Alter by incorporating some repeated patterns as desired.

Alternate the large-group situations of performing with small-group and individual activities that contribute to an open-class situation to keep all students active at their own rate of progress.

Related Activities

Study the visual art examples in the text for:

—movement
—color
—design
—repetition
—contrast

Discuss the feelings conveyed by the photographs on page 3. What adjectives can you find to describe them? To which musical works in the text would you assign the same adjectives?

Read appropriate passages from Sholokhov's novel, *And Quiet Flows the Don.*

Report on the ancient rites of the Druids at Stonehenge.

Investigate current happenings in the world of music. How many different musical events of the past month can the students enumerate? What events have importance locally, nationally, internationally?

Report on jazz and rock musicians of current significance.

Write your own text on the theme "My Brother American—who is my brother?" Set it to music if possible.

Find examples of poetry and visual art in your school library that convey some sound, beat, or feeling to you.

UNIT 2 Music and You

Learning Objectives

People have their own individual tastes in music. At different times in our lives and in various situations our performance and taste in music may differ. In this way, our likes and dislikes in music reflect our personalities and general development, for human beings constantly grow and change. The quality of growth and change is highly dependent upon how open, how selective, how curious, and often how courageous one has been in seeking and exploring new experiences. Since experience with the arts is an integral part of life, it causes us to become more aware, more sensitive and more complete. All people desiring to develop into the best that they can be welcome new and exciting experiences in the arts as a significant contribution to such development.

The questions of preference, taste, value, cooperation, and volition fall into the affective realm of educational objectives. Experts in the area of behavior and testing have disagreed about the possibilities for assessing behavior in the affective realm. However, the assessment of affective behavior may be accomplished both through self-evaluation and teacher evaluation. Many of the objectives of this unit are affective in nature.

If *affective* growth is present, students should:

1. Value their musical experiences in terms of personal satisfaction.
2. Evaluate realistically their musical accomplishments.
3. Cooperate with others in musical undertakings.
4. Show alert response.
5. Evaluate musical works and performance in terms of personal reaction.
6. Attend musical performances without being required to do so.
7. Demonstrate self-confidence in their approach to musical activities.
8. Show self-direction in musical activities.
9. Seek information about music.
10. Choose to participate in out-of-school musical activities.

Cognitive growth during this unit may be assessed through the students' ability to:

Symbolize musical relationships.

Identify various aspects of communication through music.

Relate contrasting approaches to music-making (composing, listening, performing).

Do not abandon the objectives of Unit 1. Continue earlier emphases as you and your students feel the need to do so. The objectives listed above represent only the new approaches for this unit.

Learnings and Skills

The materials in "Music and You" give opportunities for students to:

Identify melodic lines of vocal or instrumental character.

Distinguish between adherence to composer's wishes and the performer's responsibility for creative aspects of specific compositions.

Use various instrumental, vocal, non-tonal, and environmental sound sources.

Describe sounds.

Identify important composers and performers of today's world.

Phrase effectively.

Demonstrate comprehension of new meter signatures ($\frac{4}{8}$ $\frac{6}{8}$)

Diagram melodic lines.

Recognize glissando and electronic effects.

Use aspects of sound (range, duration, attack, decay, color) as a basis for composing.

Recognize and explain "ordering" as a unifying factor in composition as it is found in

—serial technique
—theme and variations
—other contemporary compositions

Identify human and technological elements in musical compositions.

Student Involvement

As soon as the affective elements of music are emphasized, the students become immediately involved, either positively or negatively. People have an immediate response to what they hear, but it is possible to better understand many aspects of what is heard with purposeful repetition and verbalization. Everything need not be verbalized; if teachers are sensitive enough to be aware of the moments in their classrooms which are described by Abraham Maslow as "peak experiences," they are also aware that these moments are best followed by the impact of silence rather than words.

Fuller comprehension of the learnings and skills presented in this unit will be evident as students begin to:

Discuss some of the issues presented in the unit such as:
- the role of the composers and their relationship to systems
- ways in which students might make their own model of random sounds (e.g., sneeze, tongue click, hiss, scratch, pure tone, instruments without mouthpieces, etc.)
- societal values of the arts included in any musical theatre

Demonstrate critical ability.

Divide the class so that half the class sings while the other half charts the design of the song:
- form
- phrases
- melodic line
- contrapuntal lines

or listens critically to:
- information about the composition
- phrasing
- melodic and rhythmic accuracy

Combine the altered versions in a grand "Theme and Variations," then perform.

Examine scores of vocal and instrumental music by contemporary composers, using techniques exemplified in the text.

Define, in their own way, musical terms (such as *cadenza)* by listening and then explaining what they hear.

Bring to class recordings or compositions which express humor in a musical way.

Suggest a verbal and musical phrase for the basis of a "call" pattern. Proceed with a call-and-response pattern, improvising a "spiritual" in class performance.

Related Activities

See a movie or TV version of a Broadway musical when one is available in the community. Assign specific aspects of the film for discussion, such as:
- character development
- lighting effects
- relation of spoken dialogue and musical parts
- coherence of the plot
- effectiveness of the action
- role of choreography
- appropriateness of settings

Make a cartoon which conveys a particular idea or emotion. Compare results in class discussion.

Present to the class the following sound filmstrips:

Disco Beat of the Classics; Jazz; Rock; Country Music; Now Sound of the Classics; Color. American Book Company/Keyboard Publications.

See 16mm color film, *Lines Horizontal, Lines Vertical.* (5:50 minutes). National Film Board of Canada. Music by Pete Seeger.

See the four sound filmstrips on the basics of Music: *Rhythm, Melody, Harmony,* and *Design.* American Book Company/Keyboard Publications.

Attend local concerts. Discuss these performances in class.

Additional References

Collier, James Lincoln. *Jug Bands and Handmade Music.* New York: Grosset and Dunlap, 1973.

de Lerma, Dominique-René. *Black Music in Our Culture.* Kent, Ohio: Kent State University Press, 1970.

Pooler, Frank and Pierce, Brent: *New Choral Notation, A Handbook.* New York: Walton Music Corporation, 1971.

Schafer, R. Murray. *The Composer in the Classroom.* Scarborough: Brandol Music Limited, 1965.

UNIT 3 Understanding Rhythm and Color

Learning Objectives

This unit is planned to reinforce previous learnings about rhythm through the application to new song and instrumental material which students may perform, hear, or create. Thus, the students should be able to:

1. Distinguish between *gradations* of tempo as well as make obvious contrasts of slow and fast.
2. Distinguish between qualities or styles of movement such as *legato-staccato*.
3. Recognize the underlying pulse of a composition.
4. Demonstrate the relationship between beat and background. Inexperienced students, when asked to determine the beat-pulse, respond frequently with the background pulse, due in large part to the prominence of the background pulse in rock music and its derivations. Both beat and background are pulse, a steady, throbbing movement underlying other kinds of rhythmic organization.
5. Recognize distinctions of timbre produced by
   voice
   strings
   percussion
   brass
   woodwinds
   electronic sources of sound
6. Demonstrate knowledge of accent and the effects of its displacement.
7. Clap rhythmic patterns in duple, triple, and quadruple meters accurately.
8. Write from dictation simple patterns in duple, triple, and quadruple meters based on those performed in class.
9. Conduct compositions performed by students, using single rhythmic patterns or songs from the text.
10. Compose experimental works, utilizing varying rhythm patterns, tone colors, traditional and newer sound resources including electronic sounds.

Learnings and Skills

New learnings and skills introduced in this unit include compositions of various regions, cultures, and periods in which the student can:

Determine tonalities not used previously:
F Major
E Minor

Relate his knowledge of meter signature to a meter signature not used previously: $(\frac{2}{2})$

Conduct duple, triple, and quadruple meters.

Recognize aurally and explain:
accelerando—ritardando
tempo indications (*allegro, moderato, adagio,* etc.)

Perform accents (marked or implied by meter) accurately.

Contrast accompaniment patterns:
chordal
broken chords

Student Involvement

Students comprehend concepts in rhythm such as *tempo, pulse,* and *quality* and concepts of *tonal color* with little need for extensive experience with musical terminology. Students involvement with pulse is immediate and they need only the guidance of the teacher to relate pulse to tempo and quality.

Possible approaches to student involvement in this unit include:

Composition
Use a student's name as the basis of a melodic idea which matches rhythm and tonal inflection of the name.
Improvise on basic beat patterns.
"Orchestrate" various songs in the unit.
Experiment with electronically altered sounds.

Performance
Singing
Chant words rhythmically as an aid to learning songs.

Moving

Plan choreography for a composition such as "Waiting."

Playing

Tap rhythmic patterns with drumstick, clap, snap fingers, stamp feet, or slap thighs.

Conducting

Listening

Discussion

Discuss rhythmic patterns of a song.

Compare patterns used in general compositions.

Relate possible types of social activities to songs such as "Tongo."

Related Activities

Attend a concert presented by a local symphony orchestra or visit a nearby high school during rehearsals or concerts of the band and orchestra.

Invite professional musicians in the community to demonstrate and explain their instruments.

If your school does not have a synthesizer, plan a field trip to a college or university where the students can see one in operation.

Compare the Mozart score in the text with a full orchestral score of the nineteenth or twentieth centuries.

Classify speaking voices by assigning numbers to students individually. Say "I am ——— ——— from ——— School."

girl's voice—light and high
girl's voice—deeper quality
boy's voice—light
boy's voice—decidedly low and heavy

You may find some 1½ or 3½ voices. Have all "ones" repeat a phrase, "twos" the same phrase, etc. This is a quick way to convey a concept of vocal timbre. Contrast singing and speaking timbres which may or may not be the same.

Have students plan a class program of music which will emphasize contrasts in tempo, key, and timbre.

See films related to content of unit:

Carl Sandburg, *Colors in Music*. Encyclopedia Britannica Films. (b&w), 30 minutes.

Colors in Music. University of Rochester (b&w), 29 minutes.

Music and Emotions. University of Rochester (b&w), 29 minutes.

Read Hector Berlioz's "The Orchestra and the Conductor" in Leroy Ostransky's *The World of Music*.

Additional References

Baines, Anthony. *Musical Instruments Through the Ages*. Baltimore: Penguin Books, 1961.

Bartholomew, Wilmer T. *Accoustics of Music*. Englewood Cliffs, N.J.: Prentice-Hall, 1963.

Garland, Phyl. *The Sound of Soul*. Chicago: Henry Regnery Company, 1969.

Ostransky, Leroy. *The World of Music*. Englewood Cliffs, N.J.: Prentice-Hall, 1969.

Sootin, Harry. *Science Experiments with Sound*. New York: Grosset and Dunlap, 1964.

UNIT 4 Exploring Line, Texture, and Design

Learning Objectives

Units 3 and 4 both include concepts and activities related to basic factors in understanding music. As a result, the students should be able to:

1. Identify aurally characteristics which contribute to the formation of a melodic line:

pitch
contour
range
interval movement (step, skip, or combination) cadence points

2. Distinguish aurally major, minor, and modal sounds.

3. Explain factors which affect the character of a melody.

4. Demonstrate understanding of melodic movement.

5. Distinguish aurally between triads and seventh chords.

6. Distinguish between the bases of formal relationships in

music	(sound and silence)
dance	(movement and rest)
poetry	(words and silence)
sculpture	(mass and space)
painting	(light and shade, color)

7. Identify organizing principles comparable in the various arts such as:

rhythm
line
repetition
contrast
alteration
unity
variety

8. Distinguish thick and thin musical textures.

9. Identify monophonic, homophonic, and polyphonic passages aurally and visually.

10. Identify tonal, polytonal, and atonal music.

11. Identify recitative style.

12. Use musical vocabulary in discussing elements of musical compositions.

Learnings and Skills

New learnings and skills relate to *melody* or line (a series of tones ordered in time); to *harmony* or texture (the simultaneous sounding of tones); to *form* or design (the scheme or organization of a composition). The student has the opportunity to:

Recognize melodic concepts:

When tones change in a melody, they give a melody direction.

When the register changes, the effect of the melody is sometimes different.

When the contour of a melody is different, the expressive quality of the melody is affected.

The range and variety of pitches used contributes to the effect of a melody.

Frequent cadences which mark "rest points" contribute to the character of a melody.

Recognize harmonic concepts:

Harmony develops from converging melodic lines or the chordal treatment of a single melodic line.

Harmonic texture may be described as *thick* (the presence of many simultaneous sounds) or *thin* (the presence of a few simultaneous sounds).

The terms "consonance" and "dissonance" have varying connotations in relation to historical practice.

There may be harmonic points of rests, also called *cadences.*

The process of moving from one key to another is called *modulation.*

Recognize concepts of form:

basic principles:
unity
variety
organizing techniques:
repetition
contrast
alteration (variation)
possible combinations of techniques:
forms based on *repetition* (strophic: A-A-A)
forms based on *repetition* with contrast
two-part—A B
three-part—A B A
rondo—A B A C A
five-part—A B A B A
forms based on repetition with *alteration* (theme and variations: A A^1 A^2, A^3)
forms based on repetition with *contrast, variation,* and *development*
Sonata Allegro
fugue
free forms
forms combined within a larger form

song cycle	suite	cantata
opera	sonata	mass
oratorio	symphony	

Learnings to develop concepts presented in earlier units will help the student:

Identify new key signatures:
A-Flat Major
D Minor
G Minor
Explore design in music:
canon
round
fugue

Recognize keys, meters, harmonic concepts, and forms encountered previously.

Comparison Chart

TITLE:	Composition 1					Composition 2				
Characteristics:	1	2	3	4	5	1	2	3	4	5
Originality										
Eclecticism										
Rhythmic Variety										
Beat										
Patterns										
Melodic Interest										
Counterpoint										
Textural Variety										
Harmonic Background										
Dynamic Range										
Clarity of Form										
Performance Technique										
Performance Effectiveness										
Conveyance of Mood										
Interesting Timbres										
Individuality of Style										
Style Representative of Period										
Style Representative of Place										
Consistency of Style										
Use of Nuance										
Lyrics or Program										

Student Involvement

Graph student responses. After the students have become familiar with major musical characteristics (rhythm, melody, harmony, tone color, form) and their component parts (rhythm-pulse, duration, tempo, pattern, etc.), take time to graph responses to these elements by comparing two musical works.

Compare:

two compositions by Mozart or any composer of your choice

two compositions by John Lennon, Bob Dylan, the Jefferson Airplane or others of your choice

Do not compare:

Mozart with Dylan

Brahms with Mozart

The latter are possible, but are less valid comparisons in terms of the "value" of the composition. Discuss the variations in graphs from person to person.

Spell and play chords. Change major chords to minor to major, etc.

Sing intervals. Make a list of mnemonic devices from current popular songs or old favorites:

5 1

Perfect fourth: "*The eyes* of Texas are upon you"

or

1 5
Perfect fifth: "*Don't throw* bouquets at me"
or
1 #4
Augmented fourth: "*Ma-ri*-a"
or
3 5
Minor third: "*To-dream* the impossible dream"

Write melodies such as "Shalom Haverim," "Kol Dodi," or "Ah, vous dirai-je, Maman" in augmentation and/or diminution.

Related Activities

See black and white 16mm. film, *Mexican-American Border Songs*. National Educational Television. 29 minutes. Also: *Music as Sound*. University of Rochester. 29 minutes.

Additional References

Ernst, Karl and Gary, Charles. *Music in General Education*. Washington, D.C.: Music Educators National Conference, 1965.

Fontaine, Paul. *Basic Formal Structures in Music*. New York: Appleton-Century-Crofts, 1967.

Janson, H. W. with Cauman, Samuel. *History of Art for Young People*. New York: Harry Abrams for American Book Co., 1971.

Tovey, Donald Francis. *The Forms of Music*. New York: Meridian, 1959.

Tyndall, Robert. *Musical Form*. Boston: Allyn and Bacon, 1964.

UNIT 5 Playing Instruments

Learning Objectives

This unit contains instructions and materials with which students may work without the help of the teacher. The students will recognize songs which they already know. Some may wish to work on "Playing Instruments" independently while class activities center around other units. If you choose to introduce the unit as a large group activity, there is additional bibliography for students who are able to go on with other songs but still need fairly simple materials.

In selecting enrichment materials for this unit, it would be helpful to choose music in the keys presented here so the students will have added experience with the same chording patterns for new melodies. Some of the materials suggested are not melodies for chording, but include compositions to which the students may transfer their knowledge of notation, chords, and the keyboard structure.

For full comprehension and musical satisfaction, this unit should enable students to:

1. Play with precise rhythm, accurate pitch, and well-produced tone.
2. Illustrate expressive characteristics in their playing.
3. Study the keyboard as a compositional medium.
4. Demonstrate self-confidence in playing an instrument.
5. Demonstrate ability to direct themselves in musical activities.
6. Apply their instrumental experience to new situations.

Learnings and Skills

Certain learnings and skills are related to the content of other units in the book, but are given a new practical dimension through instrumental performance. Here the students should:

Relate the structure of the instrument to musical notation.

Identify key signatures.

Identify meter signatures.

Relate note values to meter indications.

Perform accurately duple, simple and compound, and triple meters.

Perform syncopations.

Perform melodic notation correctly.

Identify and perform specific chord complexes.

Transfer chord symbols to other songs written in the keys used in this unit.

Identify the differences in sound between major triads and major-minor seventh chords.

Identify the terms for texture—monophonic, homophonic, and polyphonic–and relate these terms to their work at the keyboard.

Demonstrate knowledge of the working principles of instruments.

Demonstrate knowledge of the history of keyboard instruments.

Student Involvement

Playing an instrument requires constant involvement on the part of the students—large muscles, small muscles, eyes, ears, mind; a constant discipline of transferring former associations to new contexts—physical, mental, emotional; a constant reinforcement of the pleasing effects of accurate response. Students' desire for involvement will continue if:

Progress, no matter how slight, is encouraged.

Mistakes are minimized, but not allowed to continue.

Opportunities are provided for transferring principles learned.

Materials relevant to students' interests outside the classroom are used.

Related Activities

Listening

Listen to recordings of compositions by musicians recognized as skilled in composing for piano.

Ludwig van Beethoven, *Sonata No. 14 in C♯ Minor* ("Moonlight"). Opus 27, No. 2, Colosseum Recording No. Co. M1007.

This is the sound of Beethoven's last piano, restored after several years of careful work.

Frederic Chopin, *Grand Fantasy on Polish Airs.* Op. 13, Victor LSC 3055; *Grand Etude. Op 10, No. 12* in C Minor ("Revolutionary"), Columbia MS 6541.

Robert Schumann, *Die Davidsbündler.* Opus 6, Deutsche Grammophon Gesellschaft 139316.

Franz Liszt, *Piano Concerto No. 1 in E Flat Major.* Victor LSC 2068.

Johannes Brahms, *Rhapsody in G Minor.* Opus 79, No. 2, Angel 35027.

George Gershwin, *Preludes* for Piano. Concert Disc 217.

Béla Bartók, *Sonata for Two Pianos and Percussion.* Turnabout 4159.

The Story of the Piano. Book Box Unit, B68M-6. American Book Company/Keyboard Publications.

Listen to recordings of well-known keyboard performers:

Six Legendary Pianists. Seraphim 6045.

Lorin Hollander at Fillmore East. Angel S-36025.

Famous Composers Play. Telefunken 38.

Famous Pianists at the Turn of the Century. Telefunken 37.

Wanda Landowska, *Art of the Harpsichord.* Victor LM 2194.

Compare performances of a single work by two or more performers:

Beethoven, *Sonata No. 8 in C Minor.* Opus 13 ("Pathétique")

by Walter Gieseking	Angel 35025
Glenn Gould	Columbia MS 6945
Vladimir Horowitz	Columbia MS 6541
Arthur Rubinstein	Victor LSC 2654

Live Performances

Attend a concert by a visiting artist. If possible, secure a program in advance of the concert and listen to the compositions which will be played.

Invite a pianist of good local reputation to perform at school. If there is a skilled organist in the community, arrange for the class to hear the organist demonstrate the resources and construction of the organ.

Films

Keyboard

Arthur Rubinstein, 2 films. Black and white 26 minutes. Mills Picture Corporation.

Music in the Wind (organ). Black and white, 10 minutes. Sterling Educational Films.

New Horizons: The Building of a Piano. Color, 14 minutes. Baldwin Piano Company.

Piano Encore. Color, 10 minutes. Films Incorporated.

The Harpsichord. Black and white, 10 minutes. Almanac Films.

The Piano (We Make Music Series). Color. Film Associates of California.

Young Performers (Leonard Bernstein Concert Series). Black and white, 52 minutes. Southern Bell Telephone.

Guitar

Andres Segovia. Black and white, 30 minutes. Encyclopedia Britannica Films.

Carl Sandburg. Black and white, 30 minutes. Encyclopedia Britannica Films.

Classic Guitar: Miniature Orchestra. Black and white, 23 minutes. National Educational Television.

The Guitar (We Make Music Series). Color, 30 minutes. Film Associates.

Filmstrips

The Guitar. Color. Sound filmstrip. American Book Company/Keyboard Publications.

Art

Pierre-Auguste Renoir. *Girls at the Piano.* Society for Visual Education, No. 74.

Jan Steen. *The Music Lesson.* Peter Adelberg, European Art Color Slide Company.

Readings

Vincent d'Indy, "Cesar Franck is Inspired" in Barzun, Jacques, Ed. *Pleasures of Music,* p. 284.

Robert Schumann, "A Meeting of the House of David" in *Pleasures of Music,* pp. 98–102.

West, Jessamyn, *Cress Delahanty.* New York, Harcourt, Brace, 1953. Cress' music lesson is found in chapter entitled "Thirteen: Winter," pp. 130–132.

Books

Baines, Anthony. *Musical Instruments through the Ages.* Baltimore: Penguin Books, 1961.

Bellow, Alexander. *Illustrated History of the Guitar.* Rockville Center, New York: Belwin-Mills Publishing Corporation, 1970.

Bessaraboff, Nicholas. *Ancient European Musical Instruments.* Boston: Harvard University Press, 1941.

Grunfeld, Frederic V. *The Art and Times of the Guitar.* New York: Macmillan Company, 1970.

Hoover, Cynthia A. *Harpsichords and Clavichords.* Washington, D.C.: Smithsonian Institution Press, 1969.

Noble, Robert. *Three Chords and Beyond.* London: Novello and Company, 1967.

Pace, Robert. *Piano for Classroom Music.* Englewood Cliffs, N.J.: Prentice-Hall, 1956.

Pelz, William. *Basic Keyboard Skills.* Boston: Allyn and Bacon, 1963.

Sheftel, Paul. *Exploring Keyboard Fundamentals.* New York: Holt, Rinehart and Winston, 1970.

Music

Agay, Denes. *The Young Pianists' Library* (No. 1-A, *From Bach to Bartók*). New York: M. Witmark, 1960.

Bartók, Béla. *The First Term at the Piano.* New York and London: Boosey and Hawkes, 1950.

Birnie, W. A. H. *et al. Family Song Book.* Pleasantville, N.Y.: Reader's Digest Association, 1969.

Bob Dylan Song Book. New York: M. Witmark, 1970.

Clark, Frances and Goss, Louise. *Piano Literature of the 17th, 18th, and 19th Centuries* (4 vols.). Evanston, Ill.: Summy-Birchard Company, 1954.

Kraehenbuehl, David. *Jazz and Blues* (6 vols.). Evanston, Ill.: Summy-Birchard Company, 1954.

Kraehenbuehl, David, *et al. Themes from Masterworks.* Evanston, Ill.: Summy-Birchard Company, 1963.

Noad, Frederick. *The Guitar Songbook.* London: Collier-Macmillan Ltd., 1969.

Podolsky, Leo. *Guild Repertoire.* Evanston, Ill.: Summy-Birchard Company, 1959.

Solomon, Maynard, (Ed.). *American Ballads and Folk Songs from the Joan Baez Song Book.* New York: Ryerson Music Publishers, 1964.

Thompson, John. *First Year Classics.* Cincinnati, Ohio: Willis Music Company, 1951.

UNIT 6 Ethnic Worlds

Learning Objectives

This unit should enable students to:

1. Distinguish between musical systems of tonal, microtonal, pentatonic, and modal characteristics.

2. Identify rhythmic, melodic, and harmonic characteristics of various ethnic musics.

3. Identify instruments associated with a particular culture by name and by sound.

4. Identify music of composers who have utilized folk songs or folk style in their compositions.

5. Compare and contrast the uses of music in contemporary American society with uses in societies of other civilizations.

Learnings and Skills

The group of countries included in *Ethnic Worlds* is representative, not all-inclusive. The music of some countries, such as the U.S., reflects the musical sound or *idiom* of parent countries, yet the words illustrate the unique language of the settlers themselves. The U.S. owes its musical heritage to music of the native Americans and of various Western European and African countries; thus, it contains a fusion of folk styles. A parallel is seen in the music of Australia, with its English, Scottish, Irish and aboriginal influences.

In contrast, other civilizations like those of India, China, and Japan, have a totality of sound—in musical idiom, language, and instruments—that has existed for hundreds of years, and still exists as a distinct sound. Western composers often use such distinctive sounds from ethnic traditions to create special exotic effects in their music. Contemporary non-Western composers, in like fashion, use the music of the West as an exotic source–new to the ears of their people.

Among their learnings and skills students should:

Use the word *ethnic* for *any* distinctive culture, not only those that are non-Western or non-American. American music is as ethnic as Japanese or African music.

Identify microtonal sound in a composition.

Identify modal sound in a composition.

Identify pentatonic sound in a composition.

Distinguish between triadic and organal harmonies in folk songs.

Recognize characteristics of ethnic music in contemporary youth music.

Learnings related to specific areas:

Welsh Music

For many years musicians thought the tune of a harp was most characteristic of Welsh melody. Later studies of old folk songs have shown that modal folk songs show much more of the ancient, true character of Welsh national music. Since the folk songs of Wales were almost entirely unrecorded until the beginning of the nineteenth century, the original words for the melodies have been lost in many cases. The singers often sang different sets of verses, some on topics of current interest, to a favorite air.

During the Tudor period (c. 1485–1600), Welsh musicians were in great demand at the English court, with the result that many of the chief musicians left Wales and contributed to the development of music in England. At the same time, professional musicians of Wales became more English in their expression, neglecting their instrumental and vocal traditions.

The instruments particularly associated with Welsh music, in addition to the harp, are the *crwth* and the *pibgorn*. The crwth is a lyre that was used with a bow from the thirteenth century on; it gradually acquired a fingerboard. It was held like a fiddle and had six strings: two octave courses and a pair of bourdons, also tuned to an octave, which were struck with thumb or bow as a kind of bass accompaniment. The name of the pibgorn was derived from Welsh words meaning 'pipe" and "horn" and was a small reed-type instrument with cylindrical tube and expanding bell. Sometimes it was made of elder wood, sometimes of the shinbone of a sheep or deer. One musician described it as "1 foot, 8½ inches long, six holes in front and a thumbhole behind with the scale of F Major."

Music of Latin Countries

It is not easy to identify features which are Latin or, more particularly, Spanish. There are frequent triple meters and compound meters, but there are also some which are duple and quintuple. Augmented and minor seconds are often found in the melodies. There is also polyphonic singing in parallel thirds and sixths, sometimes with drone accompaniment. Features such as ornamentation in the melody are probably of Arabic origin; there are many other Arabic traits in Spanish music such as the harsh, nasal, rather tense voice production.

Latin-American folk music presents a complex picture, characterized by a combination of the complicated, driving rhythms of West African and Hispanic traditions. Some countries, like Brazil, gravitate toward the African influence, while others (Colombia and Argentina among them) have preserved a very old Spanish heritage.

Mexican folk music is largely in the Spanish tradition, but an important difference lies in the prominence of instruments in Mexico. The *mariachi* orchestras—three to ten or twelve players of violins, guitars, mandolins, and double basses—play traditional or popular tunes in city streets. In recent years, brass instruments have been added.

The Spanish tunes in Latin American folk songs are usually songs composed in the styles brought from Europe. European folk songs are often unaccompanied, while Latin-American melodies have a thin texture until they are vitalized with an accompaniment.

Music of Africa

Although much homogeneity of style is apparent in African music, there are also many differences among the various regions south of the Sahara. The four contrasting areas are:

The Khoi-San (Southwest). Bushmen and Hottentots

The Eastern Cattle Area: Masai and Watutsi

Guinea Coast: Ghana, Liberia, Nigeria

The Congo

In general, Africans participate more actively in singing, dancing, playing, and composing than do most Westerners. Music accompanies all kinds of activities such as hunting, harvesting, boating, and drawing water for cattle; it is important in festivities and rituals—at the birth of a child, in death, in preparation for a marriage, in homage to a chief. There is a highly trained group of professional musicians for whom music is a livelihood. Music may even appear in litigation as individuals argue about ownership of territory or honorary titles.

The tone languages of Africa have stimulated much speculation among ethnomusicologists concerning the relationship between words and music, for many of the syllables used vary in meaning with the pitch at which they are spoken.

Music of India

The people of India have been taught that the art of music was created by the Hindu trinity—Brahma the Creator, Vishnu the Preserver, and Shiva the Destroyer. Shiva's movements are the source of all movement.

There are two systems of music in India. The music of North India is called Hindustani music, and music of South India is called Karnatic. They require different instruments and their nomenclature is different. Yet, their basic concepts are the same and have been cultivated in India for centuries.

It was a common practice in former times to teach young people their lessons in tones of music. Every Hindu was taught to praise and pray to his divinity by certain intonations. One of the oldest collections of such hymns, the *Rig Veda,* contains texts such as the canticle to Savitar, the Sungod, part of which is in the student text.

The basis of India's musical system is represented in the book, *Songitarathnakara* (The Ocean of Music), written in the thirteenth century. Among its basic musical principles are:

1. Division of the octave into:
   Consonances—the octave, the fifth, the fourth
   Dissonances—semitones
   Assonances—all other divisions

2. The tonal subdivision into microtones (fractions of tones) called *Sruti.* Within an octave there are 22 tones which are not mathematically alike and are not used in succession.

3. A series of *srutis* in uninterrupted succession, called a *Svara.* In Indian terminology the svara is like the sol-fa scale:

sa	do
ri	re
ga	mi
ma	fa
pa	sol
dha	la
ni	ti

4. A scale-melody form called *Raga.* A raga is both the basic scale and the basic melodic structure.

5. A system of rhythmic patterns called *Tala.* A tala is a rhythmic cycle consisting of from 3 to 128 beats marked off by accents into smaller rhythmic groups. *Sam* is a strongly emphasized beat. *Tali* are other important beats. *Khali* are the unstressed beats. The beat of the tala in North India is *Matra;* in South India, Akshara. However these are not equivalent in duration.

Some frequently used talas of North India are:

Dadra—six beats 3-3
Rupak—seven beats 3-2-2
Kaharva—eight beats 4-4
Jhaptal—ten beats 2-3-2-3
Shooltal—ten beats 4-2-4
Ektal—twelve beats 4-4-2-2
Dhamar—fourteen beats 5-5-4
Ada Chantal—fourteen beats 2-4-4-4
Jhumra—fourteen beats 3-4-3-4 (very slow compositions)
Chanchar—fourteen beats 3-4-3-4
Teental—sixteen beats 4-4-4-4

Some talas have half-beats, but they are not very traditional. They are really fast versions of talas with an odd number of beats.

6. A formal arrangement.
   Alap–the rhapsodic, free-rhythm introduction with which each Indian form begins. Its function is to reveal gradually the notes of the raga and its melodic characteristics.

Pallavi	
Anna pallavi	The four sections of
Caranam	a concert piece.
Pallavi	

7. Drone—an essential element which serves as a constant reminder of the starting point.

8. Instruments of Indian origin are the:

   vina—a South Indian stringed instrument, traditionally associated with Saraswati, the Goddess of Wisdom. It is a fretted instrument with 4 melody strings, 3 drone strings, and 2 resonating gourds. The artist may use his fingers or a plectrum to pluck the strings. The tone is gentle and sweet, capable of many subtle shadings.

sitar—the most popular stringed instrument of North India. The frets are movable and there are 5 melody strings, 2 drone, and 13 sympathetic vibrators which give a full sound.

sarod—a lutelike instrument which may be either plucked or bowed. The unfretted fingerboard is made of metal and there are 16 sympathetic strings.

sarangi—a bowed stringed instrument with 4 melodic strings and 40 sympathetic strings. It is used as a dance-music instrument.

tambura—a plucked drone instrument with 4 strings and no frets.

shahnai—an oboelike instrument played on auspicious occasions such as a marriage.

murali—the flute associated with Lord Krishna (a favorite theme in Indian art).

mridanga—the most highly developed percussion instrument, played on both ends with bare hands in South India. Each head is a composite of several layers of hide and two kinds of tuning paste, making possible a great variety of tonal inflections. There are similar patches on the kettle-shaped *baya* and *tabla* which are played together.

Japanese Music

The Japanese folk song is perhaps best known to the western world, but music is also a vital part of Japanese theatrical tradition in the Noh drama, the Kabuki Theatre, and the Bunraku, or puppet theatre.

Noh music consists of singing by the main actors or chorus and *hayashi* accompaniment; four instrumentalists who play a flute (*nokan*), a shoulder drum (*ko tsuzumi*), a side drum (*o tsuzumi*), and a floor drum (*taiko*).

Kabuki is a combination of melodrama and colorful dancing. The music includes an onstage ensemble with a hayashi group and *shamisen*-accompanied songs. The second music is a narrative, *jojuri,* and the third is the off-stage *geza,* which sets the mood and gives action clues.

Bunraku music is called *gidayu* after a famous singer and is shamisen-accompanied. The gidayu performer must be as great an actor as he is a singer.

The instruments in a Japanese court orchestra (*gagaku*) include:

a short double-reed aerophone (*hichiriki*)
side-blown flutes
mouth organ (*sho*)
a large hanging barrel drum (*gakudaiko*)
small hanging gong (*shoko*)
a small barrel drum (*kakko*), or a large hourglass-shaped drum (*san no tsuzumi*).

Sometimes these are added:

the 13-stringed zither (*koto*)
a pear-shaped lute (*biwa*)

In *gagaku,* the way in which you play is as important as the notes which are performed. The rhythm seems to move in deep "breaths" as the performers listen and feel the music together.

There are many composers who have used Japanese music and life as a source for compositions which are not entirely Japanese in sound, although melodies may be pentatonic and harmonies at times may move in fourths and fifths rather than in thirds.

Music of the United States

In the large cities of the United States, the old songs of minority groups of European traditions, who settled in special areas, are frequently found almost undisturbed. Sometimes, European traditions may be changed in accordance with pressures from the culture in American cities. Singing clubs and dance groups are often formed to keep musical traditions alive.

American folk songs come partly from popular songs and broadside ballads of the British Isles. The principal differences between American and Anglican songs are in the words rather than in the music. The British tradition is one of solo singing rather than group singing, like the African tradition. Both are a part of folk music in the United States. North America preserves more of the British musical tradition than Latin America has retained of the Hispanic tradition.

There are some differences in the songs of various regions with relaxed, open-voiced tone in the North contrasted with a tighter Southern voice. The "caller" is a distinctive feature of American dances, and the "playparty sing" is also a distinct Americanism which arose from the aversion of some religious leaders to dancing. Instruments typical of the American folk tradition are the banjo, dulcimer, guitar, violin, mandolin, and harmonica (mouth organ). African influence has contributed the use of rhythmic handclapping, "hot" rhythm, and the tendency to use strong metrical and polymetrical effects.

American folk music is constantly changing—adding new features, losing old ones. As long as each year brings discoveries of formerly unknown styles and instruments, folk music remains a living art.

Student Involvement

Perhaps the single most important involvement in understanding the various ethnic musics is *rhythm.* Students should be involved physically in a variety of ways as they attempt to understand the rhythmic patterns, i.e.:

The metrical quality of the European folk songs
The complicated polyrhythms of Africa
The additive patterns heard in India
The syncopations of American folksong

Follow the suggestions given page by page for rhythmic involvement. Do not underestimate the importance of dance in ethnic tradition.

The recognition of unusual instrumental *timbres* comes from repeated experiences with those timbres. The guitar, the balalaika, the gusle, the banjo, the fiddle, the vihuela, and the harp may sometimes be confused, but each has its distinctive sound when timbre is combined with the music of the country of its origin. One of the best ways of learning about timbres and instruments is to construct them. Use materials of good quality and allow sufficient time for experimentation.

The *traditions* associated with the music are also an important approach to involvement. A lawyer's child may not have the slightest interest in polyrhythms, but may become fascinated with the fact that music is a part of some legal procedures in Africa. A student with social orientations may be intrigued with the use of songs as social protest, not only in our own time, but for hundreds of years in many ethnic traditions. Involve students in concrete reenactments of ethnic traditions; produce a Balinese shadow play; research and stage a Chinese opera; or plan a Japanese puppet show. The possibilities are limited only by the imaginations of your students. If you have minimal musical resources available, compose your own music, using the musical characteristics presented here as a guide to compositional style to achieve a degree of authenticity. There are many fine authentic sources for the extension of involvement in ethnic music; some of these are listed in the "Additional References" section for this unit.

Improvise on the materials available in the unit, selecting the appropriate type of improvisation for the musical style, i.e.:

Add melodic ornamentations.

Select motives to use as call-and-response improvisations.

Determine how many rhythmic variations can develop from a given phrase.

Add harmonies in triadic or organal fashion.

Related Activities

Ethnic music is an ideal entree to the exploration of community musical resources. It is perhaps natural, if one lives on the west coast of the United States, to explore in depth the music of China or Japan, where there are many opportunities to hear live performances and to visit exhibitions of Oriental artifacts. However, one also may find a Scottish bagpiper in an unlikely metropolitan area in Florida or a beautiful Sari-attired librarian in a small college who plays the violin in the Karnatic tradition of India. When you are fortunate enough to have one near, a university ethnomusicologist is still another source of information and stimulation for young people, since he invariably has a vivacious approach that gives music a whole new dimension.

Make a field trip to an accessible university or museum where there is a collection of ethnic instruments or a performance by a visiting artist.

Invite available performers to your school.

If feasible, plan with social studies teachers a tentative parallel development for ethnic emphasis. Such planning should never be rigid, for the "live moment" is worth a dozen planned but artificial encounters. Be alert to what is current and choice in your community.

Investigate the literature and art of the country whose music you are studying particularly in regard to the knowledge each communicates about music.

See and hear the four sound filmstrip units: *Roots of Our Culture*: Music, Art and Architecture; Social Studies, and Literature. The immigrants' contribution to American culture is a fascinating study. American Book Company/Keyboard Publications.

Sound filmstrips on *Africa, American Indian, Brazil, Mexico, Puerto Rico, Argentina, U.S.S.R., China, Japan,* and the *Middle East* are available from the same source.

Five filmstrips on *UNICEF. Art.* W. Schloat. Plan a trip to a specific country. Make an itinerary which includes concerts and ethnic music. Read about the country and its music. Bring recordings, art, books, maps to share. (A book on world culture will give an overview.)

Additional References

These may be used as source material for the teacher or reports by students to expand the material presented in the units. They also offer opportunity for expansion beyond the countries included in this book.

Books

Chase, Gilbert. *The Music of Spain*. New York: Dover Publications, 1959.

Clifford, William. *The Whole Wide World*. New York: Crown Publishers, 1965.

Coomaraswamy, Ananda, K. *The Dance of Shiva*. New York: Farrar, Straus, and Giroux (Noonday Press), 1957.

Gomme, Alice B. *The Traditional Games of England, Scotland and Ireland* (2 vols.). New York: Dover Press, 1964.

Haywood, Charles, Ed. *Folk Songs of the World*. New York: John Day (Bantam), 1968.

Idelsohn, A. Z. *Jewish Music in its Historical Development*. New York: Schocken Books.

Karpeles, Maud, Ed. *Folk Songs of Europe*. New York: Oak Publications, 1964.

Landeck, Beatrice. *Echoes of Africa in Folk Songs of the Americas*. New York: David McKay, 1969.

Library of Congress, Washington, D.C., 1959 (listing of folk songs from archives).

Lloyd, A. L., Ed. *Folk Songs of the Americas*. New York: Oak Publications, 1965.

Lomax, Alan. *A Staff Report on Cantometrics*. Washington: American Association for the Advancement of Science.

Lomax, Alan. *Folk Songs of North America*. New York: Doubleday, 1960.

Music Educators Journal. World Cultures Issue. Vol. 59, No. 2 (October, 1972)

Nettl, Bruno. *Folk and Traditional Music of the Western Continents*. Englewood Cliffs, N.J.: Prentice-Hall, 1965.

Pingle, Bhava'nra'v A. *History of Indian Music*. Calcutta: Susil Gupta, 1962.

Rubin, Ruth, Ed. *A Treasury of Jewish Folk Song*. New York: Schocken Books.

Scott, John A. *The Ballad of America*. New York: Grosset and Dunlap, 1966.

Seeger, Pete. *The Incompleat Folksinger*. New York: Simon and Schuster, 1972.

Shankar, Ravi. *My Music, My Life*. New York: Simon and Schuster, 1968.

Southern, Eileen. *The Music of Black Americans*. New York: W. W. North, 1971.

Tooze, Ruth, and Krone, Beatrice. *Literature and Music as Resources for the Social Studies*. Englewood Cliffs, N.J.: Prentice-Hall, 1965.

Recordings

Listed below are recording companies and distributors who handle collections of ethnic music. Certain companies tend to specialize in the music of particular areas. The following companies are especially helpful sources for music of countries specifically listed.

American Society for Eastern Arts (ASEA). 405 Sansome St., San Francisco, California 94111 (also for books)

UNESCO Collection. *A Musical Anthology of the Orient and Africa* by the International Institute for Comparative Music Studies and Documentation. (24 vols.) Includes Laos, Cambodia, Afghanistan, Iran, North and South India, Tunisia, Tibet, Japan, Turkey, Ethiopia.

Capitol Records, 1750 N. Vine St., Hollywood, California 90028. Folk Songs of the Old World, (2 vols.), P8387-8388 (America, Austria, Finland, Germany, Hungary, India, Israel, Ireland, Italy, Japan, Mexico, Norway, Philippines, Poland, Russia, Sweden).

Everest Records, 10920 Wilshire Blvd., Suite 410, Los Angeles, California 90024.

Anthology of Music of Black Africa, Everest 3254/3

Also: China, Spain, etc.

Folkways Records, 121 W. 47th St., New York, N.Y. 10036.

Music of Equatorial Africa, Folkways 402

Bantu Choral Folk Songs, Folkways

Folk Music of the Western Congo, Folkways P427

Drums of the Yoruba of Nigeria, Folkways P441

Africa South of the Sahara, Folkways FE 4503

Songs of the Watusi, Folkways P428

Folk Music of Greece, FE4454

International Library of African Music, Johannesburg, South Africa
The Sound of Africa.
Nonesuch Records, 51 W. 51st St., New York, N.Y. 10019
Bulgaria, India, Japan, Mexico, Russia, Greece, Scotland, Spain
Odeon Records
Music of China, India, Germany, France, Spain, Sweden, Yugoslavia, Middle East, Korea

RCA Victor Records
Happy Folk Dances, LMP 1620
Let's Square Dance, LE 3002, 3003, 3004
Special Folk Dances, LPM 1619

Instruments

Inter Culture Associates, Box 277, Thompson, Connecticut 06277.

UNIT 7 Temporal Worlds

Learning Objectives

Temporal Worlds is planned to help students recognize the musical characteristics of six major historical periods, and relate past musical developments to the ever-changing contemporary world. In this unit students should:

1. Identify the sound of a stylistic period through the use of call charts.
2. Use source materials such as letters and other writings to find clues to the composers intentions for their music.
3. Experiment with some devices of musical style used by the composers presented in the unit and throughout the book.
4. Identify rhythmically, through discovery charts and dances, the changing rhythmic emphases of various periods.
5. Identify, in discovery charts, specific stylistic effects such as ritard, da capo form, instrumental timbre, etc.
6. Identify characteristics of styles, idioms, and media.
7. Identify a musical excerpt in terms of:

style	form
period	composer

8. Relate music to other aspects of civilization

political	geographic
social	scientific
economic	philosophical
cultural	

9. Evaluate musical works and performances.
10. Analyze compositional techniques in various periods.

Learnings and Skills

Among their learnings and skills students should:
Study scores and detect by ear stylistic changes in instrumental forms:

Gabrieli, *Canzona Quarti Toni A 15*
Corelli, *Sonata for Violin and Piano*
Bach, *Brandenburg Concerto No. 5 in D Major*
Vivaldi, *Concerto in D Major, Op. 10, No. 3*
Beethoven, *Sonata in A Major*
Brahms, *Concerto No. 1 in D Minor for Piano and Orchestra*
Chinese composers, *Youth*

Identify characteristics of individual composers.

Dowland	Mozart	Chopin
Gabrieli	Beethoven	Debussy
Corelli	Schubert	Bartók
Bach	Brahms	Schönberg
Vivaldi	Tchaikovsky	Stravinsky
Handel	Berlioz	Cage

Identify modes visually and aurally.

Look at key signature of "L'Homme Armé". Key possibilities are F Major and D Minor.

Final note is G, therefore this is probably modal, G major would have an F♯ sharp and a B♮; G minor would have an E flat. Since this has B♭ and E♮, it has the Dorian characteristic of the raised sixth in relation to the minor scale.

Look for the characteristic changed note:
The Phrygian mode is minor, with a lowered degree of the scale. The keyboard pattern for Phrygian is e^1 to e^2 on the white keys.

The musical pitches used in the song are based on this scale:

G A B♭ C D E F G

Therefore, this is Dorian, transposed to G.

Modal key detection procedures for dorian mode:

Pattern scale for Dorian:

D E F G A B C D

(d[1] to d[2] on white keys of piano)

for D minor:

D E F G A B♭ C D

Modes

	Range on white keys of piano	Final	Dominant	Characteristic
		Identification by		
1. Dorian	d-d	d	a	(from minor) raised 6th
2. Hypodorian	a-a	d	f	
3. Phrygian	e-e	e	c	(from minor) lowered 2nd
4. Hypophrygian	b-b	e	a	
5. Lydian	f-f	f	c	(from major) raised 4th
6. Hypolydian	c-c	f	a	
7. Mixolydian	g-g	g	d	(from major) lowered 7th
8. Hypomixolydian	d-d	g	c	
Ionian	c-c			like major
Aeolian	a-a			like natural minor
Locrian	b-b			

Patterns:

Mode I (Dorian)
D E F G A B C D

Mode III (Phrygian)
E F G A B C D E

Mode V (Lydian)
F G A B C D E F

Mode VII (Mixolydian)
G A B C D E F G

Student Involvement

The materials suggested in this unit should be a point of departure for *active* listening. At the outset of the unit, select a *short* composition (two to three minutes) to play for the class. Ask the class to make at least one observation about the music in terminology which is musical if possible; if not, then in any words the students have at their command. Play the composition two or three times if necessary and discuss the observations.

Group the comments on the board as they are made, putting like comments together, then determine a major heading for the column, e.g., "flute, drum, guitar, trombone, person's voice." Unsophisticated students usually will hear more that relates to timbre, to rhythm or to extra-musical associations than characteristics of form, style, or harmony. Therefore, they can be guided in understanding (1) their musical needs, (2) terms that are musically accurate and important, (3) the value of their observations. One person may only make a programmatic association, and another may hear six or seven musical instruments, a metrical distinction of the beat, something that "sounds like Mozart," and a legato melody. However, they learn to respect and value the exchange of opinion which, after all, is the only educationally valid reason for meeting to study in groups.

It is the teacher's challenge to bring order from aural chaos, to help the students organize their listening and verbalization skills. When these abilities are added to performing, students will begin to understand why the rhythms of the Baroque period are such a contrast to those of the Romantic period; how forms, instrumental groups, and melodic sound have developing characteristics; and why their beloved "rock" or rock-derived music is an eclectic art.

After you have consistently presented the stylistic periods in the unit, ask the students as an evaluation to identify musical selections by period. It would be better to identify a twentieth century piece as "romantic" if it *sounds* romantic and the student explains this satisfactorily. The eventual goal is to know the music so well that it is identifiable because of familiarity not only with the general style of the period but with the composer and the music itself. Listening becomes an exciting game if the students have not been rebuffed at the outset.

Related Activities

Using the Comparative Style Chart (pp. 194–195)

The way in which you present the vast amount of material in the charts depends upon the time you have as a teacher. This may range from a twelve-week exploratory experience with music and a maximum of thirty 50-minute periods to a class which meets five days a week for a semester or for an entire year. You may also be using materials on an individual or small-group basis. The charts can be adapted to all approaches; they may be used in relation to all music in the book, not only to the music included in this unit.

For a first experience with the charts:

Select a composition typical of the period you plan to emphasize.

Explain the two uses of the chart:

Vertical—gives characteristics of a period.

Horizontal—gives a development throughout history of a particular musical element.

Ask students which words in the column are unfamiliar and explain these new terms.

Play the composition and ask students to decide which of the terms discussed is most prevalent in the music as they listen.

Discuss their reactions and replay specific passages if needed.

Materials need not be limited to the contents of this unit. Additional suggestions for exploring the music of each period are made at the end of this section and in the classified index.

Related Activities to Clarify Historical Trends in Music

Make an orchestral diagram showing the additions to the symphony orchestra in each period of history, using color to distinguish the various periods. Read Berlioz' "recipe" for a symphony orchestra in H. Schwarz's *Story of Musical Instruments.*

Make a map of musical centers for each historical period. These could be events in your appendix charts and/or people and places such as those in the following list:

Medieval

Papal court in Avignon
Eleanor's court in Aquitaine
Troubadours in southern France
Meistersingers in Nürnberg
Blondel at English court
Liturgical drama in Rome
St. Francis at Assisi
Guido in Arezzo

Renaissance

Elizabeth I's court in London

St. Mark's in Venice
Cathedral in Antwerp
Lorenzo de Medici's court in Florence

Baroque

Handel in Dublin
Scarlatti in Madrid
Bach in Lübeck
Vivaldi in Italy

Classical

Mozart in Salzburg
Beethoven in Bonn
Schubert in Vienna
Haydn at Esterhazy
Orchestra at Mannheim
Concert at Versailles
Frederich the Great as a flutist in Berlin
Mozart at coronation of Leopold II in Prague
Haydn awarded doctorate in London

Romantic

Berlioz' orchestra in Paris
Mazurka in Warsaw
Brahms at piano in Vienna
Bruckner organ near Lenz
Festspielhaus in Bayreuth
Wagner in Lucerne
Schumann in Leipzig
Verdi in Milan
Tchaikovsky in St. Petersburg

Contemporary

Musical comedy in New York City
Rock in Woodstock
Casals in Puerto Rico
Opera in Seattle
Chavez in Mexico
Ballet in Moscow
Shankar in N. India
Opera in Milan
Britten in London
Eisteddfod in Wales
Marionettes in Salzburg
Xenakis in Greece
African music in Ghana
Folk dance in Israel
Bartók in Hungary
Stravinsky in California
Jazz in New Orleans
Country music in Nashville
Polynesian music in Hawaii

Musical Events

Turn your school into a community arts center and stage a juxtaposition of "Temporal Worlds." Arrange simultaneous musical events—in the cafeteria, in a classroom, or in the central hall. They might include a madrigal concert, a rock concert, a session with electronic composing, a dance-theatre-music production, a chamber music production, a chamber music group, a happening.

Have students experiment with reading an excerpt from "Where are we going and what are we doing?" in John Cage's book, *Silence* (pp. 228–231). John Cage's world of music revolves around his frank avowal that "no sound is displeasing to my ears." His conception of music is the broadest possible organization of sound. Invited to speak in January 1961, for students in Brooklyn, he was told that the questions above were their burning interests.

> Cage's texts were to be heard as four simultaneous lectures. Perform these aloud after the students have discovered the individual threads. The lectures were designed to be used in whole or in part, horizontally and vertically. A performance must be given by a single lecturer who may read "live" any one of the lectures; variations in amplitude may be made. The whole lecture is recorded in four single-track tapes (45 minutes each) by C. F. Peters.

Role-playing

Read excerpts from letters of composers as class dialogues:

Exchanges between composers and their families, e.g., Mendelssohn and his sister; Mozart, his father and sister.

Exchanges between friends: Brahms and Theodore Billroth; Brahms and Clara Schumann; Tchaikovsky and Madame von Meck.

Exchanges between composers.

Score-reading

Secure pocket-size copies of musical scores for use with recordings. If multiple copies are not available to attempt score-following as a large class, use this activity for individual participation. Explain the arrangement of orchestral parts in a traditional orchestral score. Contrast with the innovative scores in earlier units of this book.

Composer—G. F. Handel **Discovery Chart** *Title*—V'Adoro Pupille

---

1
A
M KC
. . . .

11
. . . .

21
. . . .

---

31 B
I. m M
. . . .

41
m M m A
. . . . M . . . . . .
. . .

51
KC
. . . .

61
. . . .

71
. . . .

81
. . . . .

91

101

111

Symbols
. = Beat
KC = Key Change (M to m)
= First section
M = Major
m = minor
B = Contrasting section
I = instrument alone

Instructions for the Use of the Discovery Charts

The discovery chart on p. 35 will help students understand what is happening and when it happens in the music being played.

Start by following the beat.

1. Does the music move in two's, in three's or in four's?
2. Use a dot for each beat pulse. You can show the strong pulses by small strokes.
3. Each square represents one measure of music. As you feel each strong beat (or "1" in the measure) move to a new measure.
4. How many measures long is this composition?

Now that you have the feeling of the beat, listen for the sounds of various instruments.

Use an "F" for flute and put an "F" in each measure in which you hear a prominent flute part begin.

Follow the example in the book for the first time. Later, you can make your own charts, using a blank chart for some of the music you will hear. Try this with short, well-known compositions such as "The Blood, Sweat, and Tears" version of *Variations on a Theme by Satie.*

Be consistent from one selection to another in the abbreviations which you use. This will make it easier for the student to concentrate on what he hears.

Suggested abbreviations:

F	Flute
C	Clarinet
O	Oboe
B	Bassoon
T	Trumpet
FH	French Horn
Tn	Trombone
Tu	Tuba
V	Violin
Va	Viola
Vc	Violoncello
SB	String Bass
H	Harp
P	Percussion
M	Major
m	minor
M1	modal
MC	Meter change
I	Imitation
R	Repetition
A	Alteration

Additional References

General

Baines, Anthony. *Musical Instruments through the Ages.* Baltimore: Penguin Books, 1971.

Bonanni, Filippo (Harrison and Rimmer, Eds.). *The Showcase of Musical Instruments.* New York: Dover Publications, 1964.

Davison, Archibald T. and Apel, Willi. *Historical Anthology of Music.* Cambridge: Harvard University Press, 1950.

Gillespie, John. *The Musical Experience.* Belmont, California: Wadsworth, 1968.

Grout, Donald S. *A History of Western Music.* New York: W. W. Norton and Company, 1960.

Harman, Alec and Mellers, Wilfred, Eds. *Man and His Music* (4 vols.). New York: Schocken Books, 1971.

(1) *Medieval and Early Renaissance*
(2) *Late Renaissance and Baroque Music*
(3) *The Sonata Principle*
(4) *Romanticism and the 20th Century*

Hill, Ralph, Ed. *The Concerto.* Baltimore: Penguin Books, 1956.

Hill, Ralph, Ed. *The Symphony.* Baltimore: Penguin Books, 1956.

Strunk, Oliver. *Source Readings in Music History.* New York: W. W. Norton and Company, 1950.

Medieval Period

Reese, Gustav. *Music in the Middle Ages.* New York: W. W. Norton and Company, 1940.

Seay, Albert. *Music in the Medieval World.* Englewood Cliffs, N.J.: Prentice-Hall, 1965.

Renaissance Period

Reese, Gustav. *Music in the Renaissance.* New York: W. W. Norton and Company, 1947.

Baroque Period

Bukofzer, Manfred. *Music in the Baroque Era.* New York: W. W. Norton and Company, 1947.

Greenfeld, Frederic. *The Baroque Era.* New York: Time-Life Publishing Corporation, 1967.

Palisca, Claude V. *Baroque Music.* Englewood Cliffs, N.J.: Prentice-Hall, 1968.

Classical Period

Gillespie, John. *The Musical Experience.* Belmont, California: Wadsworth Publishing Company, 1969.

Landon, H. C. R., Ed. *Studies in Eighteenth Century Music.* New York: Oxford University Press, 1971.

Pauly, Reinhard, *Music in the Classic Period.* Englewood Cliffs, N.J.: Prentice-Hall, 1965.

Romantic Period

Einstein, Alfred, *Music in the Romantic Era.* New York: W. W. Norton and Company, 1947.

Twentieth Century

Austin, W. W., *Music in the Twentieth Century.* New York: W. W. Norton and Company, 1966.

Belz, Carl, *The Story of Rock.* New York: Oxford University Press, 1969.

Cage, John, *Silence.* Cambridge, Mass.: The M.I.T. Press, 1961.

Collaer, Paul, *A History of Modern Music.* New York: Grosset and Dunlap (Universal Library), 1961.

Eisen, Jonathan, *The Age of Rock.* New York, Random House: 1969. (Vol. I and II).

Fox, Sidney, *The Origins and Development of Jazz.* Chicago: Follett Educational Corporation, 1968.

Hansen, Peter, *An Introduction to 20th Century Music.* Boston: Allyn and Bacon, 1969 (Second Edition).

Hodeir, Andre, *Jazz: Its Evolution and Essence.* New York: Grove Press, 1956.

Machlis, Joseph, *Introduction to Contemporary Music.* New York: W. W. Norton and Company, 1961.

Salzman, Eric, *Twentieth Century Music: An Introduction.* Englewood Cliffs, N.J.: Prentice-Hall, 1967.

Trythall, Gilbert. *Principles and Practice of Electronic Music.* New York: Grosset and Dunlap, 1973.

Yates, Peter, *Twentieth Century Music.* New York: Random House, 1967.

Recordings

General

The Story of Great Music. New York, Time-Life Publishing Company, 1966ff.

Contemporary—*Prelude to Modern Music*
The Early Twentieth Century

Romantic—*The Romantic Era*
The Opulent Era
Age of Revolution

Classical—*Age of Elegance*

Baroque—*The Baroque Era*

Medieval

Compositions which use the "Dies Irae" sequence:

a. Berlioz, Hector. *Symphonie Fantastique* (5th Movement).

b. Mozart, W. A. *Requiem* (Dres Irae).

Medieval Music and Songs of the Troubadours. Everest Recording 3270.

Music of Medieval France. Bach Guild Recording BGS-70656.

The Play of Daniel. Decca Recording DL 79402.

Renaissance

Dowland, John. "Queen Elizabeth's Galliard," *Lute Music from the Royal Courts of Europe.* RCA LSC-2924.

Lute Dances. Pleiades S.I.U.-P. 253.

Morley, Thomas. *Madrigals.* Everest Recording S-2397-5520.

Palestrina, Giovanni Pierluigi. *Missa Papae Marcelli.* Angel S-36022.

Baroque

Bach, J. S. *Bach Organ Favorites.* Columbia MS 6261.

Bach, J. S. *Suite No. 3 in D Major.* Deutsche Grammophon 138976-7 or London 6243.

Bach, J. S. *Sheep May Safely Graze.* Columbia MS6058 or London 25141.

Bull, John. *Queen Elizabeth's Pavan,* VOX SVBX-572.

Corelli, Arcangelo. *Suite for Strings.* Columbia MS-6095.

Corelli, Arcangelo. *"Christmas" Concerto Grosso.* Op. 6, No. 8, Bach 70696.

Gabrieli, Giovanni. *Baroque Brass.* RCA LSC 2938. (Also, Purcell, Bach, Des Prés, Monteverdi).

Gabrieli, Giovanni. *Processional and Ceremonial Music.* Nonesuch Recording H-71118.

Handel, George Frederic. "Amen" Chorus from *Judas Maccabaeus.* Westminster 301.

Vivaldi, Antonio. *Four Seasons,* Op. 8. Decca 79423.

Classical

Beethoven, Ludwig van.

Sonata for Piano in F Minor, Op. 2, No. 1. London 6389.

Sonata for Piano in F Minor, Op .57, Vic. LSC-

Haydn, Franz oJseph. *The Creation.* Columbia 2812. M2S-773.

———.*"Drum Roll" Symphony,* No. 103 in Eb. Westminster 18327.

———. *"London" Symphony,* No. 104 in D. Westminster 18327.

———. *"Oxford" Symphony,* No. 92 in G. Epic BC-1156.

Mozart, Wolfgang Amadeus. *String Quartet in C.* K.465.

———. *Mass in C.* K.317. Turnabout 34063.

Rousseau, Jean-Jacques. Overture to *Le Devin du Village.* Baroque Records BU 2843.

Romantic and Impressionist

Brahms, Johannes. *How Lovely Are Thy Dwellings.* Columbia M2S-686.

———. "Wie Bist du Meine Königin?"

———. *Symphony No. 3 in F Major.* Columbia MS-6909.

Debussy, Claude. *La Mer.* Columbia MS-7361.

Mendelssohn, Felix. *Symphony No. 4 in A Major.* Columbia MS-6931.

Ravel, Maurice. *Pavane pour une Infante défunte.* VICS-1199.

———. *Alborada del Gracioso.* VICS-1199.

Saint-Saens, Charles Camille. *Symphony No. 3.* Angel S-35924.

Schumann, Robert. *"Spring" Symphony No. 1* in Bb, Op. 38. Angel S-36353.

Smetana, Bedrich. *The Moldau.* Deutsche Grammophon 139037.

Contemporary

Bartók, Béla. *The Wooden Prince.* Vox Recording PL 12040.

Berio, Luciano. "Differences." Time Records S/8002.

Britten, Benjamin. *Noye's Fludde.* London Recording OS 25331.

Cage, John. *Cartridge Music.*

Chicago Transit Authority. Columbia GP 8 CS 9809.

Ives, Charles. *Circus Band March.* Vanguard C-10013.

Milhaud, Darius. *La Création du Monde.* Nonesuch 71122.

Orff, Carl. *Carmina Burana.* Columbia MS 6163.

Stockhausen, Karlheinz. *Gesang der Jüngling.*

Stravinsky, Igor. *Pulcinella.* Columbia MS 6881 and Columbia MS 7093.

The Beatles. *Sergeant Pepper's Lonely Hearts Club Band.* Capitol ST 2653.

The Jefferson Airplane. *Surrealistic Pillow.* RCA LSP 3766.

Visual Aids

16mm Films

The Sound of an Orchestra. Leonard Bernstein, Black and white. Bell Telephone Company.

We Make Music Series. Color. Film Associates. Each film deals with the historical development of an instrument as well as with its structure and literature.

Discovering the Music of the Middle Ages. Color, 20 minutes. Bailey Films Associates, 1968.

The Renaissance. Encyclopedia Britannica Films.

The Chronicle of Anna Magdalene Bach. 93 minutes. New York Presentations.

Discovering Jazz. Color, 21 minutes. Bailey Film Associates, 1969.

New Sounds in Music. Color, 22 minutes. Churchill Films, 1968.

Filmstrips

Pathways to Music. Color, sound filmstrips. Units on the Renaissance, Baroque, Classic, Early and Late Romantic, Inpressionistic Eras. Also *Twentieth Century Music and Art.* American Book Company/Keyboard Publications.

UNIT 8 Music for Chorus

Learning Objectives

This unit is composed of slightly more difficult selections than those contained in the preceding units of the book. The compositions are suitable for choral groups of varying composition, or for various groupings of voices within a large group of junior high students with a wide range of voice classifications.

The choral *experience* should be the ultimate objective of this unit rather than the choral *rehearsal.*

Although the experience contains many of the emphases of the rehearsal, the former is a more inclusive opportunity for the student to develop a full awareness of the physical, intellectual, and aesthetic facets of choral music. There should be frequent interplay among classroom listening and singing activities, and choral performances and instrumental performances rather than isolated developments. Too often the choral experience has been limited to the perfecting of group rehearsal techniques when the students should also be concerned with personal vocal mastery and an awareness of complete musical content—the whole effect produced by the combinations of tones, rhythms, form, and expressive characteristics.

As a result of the choral experience, students should be able to:

1. Watch the conductor when one is required.
2. Sing with well-produced tone, accurate pitch, and precise rhythm.
3. Master the basic techniques of tone-production: breathing, relaxed jaw, projection, freedom of tone, variation of tone-colors.
4. Master the basic techniques of diction: pure vowels, lingual flexibility, and consonant articulation.
5. Produce a feeling of musical line.
6. Perform with consistency throughout their vocal range.
7. Use expressive characteristics in individual performances.
8. Demonstrate ability to achieve blend and balance in group performances.
9. Read the musical score with the degree of accuracy appropriate to their individual background.
10. Recognize the melodic nature of parts other than the basic melody.
11. Perform alone or in groups in relation to their ability and confidence.
12. Perform with a realization of style appropriate to the music.
13. Apply musical understandings to the memorization process.
14. Discuss briefly the compositions being performed in terms of style, period, form, composer, and musical devices used.
15. Discuss choral and vocal performances.
16. Evaluate choral compositions and performances.
17. Relate choral music to other kinds of music and other aspects of civilization.
18. Arrange a song for the choral group.
19. Compose for the choral group.
20. Participate in out-of-school choral activities when possible.

Learnings and Skills

Skill development for all students in this unit should focus on seven of the learning objectives listed above. Eight specific points related to these appear in the student book, page 225. All students should demonstrate knowledge related to style, musical devices, and composers.

Some of the objectives refer to partly affective behaviors which contribute immensely to the total choral experience, while others demand specific activities which all students may not wish to pursue. Some students may have no need to arrange for the choral group, but others may be served well by the additional opportunity to develop such musical skills. The importance of relating choral music to other phases of musical life and life in general should not be minimized. What *is* the role of choral music in the shock-wave changes of the twentieth century? Look to the future for answers. In *your* classroom the answers for the future are not in the pages of a text, but in the minds of your students. Only you can be alert for the moment when such a question is vital to their understanding of the music being performed.

Suggested evaluations of learnings and skills are:

Objective: Accurately reproduce musical score.
Evaluation: Students sing in small groups for class or teacher.

Objective: Appropriately phrase, regarding music and text.
Evaluation: Students suggest, individually, points at which music should be phrased.

Objective: Freely produce musical tone.
Evaluation: Teacher observes students for proper breath support, freedom from muscular tension in area of throat, freedom from strained facial expression.

Objective: Effectively communicate the mood and text of the composition.
Evaluation: Students, in turn, observe group to determine whether words and spirit are evident.

Student Involvement

Like the instrumental unit, the choral unit is essentially developed around students involvement through performance. However there are many kinds of involvement which should be utilized in the total choral experience.

Encourage students to conduct:

1. interpreting the score as faithfully as possible.
2. experimenting with tempi and dynamics.

Use small groups of student evaluators or individuals to check blend, balance, dynamics, and diction.

Suggest that students bring in poems or sentences, e.g., "Song of the Pop-Bottlers" by Morris Bishop in Phyllis McGinley's *Wonders and Surprises*. Philadelphia, J. B. Lippincott, 1968.

Have students make a chart of voice ranges and classifications for their particular class.

Suggestions on voice classification

1. By speaking voices:

   A quick, but not conclusive determination of timbres may be used as a preliminary step in grouping voices. Have students say their names and addresses clearly. Classify them 1, 2, 3, 4. 1 will be soprano, etc. It is an interesting approach to timbre, but not a decisive classification. It helps determine groups.

2. By small groups:

   Students frequently are more at ease singing and vocalizing in groups. They acquire confidence in singing with others, and the teacher is able to determine individual needs more easily.

3. By individual auditions:

   When a student is comfortable singing in the small group, have that student sing a verse of a familiar song individually. The 3-note arpeggio on "ah" gives a more accurate idea of quality as well as range (1-3-5-3-1), while the octave arpeggio (1-3-5-8-5-3-1) is the quickest way to determine extent of range.

All three should be included.

Chart of voice ranges

Related Activities

Relate composers such as Mozart, Haydn, Palestrina, and Byrd, who appear in this unit, to other compositions by these musicians presented in the book. Additional suggestions for listening activities follow:

Listening:

Mozart, W. A. *Vesperae Solemnes de Confessore,* C Major, K. 339 (Solemn Vespers). Vox Recording PL 10-260.

Haydn, Franz Joseph. *The Creation:* Opening, "Chaos"; "Darkness Covered the Earth"; "Let There Be Light"; "The Marv'lous Work." Deutsche Grammophon Gesellschaft 2707044.

Palestrina, Giovanni Pierluigi da. *Missa Papae Marcelli,* "Sanctus." Angel S-36022.

Billings, William. *Hymns and Anthems.* Old Sturbridge Singers, Folkways 32377. Gregg Smith Singers, Columbia MS 7277.

Vaughan-Williams, Ralph. *Symphony No. 1* ("Sea"). Angel S-3739.

Hindemith, Paul. *Chansons.* Nonesuch 71115.

Britten, Benjamin. *A Ceremony of Carols.* Decca 710060.

Thompson, Randall. "Alleluia" on *First International University Choral Festival.* RCA Victor LSC-7043.

Byrd, William. "Ave Verum Corpus." Argo Recording 5226.

Films:

Stravinsky, Igor. *Symphony of Psalms.* Black and white, 49:28 minutes. National Film Board of Canada.

NEW DIMENSIONS IN MUSIC

SOUND, BEAT, AND FEELING

NEW DIMENSIONS IN MUSIC

ROBERT A. CHOATE
BARBARA KAPLAN
JAMES STANDIFER

SOUND, BEAT, AND FEELING

American Book Company

ROBERT A. CHOATE, *Formerly Dean, School of Fine and Applied Arts*
Boston University, Boston, Massachusetts

BARBARA KAPLAN
Auburn University, Auburn, Alabama

JAMES STANDIFER, *Chairperson, Department of Music Education*
The University of Michigan, Ann Arbor, Michigan

CREDITS

Cover Photographics by Jerome Kresch
Book Design by Bob Antler
Fine Art Acknowledgments on page 288

Teacher's Annotated Edition

ISBN: 0-278-44845-3

1 3 5 7 9 11 12 10 8 6 4 2

AMERICAN BOOK COMPANY

New York Cincinnati Atlanta Dallas San Francisco

ISBN: 0-278-44820-8

1 3 5 7 9 11 13 15 16 14 12 10 8 6 4 2

Contents

From the viewpoint of the arts, the following are broad suggestions of ways the sources in this text may be focused to afford a humanistic emphasis:

1. Develop understanding of the many kinds of symbolic languages people use.

2. Develop an awareness of the ways the arts are used in our society and by other cultures.

3. Develop understanding of the functions of the arts in societies.

4. Investigate the social roles and contributions of artists in our society.

5. Participate actively in music and the other arts.

UNIT 1

Morris Louis: *Third Element*. 1962
The Museum of Modern Art

Sound, Beat, and Feeling

The Humanities and Related Arts

The humanities are those studies of people as human beings—the expressions of their thoughts, their feelings, their needs, their dreams, and their aspirations.

In contrast to traditional historical and data-oriented studies, the new humanities includes a broad range of issues and problems derived from anthropology and sociology, from the physical and natural sciences, languages and literature, fine arts, and from the study of non-western cultures.

The unique qualities in music make a kaleidoscope of:

Sound	**Beat**	**Feeling**
Pitches	Beat/Pulse	Mood
Timbres (colors)	Accent	Dynamics
Pitch Patterns	Patterns (duration)	Tempo
	Tempo	Intensity
	Flexibility	

Characteristics of one art can be found in other arts. Painters, sculptors, and architects are concerned with textures. Words are used by poets, playwrights, and some composers. Designs are the concern of dancers, painters, architects, and sculptors. Textures, designs, and words all may be a part of music.

The unique quality of each art comes from its own material. Impact depends on the use of this material. The best works of art are those which use the characteristic material of its medium in the most skillful and expressive way.

Key: C
Starting Tone C (1-do)

Meter: 4 (quarter note)
Form: A B A

Record 1, Side A, Band 1

TURN! TURN! TURN!

Words from Ecclesiastes
Adaptation and Music by Pete Seeger

This song may be effectively accompanied by guitar chords.

This contemporary folk song is set to a text from the ancient book of Ecclesiastes. Which attributes of **sound, beat,** and **feeling** has it captured?

V–I

LEARNINGS AND SKILLS Find the dominant-tonic cadences. (V-I) In addition to the important harmonic cadences, find cadences in the melody that may or may not coincide.

Verse

G$_7$ C G$_7$ C

A time to be born, a time to die; a time to plant, a time to reap; A time to

mp

V I

G$_7$ C G$_7$ C (go back to the 𝄋 sign)

kill, a time to heal; a time to laugh, a time ___ to weep. ___ To ev-'ry-

V I V I V I

mf

Discuss these rhythmic patterns.

Is the pattern of sound major or minor? (major)

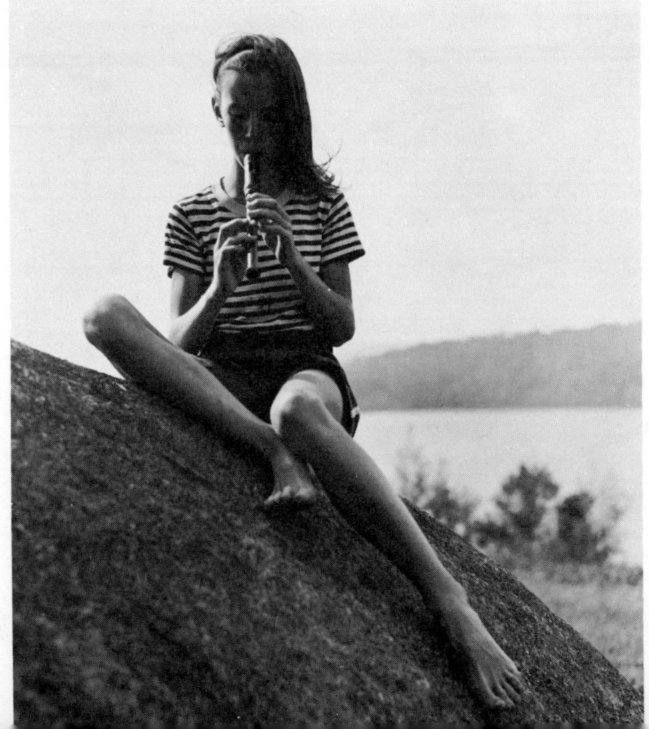

Key: C
Starting Tone: G (5-sol)

Meter: 4/♩

Form: A A' A B (AB)

Record 1, Side A, Band 2

WHERE HAVE ALL THE FLOWERS GONE?

Words and Music by Pete Seeger

This circular-question song was inspired by *And Quiet Flows The Don,* Mikhail Sholokhov's novel about Russia.

STUDENT INVOLVEMENT Help the students to discover the broken chord accompaniment to the song. Identify the broken chords as arpeggios. "What is the primary chord in the accompaniment?" (C Major: C–E–G)

Key: Am
Starting Tone: E (3-mi)

Meter: 2 3 4 / ♩

Form: ABA

Record 1, Side A, Band 3

LET'S GO DANCING

Israeli Folk Song
Tr. and Arr. by Moshe Jacobson

Experiment with the **sound, beat,** and **feeling** of this *hora* from Israel.

A
Fast
Am Am E
Let's go danc - ing ev - 'ry one, let's go danc - ing, join the fun;
Am E E E
Let's go danc - ing in a ring, let's go danc - ing as we sing,
Am E
Let's go danc - ing in a ring, let's go danc - ing as we sing, Ya -
B
Slower
Am E
lel, ya - lel li ya - lel, ya -
ya - lel, ya - lel ya - lel li
Dm E
lel ya - lel - li Ya -
- ya - lel, ya - lel ya - lel - li,
Am E
lel ya - lel li, ya - lel, ya -
ya - lel, ya - lel ya - lel - li

Dm
E
lel ___ ya - lel - li. (clap)
___ ya - lel, ya - lel ___ ya - lel, - li. (clap)

A
Fast Am
Am
E
Let's go danc - ing ev - 'ry one, let's go danc - ing, join the fun;
Am E E E
Let's go danc - ing in a ring, let's go danc - ing as we sing,
Am E E Am
Let's go danc - ing in a ring, let's go danc - ing as we sing!

This Israeli hora was arranged by Moshe Jacobson, Music Supervisor of Haifa, Israel. Play the recording for the class. Have the class sing with the recording the second time it is played.

LEARNINGS AND SKILLS The student should be able to: 1. Identify the minor tonality of the song. 2. Identify the ternary form (ABA). 3. Identify the instrumental introduction and postlude on the recording.

STUDENT INVOLVEMENT 1. After the class has listened to the recording and sung with the recording, have one student construct the A minor scale on the chalkboard (a, b, c, d, e, f, g#, a). Play or sing the A minor scale, (the harmonic minor, in this case) then play or sing the A minor scale using the g natural instead of the g#. Help the class discover the relative major scale (c, d, e, f, g, a, b, c).

2. Help the class discover the three basic sections of the song — the fast A section; the slow, two-part section; and the repeated fast A section.

RELATED ACTIVITIES Encourage the class to experiment with the sound, beat, and feeling of this hora by altering and changing the tone color, rhythms, accents, and accompaniments. Tape various versions for classroom evaluation.

Key: D
Starting Tone: D (1-do)

Meter: $\overset{2}{\text{𝅗𝅥}}$
Form: AB

Record 1, Side A, Band 4

THE HAMMER SONG

Pete Seeger's "composed folk songs" are among the most popular songs to come out of the mid-20th century.

Music by Pete Seeger

Exciting **sound, beat,** and **feeling** have made this song a favorite ballad.

With spirit

D A7 D
If I had a ham-mer, I'd ham-mer in the morn-ing, I'd ham-mer in the

D♯dim A7 D
eve-ning all o-ver this land; I'd ham-mer out dan-ger

G A7 Bm G D G
I'd ham-mer out a warn-ing, I'd ham-mer out love be-tween my

D A7 D G D A7 D
broth-ers and my sis-ters, All o-ver this land.

If I had a bell, I'd ring it in the
morning
I'd ring it in the evening all over this
land;
I'd ring out danger, I'd ring out a
warning
I'd ring out love between my brothers
and my sisters
All over this land.

If I had a song, I'd sing it in the
morning
I'd sing it in the evening all over this
land;
I'd sing out danger, I'd sing out a
warning
I'd sing out love between my brothers
and my sisters
All over this land.

Well, I got a hammer and I got a bell
And I got a song to sing all over this
land;
It's the hammer of justice, it's the
bell of freedom
It's the song about love between my
brothers and my sisters
All over this land.

STUDENT INVOLVEMENT

1. Identify the home tone (D) and show how the melody revolves around D (also called the tonic I). 2. Find other arrangements of this composed folk song and compare it with the arrangement on this page.

RELATED ACTIVITIES

Listen to the recording of "The Hammer Song." Lead the class in a discussion of the recording. Include evaluation of the following:

- performance
- accompaniment
- basic tone color
- rhythmic characteristics
- mood

Key: A Meter Record 1, Side A, Band 5

Starting Tone: E (5-sol)

DIE GEDANKEN SIND FREI

German Folk Song

This German folk song has been traced back to the sixteenth century. The **feeling** made it a battle hymn of freedom in Germany. "Die Gedanken Sind Frei" was forbidden to be sung in Germany during World War II.

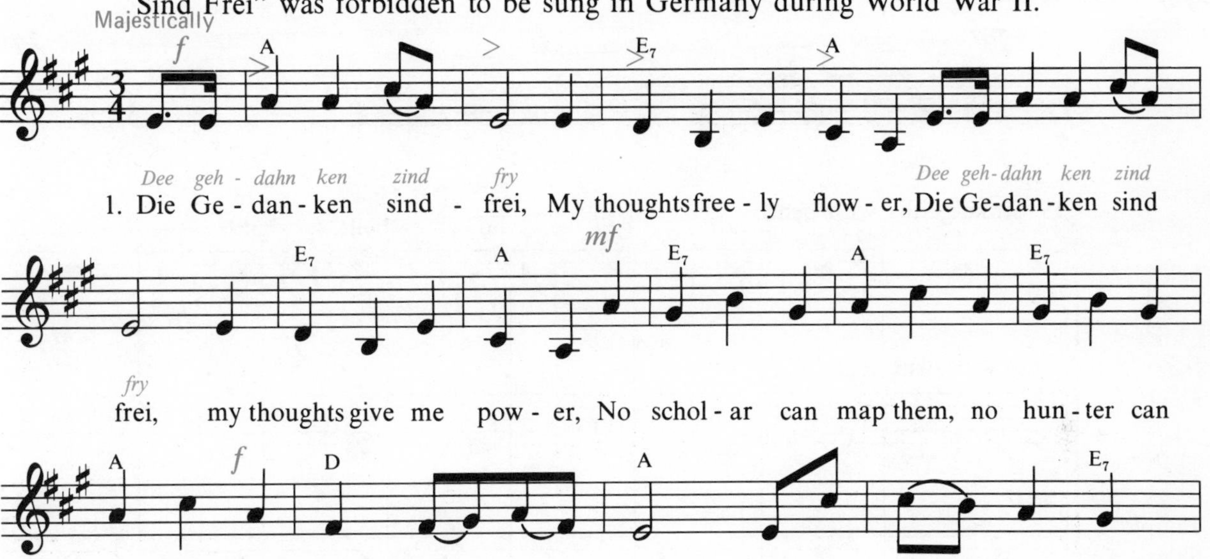

Majestically
f
A
E7
A
Dee geh - dahn ken zind fry
1. Die Ge - dan - ken sind - frei, My thoughts free - ly flow - er, Die Ge-dan - ken sind
Dee geh-dahn ken zind
mf
fry
frei, my thoughts give me pow - er, No schol - ar can map them, no hun - ter can
D

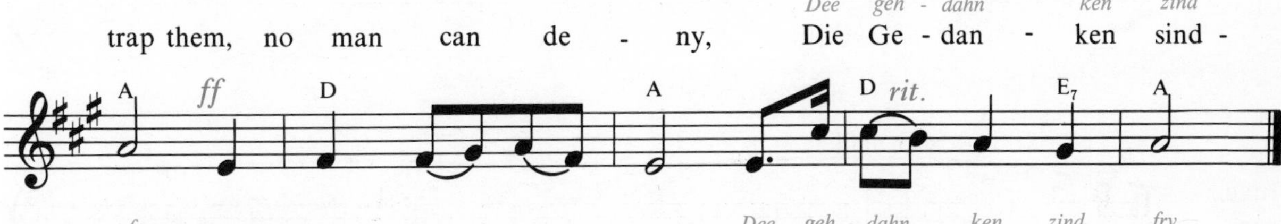

trap them, no man can de - ny,
Dee geh - dahn ken zind
Die Ge - dan - ken sind -
ff
D rit.
fry
frei. No man can de - ny,
Dee geh - dahn ken zind fry.
Die Ge - dan - ken sind frei!

LEARNING AND SKILLS

[Th]e student should be able [to:] 1. Identify the [m]ood of the song. [2.] Determine the mean[ing] that is implied in the [tex]t. 3. Set tempos and [dy]namic levels for the [so]ng (see above).

2. I think as I please,
And this gives me pleasure,
My conscience decrees,
This right I must treasure;
My thoughts will not cater
To duke or dictator,
No man can deny—
Die Gedanken sind frei!

3. And should tyrants take me
And throw me in prison,
My thoughts will burst free,
Like blossoms in season.
Foundations will crumble,
And structures will tumble,
And free men will cry—
Die Gedanken sind frei!

STUDENT INVOLVEMENT

1. Read the text aloud. Discuss with the class their interpretation of the text.
2. The song has a martial flavor. As no dynamic markings are indicated, guide the class in experimenting with various tempos and dynamic levels until they arrive at the most appropriate interpretation.

What is the beat of this music? What is the pattern of sound?

Graph the melody line on the chalkboard.

Key: modal (vocal line) Meter: 3 Record 1, Side A, Band 6
Starting Tone: A Form: free

SUNRISE AT STONEHENGE

Virginia Hagemann

Play the recording as an introduction. The instrumentation of this composition includes household objects as well as more traditional percussion instruments.

Discover the many ways in which this contemporary composer has used **sound, beat,** and **feeling** to create a mood.

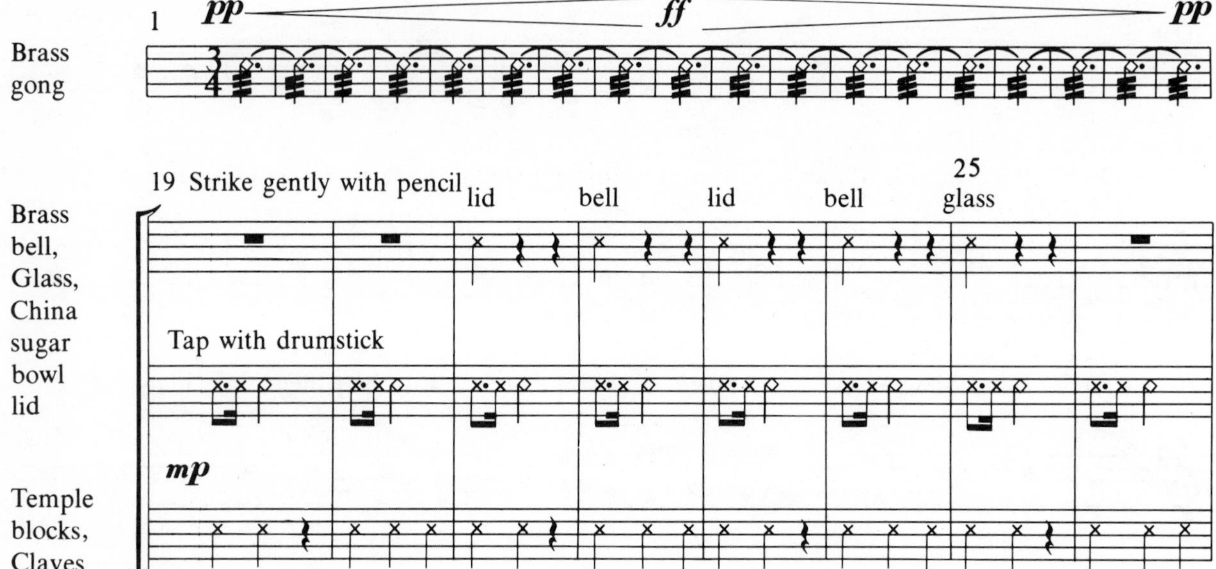

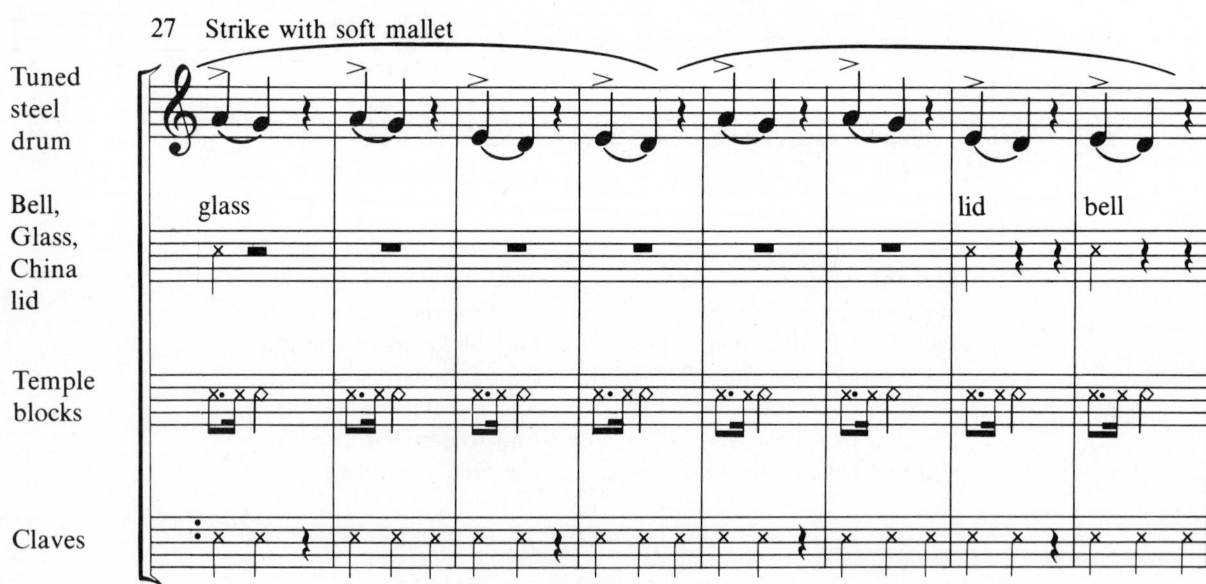

Score Reading Directions

1. Start at the end of the score reading backward to measure 55.
2. Skip measures 54 through 51.
3. Begin again at measure 50 continuing to measure 25.
4. Skip to the beginning of the score and read forward to the end.

The E and D create a dissonance.

50

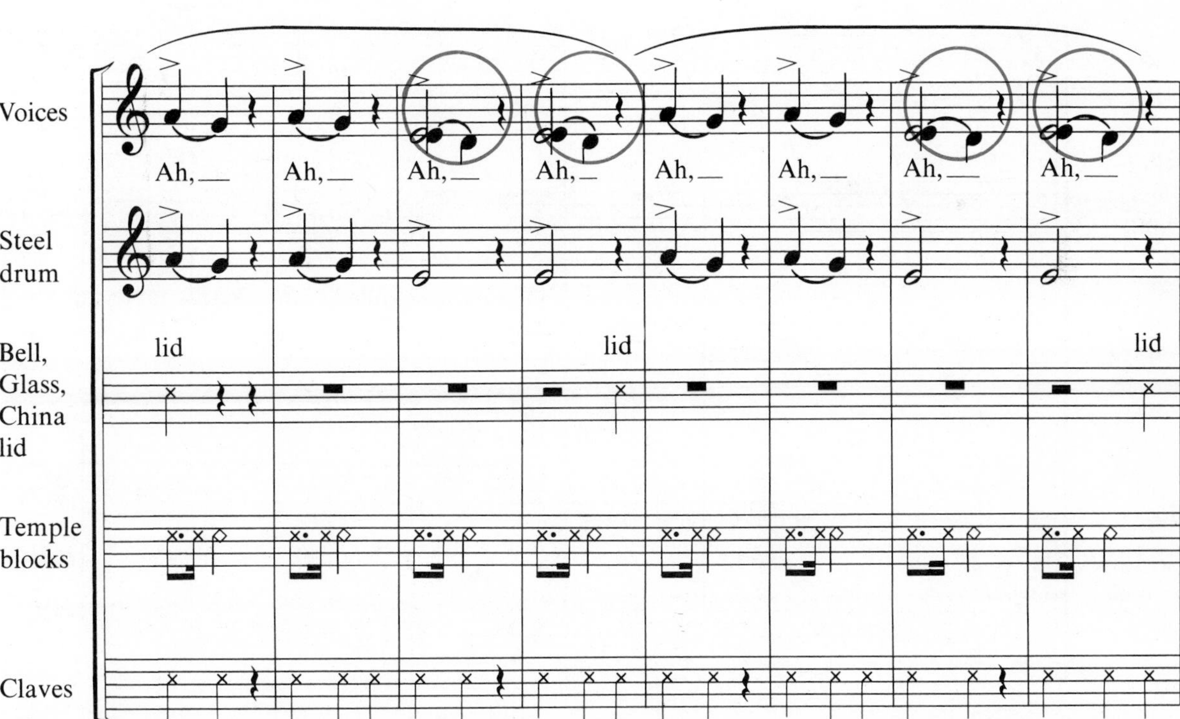

STUDENT INVOLVEMENT 1. Have the students listen to the single sound of the brass gong (measures 1-18) on the recording. Ask individuals to indicate the dynamic level changes (*pp ff pp*) with hands. Encourage the class to experiment with expressive dynamics using classroom instruments or vocal sounds. Tape and evaluate the results.

2. Encourage the students to discuss the basic problems of vocal performance in the composition. Help the class discover the dissonant sound patterns (see above).

The G and A create a dissonance.

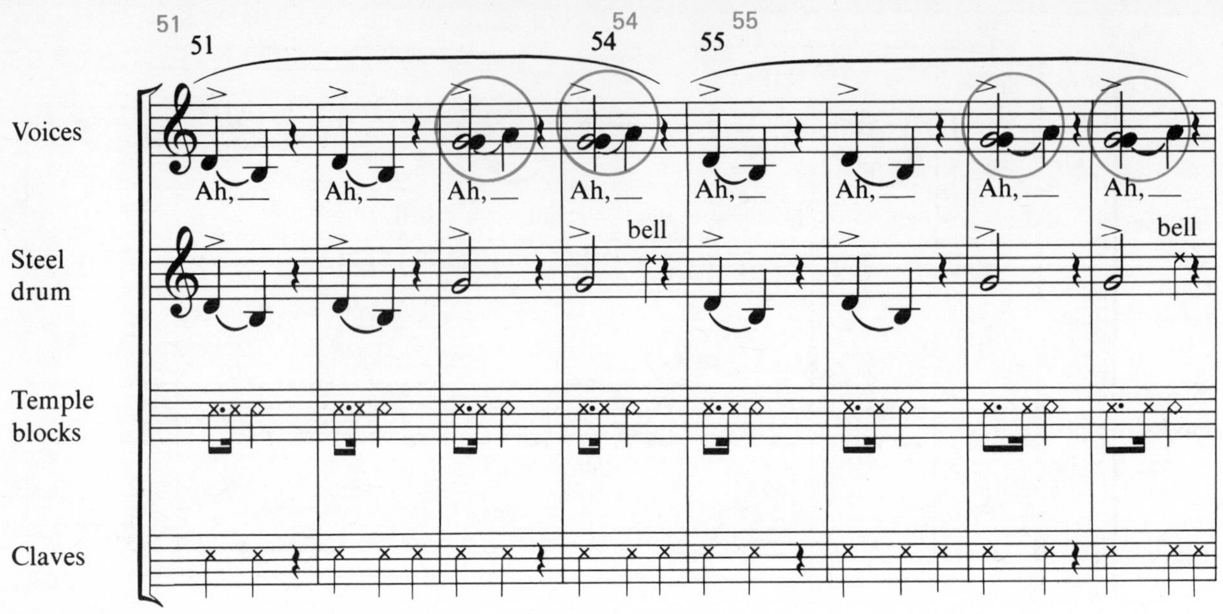

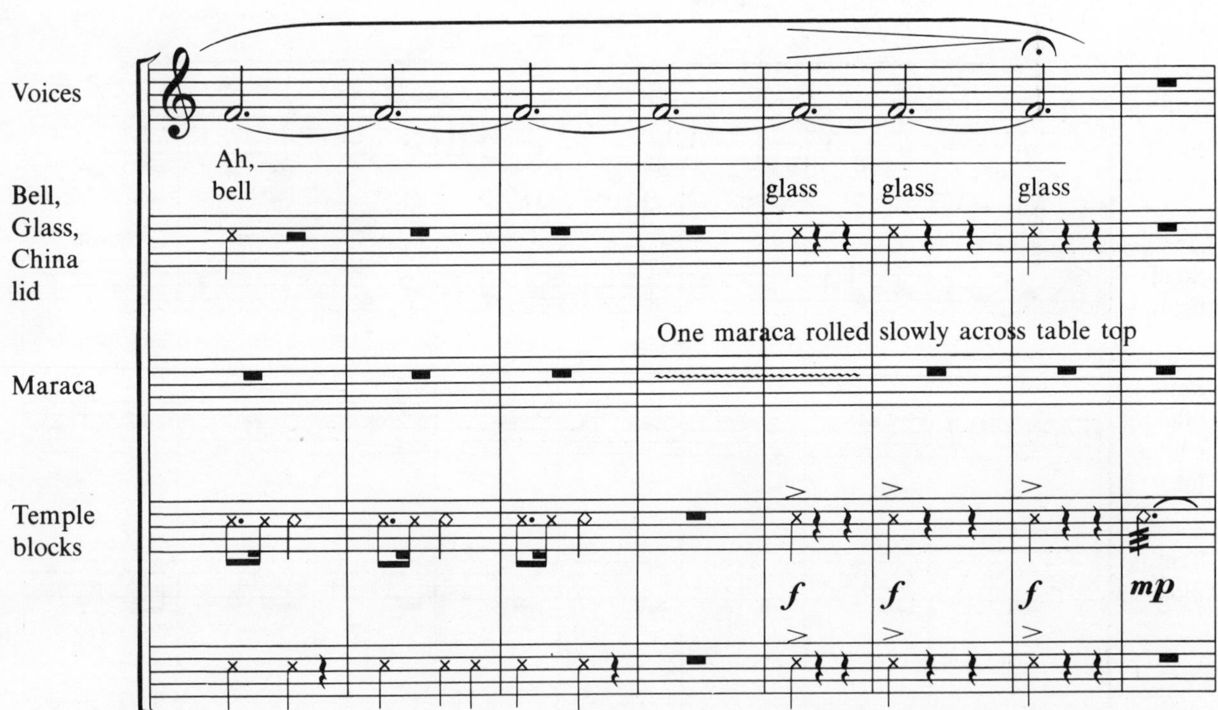

3. As preparation for the various rhythm patterns in the composition, have the class clap the individual parts followed by small groups clapping the five basic parts.
4. Use rhythm instruments to play the various parts or improvise percussion sounds of 'non-traditional' sound sources. Select one student to conduct the composition. Tape and evaluate the performance.
5. Timbre is an exceedingly important element of "Sunrise At Stonehenge." Have students discuss their perceptions of the timbre-effects resulting from the creative use of sound and silence of altered sound, and of common household objects whose sounds have been electronically altered.

STONEHENGE The most famous Neolithic monument in western Europe, Stonehenge was built between 1800 and 1400 B.C located near Salisbury, England. The stones form a circle of approximately 100 feet in diameter. This prehistoric creation of ancient man was primarily used for sun worshipers. Even today the arrangement of the giant stones forms a seasonal calendar.

Stonehenge, England
Courtesy of British Tourist Authority

LISTENING FOR SOUND, BEAT, AND FEELING

LISTENING . . .

Record 7, Side A, Band 1 (Excerpt)
Variation IV
John Cage

John Cage is one of the most experimental composers of our time. He first attracted attention with his composition for "prepared piano." One of his pieces consists entirely of four minutes and thirty-three seconds of silence! In other works Cage wires himself for sound and proceeds to make all sorts of noises, such as drinking water, slicing vegetables, and tinkling silverware.

Cage's reasons for doing this are based on his belief that the listener must supply the "sense" which exists in sound. *Variation IV* begins with an introduction which explains how the composition is "made." The listener must simply make whatever he can of what he hears and respond in ways suggested by the music.

Concepts: *Instruments* (Timbres)

Is each instrumental part independent, or dependent on other parts?
How many instruments can you identify?
What unusual sounds do you detect?

Movement

Do you feel a steady or flexible beat?
What changes of tempo do you hear?

Feeling

How do ＜ and ＞ contribute to feeling?
What other expressive characteristics do you hear?

Several characteristics may be combined as *texture:*
- Number of instruments
- Number and arrangement of sound lines and patterns
- Timbre of instruments
- The use of sound and movement patterns

What would a "thick" texture be?
A "thin" texture?
Do you hear both in this work, or is *one* of these textures prominent?

LISTENING . . . Record 7, Side A, Band 2

Ball of Confusion
Norman Whitfield and Barrett Strong

This composition uses the style of "fire and brimstone" preaching frequently heard in revival meetings. The preacher's message, which builds up to a fever-pitch presentation is concerned with the state of affairs in the world today. Listen carefully. Concentrate on hearing what is happening when the number is called.

Throughout the text there are listening examples with call charts. The numbers are called out to direct attention toward specific events in the music.

Call Number	Characteristics in Music
1	Voice alerts players: "*1 2; 1 2 3 4.*"
2	String bass (important rhythmic pattern).
3	Fuzzbox guitar; echo effects produced electronically.
4	Voice; organ enters.
5	Brass enters; voice and other tone colors < String bass figure (2) background—voice preaches message. . . .
6	All voices on "More Confusion;" <> ; *ff*
7	String bass figure (2) with percussion background.
8	Preaching text "Evolution, Revolution . . ."
9	Band plays; voices enter.
10	Ascending, thick *ff* chords; harmonica material.
11	Loud voice screams . . . ; preaches on . . . ; All voices enter: "More Confusion!" Voices; trumpet fanfare.
12	Preacher: "Fear in the air . . . "; Rhythm pattern (2) continues in percussion; low voice; "And the band played on."
13	Band plays.
14	Preacher: "Eve of destruction . . . end the war"; trumpet fanfare; low voice: "And the band played on."
15	Band plays: harmonica material in (10); electronic effects added.
16	Preacher, voices: "More Confusion." Preacher-audience interaction on "let me hear, let me hear, etc."

Key: G
Starting Tone: B (3-mi)

Meter: 4 (quarter note)
Form: AABA

Record 1, Side A, Band 7

ODE TO JOY

Words by Henry van Dyke
Music by Ludwig van Beethoven

Beethoven used the text of Friederich von Schiller's "Ode to Joy" for his Ninth Symphony. Compare the **sound, beat,** and **feeling** of this composition with Virginia Hagemann's "Sunrise at Stonehenge" and the folk song, "Die Gedanken Sind Frei."

Allegro moderato
Mor - tals, join the hap - py cho - rus Which the morn - ing stars be - gan;
Fa - ther love is reign - ing o'er us, Broth - er love binds man to man.
Ev - er sing - ing, march we — on - ward, Vic - tors — in the midst of strife,
Joy - ful mu - sic leads us sun - ward In the tri - umph song of life.

The Council of Europe has adopted Beethoven's "Ode to Joy" as the anthem of Western Europe. The council recommended that the seventeen member countries play the Beethoven work at all special occasions involving the Western European nations.

Javier Cabada, *Portrait of Beethoven*

Key: C
Starting Tone: C (1-do)

Meter: 4 / 𝅗𝅥

Form: AB

Record 1, Side B, Band 1

A MIGHTY FORTRESS IS OUR GOD

Words by Martin Luther
Translated by Frederick Henry Hedge
Melody by Martin Luther

The **sound, beat,** and **feeling** of a past age are reflected in this famous hymn. How does it resemble "Ode to Joy"? How is it different?

A might-y for-tress is_our God, A bul-wark nev-er fail - ing; Our help-er he_a-
mid_the flood Of mor-tal ills pre-vail - ing. For still our an-cient foe Doth seek to work us woe;
His craft and pow'r are great; And, arm'd with cru-el hate, On earth is not his e - qual.

Record 7, Side A, Band 3 (Bach)
Record 7, Side A, Band 4 (Stravinsky)

LISTENING . . .

Chorale, L'Histoire du Soldat
Igor Stravinsky
Chorale No. 8, Cantata No. 80
Johann Sebastian Bach

A *chorale* is a German hymn tune. Chorales are often used as subjects of larger compositions. After singing "A Mighty Fortress," compare it with the two listening selections.

Key: B Minor
Starting Tone: C# (voices) (7-ti)

Meter: $\frac{4}{♩}$
Form: AABA

Record 1, Side B, Band 2

SUMMER SONG

This song is an example of "Cool Jazz," c. 1949-55. The lush, thick harmonies consist of tones that clash and resolve to create a "jazz sound."

Words and Music by Dave Brubeck

Listen to the recording of Dave Brubeck's "Summer Song." Compare the **sound, beat,** and **feeling** of this composition with "Die Gedanken Sind Frei." How are they similar? How are they different?

With lazy motion
mf
legato
Noth - ing else ___ is like a sum-mer day;
I'm ___ for sum - mer! That's my time of year;
When ___ it's gone, ___ the mem - o - ries will stay.
Win - ter shad - ows fade and dis - ap - pear.
Life ___ so free ___ and
When ___ it's warm ___ and

Dave Brubeck did much to bring about innovations unique to "Cool Jazz." His use of polyrhythms, polymeters, syncopation, 9th chords, are particularly important.

1.
eas - y! Friend-ly clouds are float-ing high in a la - zy sum - mer sky.
peace-ful, When the
2.
rit.
after D. S. to Coda
a tempo
days are grow - ing long, I can sing my sum - mer song.
after D. S. to Coda
rit.
mf
a tempo
fish-in'
I hear laugh - ter from the swim-min' hole: Kids out fish - in'

Have the class listen to the recording. Compare the interpretation on the recording with the tempo and dynamic markings in the music.

Key: D
Starting Tone: A (5-sol)

Meter: 4 / 𝅗𝅥

Record 1, Side B, Band 3

MY BROTHER AMERICAN

Words by Verna Arvey
Music by William Grant Still

This music was written especially for this book by William Grant Still.

William Grant Still is one of the U.S.'s leading Black composers. Verna Arvey (Mrs. William Grant Still), an author, journalist, and concert pianist, wrote texts for many of her husband's compositions.

Moderately
mf
mp
My broth - er A - mer - i - can, I take your hand.
You walk be - side me
through this great land.
It mat-ters not what

The last two measures may be played for an introduction.

ritard f

col - or — or creed, You fit in - to my life: You an - swer my need. —

mf

ritard

a tempo

mf

ritard gradually to the end

My broth - er A - mer - i - can, — I take your

mp

ritard gradually to the end

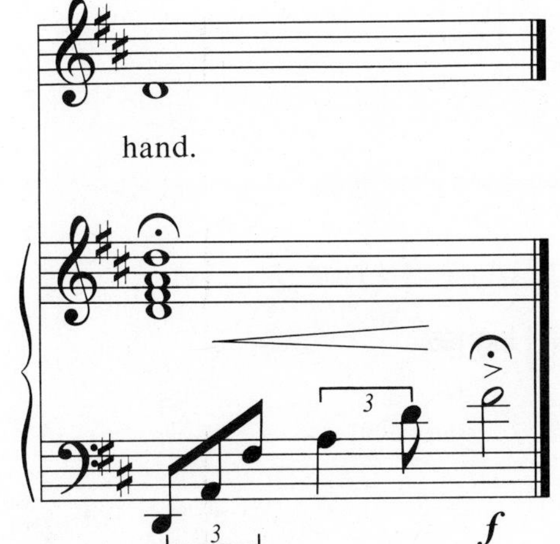

Suggest rhythm accompaniments for this song.

Listen to the sound of the piano accompaniment. Is it thick or thin? Does the melody reflect the feeling of the text? How?

RELATED ACTIVITIES 1. Encourage students to do research on William Grant Still and on other black musicians and their music (classical, folk, blues, soul, etc.) 2. Start a bulletin-board display of pictures, magazine and newspaper clippings, etc. reflecting black musicians and their music. A similar display may be made on black artists and their art.

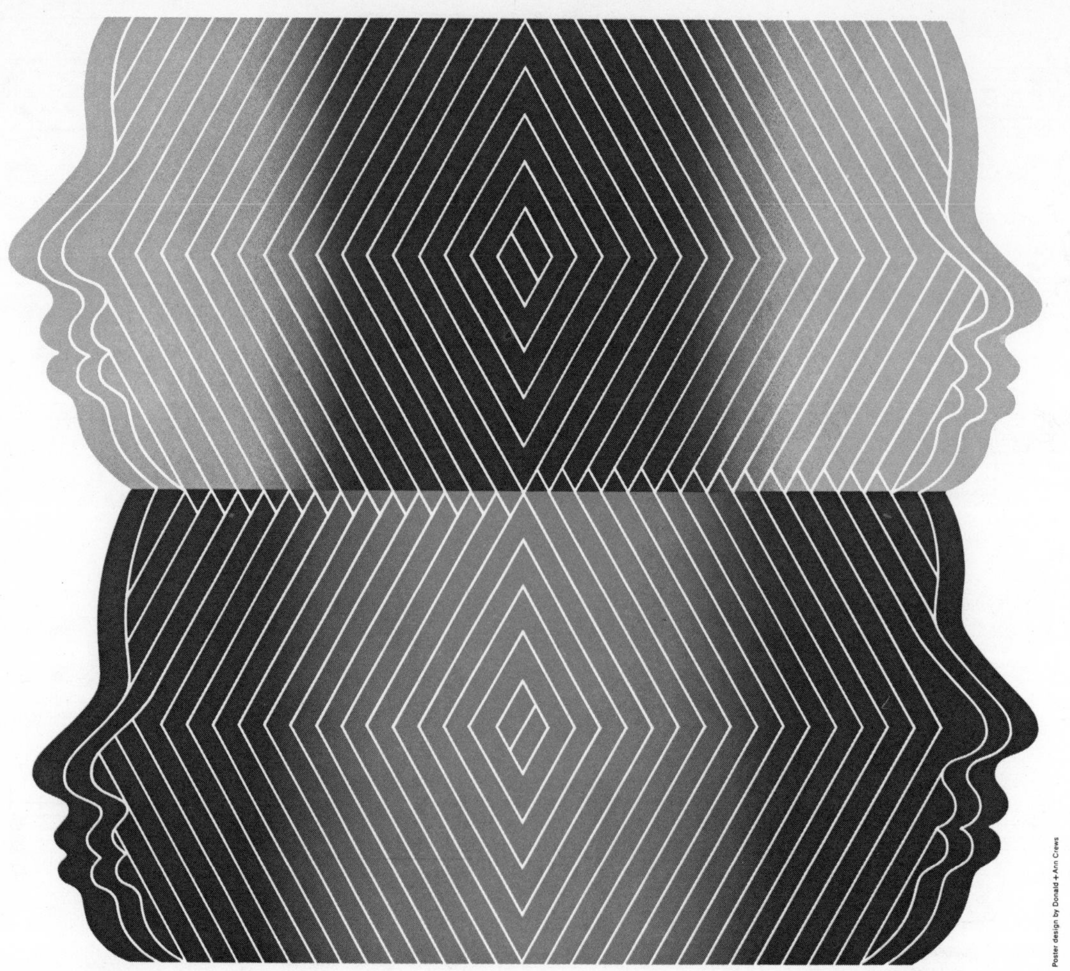
Poster design by Donald + Ann Crews

Color

Wear it
Like a banner
For the proud-
Not like a shroud.

Wear it
Like a song
Soaring high-
Not moan or cry.

Langston Hughes

ABOUT THE POET Langston Hughes (1902-1967) was a leading Black American poet and writer. He was born in Joplin, Mo. and attended college at Columbia University in New York City. His works reflect the changes in attitudes on race in the 20th century – from the despair of the blacks in The Weary Blues (1926) to the demands for social justice in his The Panther and the Lash (1967).

LISTENING . . .

At a Certain Church
Arr. by John Work
Record 7, Side A, Band 5

The hymn "I am Bound for the Promised Land" was used as the main theme of this composition. The singing tone of the piano expresses the vocal quality of the melodic line.

Call Number

1 Dissonant (clashing) chords—clanging church bell effect.

2 Piano interrupts—echo effect, clanging continues; fast notes.

3 Chords only; piano echo effect re-enters, slowing (*rit.*) to end.

4 Melody: *First Presentation:* middle register, entire verse, smooth (*legato*) sound.

5 Melody: *Second Presentation:* softer, higher register, variation of first presentation, legato, much slowing and speeding (*rubato*).

6 Melody: *Third Presentation:* summing up–similar to presentation 1; brings material from (1). Much *rubato,* changing registers, strong closing.

Can you "feel" the rubato (stretched sounds) and accents?

Try conducting various call numbers. What happens? Is it difficult to maintain a strict beat and still keep in time with the performer?

STUDENT INVOLVEMENT 1. Read poems at varying speeds and dynamic levels. 2. Identify various phrase lengths and cadences (strong and weak). 3. Discuss ways of securing tone color and rhythmic variety through the use of the speaking voice.

SOUND, BEAT AND FEELING IN WORDS AND DESIGN

Sound, beat, and **feeling** are found in life, in music, in art. Discover how these important elements are captured in the following poems.

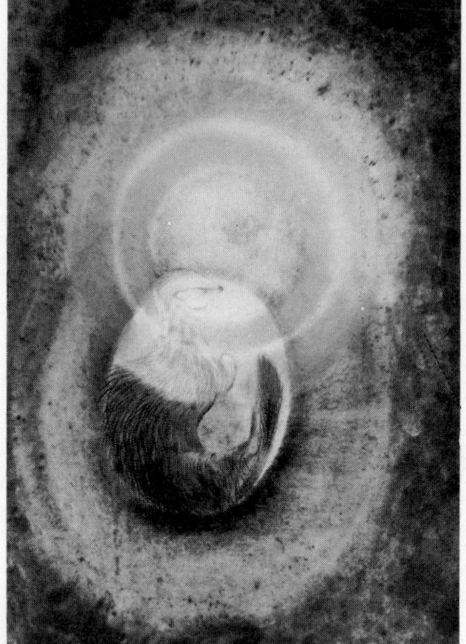

Kubla Khan

In Xanadu did Kubla Khan
A stately pleasure-dome decree:
Where Alph, the sacred river, ran
Through caverns measureless to man
Down to a sunless sea.
So twice five miles of fertile ground
With walls and towers were girdled round:
And there were gardens bright with sinuous rills,
Where blossomed many an incense-bearing tree;
And here were forests ancient as the hills,
Enfolding sunny spots of greenery. . .

Samuel Taylor Coleridge

English Poet (1772-1834)

Sun

When children see you in the summer,
Sun–
they like you.
They swim, laugh and play,
Sun–
under your warmth.
But in winter,
sun–
they lose their affection for you.
You melt their snow
sun–
they dislike you.
But why
sun–
must I always have winter?

M.B., Age 16

The Jumblies

They went to sea in a sieve, they did;
In a sieve they went to sea;
In spite of all their friends could say,
On a winter's morn, on a stormy day,
In a sieve they went to sea.
And when the sieve turned round and round,
And every one cried, "You'll all be drowned!"
They called aloud, "Our sieve ain't big;
But we don't care a button; we don't care a fig:
In a sieve we'll go to sea!"
Far and few, far and few,
Are the lands where the Jumblies live:
Their heads are green, and their hands are blue;
And they went to sea in a sieve. . .

Edward Lear

English painter and poet (1812-1888)

Morris Graves: *Hibernation* p. 26, *The Crow* p. 27 (top), *Sea, Fish, and Constellation* p. 27 (bottom)

Tone color is as essential to speech as it is to music. Each requires sound.

The Raven

Once upon a midnight dreary, while I pondered, weak and weary,
Over many a quaint and curious volume of forgotten lore,
While I nodded, nearly napping, suddenly there came a tapping,
As of some one gently rapping, rapping at my chamber door.
"'Tis some visitor," I muttered, "tapping at my chamber door—
Only this and nothing more."

Open here I flung the shutter, when, with many a flirt and flutter,
In there stepped a stately raven of the saintly days of yore;
Not the least obeisance made he; not a minute stopped or stayed he;
But, with mien of lord or lady, perched above my chamber door—
Perched upon a bust of Pallas just above my chamber door—
Perched, and sat, and nothing more.

Then this ebony bird beguiling my sad fancy into smiling,
By the grave and stern decorum of the countenance it wore,
"Though thy crest be shorn and shaven, thou," I said, "art sure no craven,
Ghastly grim and ancient raven wandering from the Nightly shore—
Tell me what thy lordly name is on the Night's Plutonian shore!"
Quoth the raven, "Nevermore."

Edgar Allan Poe

American poet and storywriter. (1809-1849)

ABOUT THE ARTIST Morris Graves (1910) was born in Oregon. His style and iconography were greatly influenced by Oriental religions and philosophy. A resident in Seattle, Washington, Graves represents a leading school of modern American art.

Have the students compare the poems of Lear and Poe with the ghetto poem, "Sun."

Seattle Art Museum

DREAMS AND FANTASIES

Sound, beat, and **feeling** can invade a world of dreams as well as the real world.

Enter de Chirico's deserted square. Float with Chagall's lovers on a birthday in Russia long ago. Track the gypsy's missing footprints in Rousseau's night vision. What kind of time do Dali's melting watches keep?

ABOUT THE ARTIST Marc Chagall (b. 1889) was born in Russia. In 1910 he went to Paris to study and to paint. The recurrent theme in many of his works is based on three subjects – birth, love, and death. His murals, stage designs, paintings, and graphics are highly imaginative. Fantasy, mystery, and romance characterize many of his works.

Marc Chagall, *The Birthday*—Museum of Modern Art, New York

ABOUT THE ARTIST Salvador Dali (b. 1904) is noted for his paintings, films, book illustrations, stage designs, and original jewelry. His world is one of dreams.

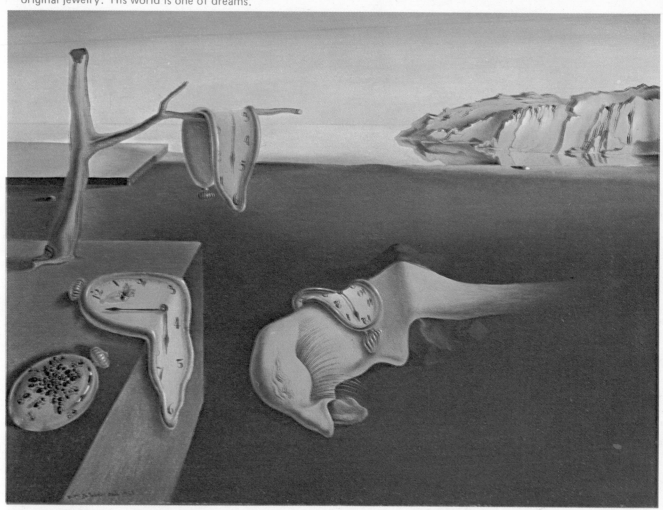

Salvador Dali, *The Persistence of Memory*—Museum of Modern Art, New York (top), Giorgio de Chirico, *The Mystery and Melancholy of a Street* (bottom left), Henri Rousseau, *The Sleeping Gypsy*—Museum of Modern Art, New York (bottom right)

ABOUT THE ARTIST Giorgio de Chirico (1888–1978) was called the father of surrealist painting.

ABOUT THE ARTIST Henri Rousseau (1844–1910) was a self-taught painter, known for his "primitive, childlike" style.

Today's music is a combination of many types of sound—soul, jazz, spirituals, blues, gospel, folk, country, and rock. For the most part, these all have one thing in common—the "BIG BEAT."

These pages visually introduce some of the headliners of pop music. Ask students to bring in recordings of their favorites. Whoever the current personalities may be, it is certain that the trend in pop sound will change again in the near future. As of this writing, "disco" is in vogue.

The Rolling Stones
Courtesy of CBS

Miles Davis

Chambers Brothers

Johnny Winter

UNIT 2

SEE GUIDE FOR UNIT LEARNING OBJECTIVES

Music and You

This unit is designed to help students:

1. Recognize different kinds of music they can enjoy.

2. Explore new sound sources and techniques used by contemporary composers.

3. Express their ideas and feelings in music.

4. Identify how composers express ideas in music.

5. Interpret composers' works.

6. Perceive how today's artists use elements of art in unique, expressive ways.

What does the word music mean to you? A folk song? Opera? Rock? Symphony? African drums? Country and Western? Hit Parade? Sitar? Bach, Beethoven, and Brahms? Electronic music? Music is all of this—and more!

People have used music to communicate and to express ideas for thousands of years. Music is a language—one which you can enjoy, study, and share with your friends. Most important, music is a personal language which can express your innermost thoughts, feelings, and emotions. Performing and listening to music are personal activities that can create pleasure and understanding of one of man's major languages.

In this unit you will have an opportunity to discuss your ideas about music, to perform, and to listen to different kinds of music. Composers, performers, and listeners are part of the music-making process—you will investigate their roles.

Encourage the class to bring recordings, articles, and music of their favorite musical personalities.

THE COMPOSER

The composer selects, combines, and organizes the elements of sound to create music. The composer must be an imaginative, technically competent, and resourceful person to write compositions of genuine artistic merit. Intensive study and fine musicianship are necessary for a composer to create original works in forms such as operas, symphonies, chamber music, or concertos.

A composer's work may depict feelings or emotions, tell a story or describe an event, or be based on purely musical ideas. The composer's handling of rhythm, melody, tone color, and texture determines whether or not the work has an appeal to the listener.

Today, many composers are experimenting with new sound sources—electronic, environmental, non-tonal sounds to make their music keep in step with the spirit of this technological age. Traditional instruments are used in new and exciting ways. Music of other cultures affords new sounds for our own musical development. Computers and tape recorders have opened limitless worlds of sound. (The invention of magnetic tape in the 1930's and the development of electronic synthesizers and computers in the 1950's have afforded new theoretical bases for music — a whole new "sound-scape.")

What Do You Think?

Obviously, yes.

- Many kinds of music are mentioned in the opening paragraph of this unit. Are all these kinds of music composed?
- How competent do you think a composer must be in order to compose the various types of music mentioned in the opening paragraph?
- What does the word improvisation mean to you? What types of music require the performer to improvise? Would you call improvisation a type of composition? Why?

Jazz and some rock require improvisation. Improvisation is a type of free and spontaneous composition.

- Many new sound sources have been labeled "noise" by some traditional musicians. One definition is ". . . the planned organization of sounds and silences by someone for some expressive purpose." Do you accept this definition? Why? Locate other definitions of music for comparison.
- Do you think the time or age in which a composer lives affects the sound and style of his or her music? How? With the exception of electrical and industrial sounds, and improvement in musical instruments, composers have had virtually the same musical sounds to work with down through the years. Why do you think composers' works sound so different, even though they have used the same basic raw materials?

From the recordings, play excerpts from the Gregorian chant (p. 70), the Vivaldi Concerto (p. 210), the Beethoven Symphony (p. 67), and Brubeck's "Strange Meadowlark" (p. 70). Let the students discuss this last question and draw their own conclusions.

MAKING YOUR OWN MUSIC

PRELUDE

Sit quietly for two minutes with your eyes closed and **listen.** Make a list of all the sounds you heard. Repeat a second time. Again list the sounds you heard. For each of the sounds you heard, identify them by a mark or symbol that represents the **sound,** not the item that made the sound, for example: footsteps = — — — — ; school bell = **0 0 0 0 ;** or a clock = / / / / . This type of devised notation takes imagination. However, you will find that it will be of assistance in notating compositional sounds later on. Much contemporary music uses imaginative notation. See an example on page 198.

bjectives:
. Learn to erceive sounds in ne environment.
. Record the ound by devising symbol for it.
. Lead to the ecessity of otation in nusic, a storage nd retrieval ystem for sound others are to erform a omposer's work.

SOUND EXPLORATION I

Select a snare drum, tympani, gong, set of cymbals, or bells. Explore each instrument one at a time. Discover the kinds of sounds you can make by striking each instrument differently and with varying force. Ask some of the students in your classroom to describe the quality of each sound—harsh, soft, bright, piercing, high, etc. Learn to control the sounds. Build a repertoire of these sounds and make a short composition on each instrument.

Example: Secure a large cymbal, preferably suspended on a stand. Strike it in varying degrees of volume with your fingers, soft mallets, wire brushes, or wood, metal or rubber sticks, or draw upward on the edge of the cymbal with a violin or cello bow. Using the sounds you like, combine them into a short composition using various tempos, dynamic levels, silence, tension, etc. Record and evaluate your composition.

Example: Create a mood background for the *haiku* by Basho on page 189. Do not try to imitate the meanings of the words; rather, try to capture the feeling or mood with an instrumental introduction and coda. Select readers for the *haiku,* perform the composition, and evaluate. This project may be extended by using other instruments in a similar fashion, composing background music for poems in the text or original poetry.

Procedure:
After experimenting as suggested, draw out the concepts stated below by questioning. Each concept may be illustrated by listening to a work if desired.

"How do we make a composition?" Let students make suggestions and experiments. Songs and works in the text may be examined to identify how composers use elements of sound and develop forms. Lead to the use of motives, phrases, repeated patterns, varying patterns, sequences, and ostinatos.

SOUND EXPLORATION II

After the excitement of the initial exploration of sounds, consider them seriously as sound sources for experimental composition. To gain proficiency, the class should be divided into four groups—for example, G-1—clap hands, G-2—snap fingers, G-3—tap feet, and G-4—slap thighs. Perform the rhythms of several well-known rounds using the selected sounds. Use different tempos, varying dynamic levels, and varying articulation. This project may be extended by including room sounds and vocal sounds.

oncepts:
1. Sound and silence are basic materials of music.
2. Sound possesses intrinsic qualities: PITCH — highness or lowness; DURATION — longness or shortness; INTENSITY — loudness or softness; and TIMBRE — unique color or sound.
3. The way a sound is produced, the speed, and volume of sounds affect the mood or expressiveness of a composition.
4. The plan, shape, or design of a work must be developed by a composer.

RANDU'S HOLIDAY

Gordon M. Uchenick

Each performer is encouraged to treat his sound very freely in an improvised style.

At a given signal, all performers move to the Number 2 block, improvising freely on the specific sound indicated by numerals 1-8 and following the directions given.

	1	2	3	4	5	6	7	8	9	10
1	8	8	5	1	6	3	5	8	8	5
2	7	3	2	2	1	1	7	3	1	4
3	7	7	5	2	5	1	2	8	4	1
4	3	6	1	1	3	2	2	7	7	4
5	7	8	8	7	1	7	5	1	1	5
6	7	3	7	7	1	1	3	3	4	3
7	5	4	5	5	5	1	5	2	3	4
8	8	8	8	5	6	5	1	6	2	5
9	1	5	2	5	8	1	3	5	2	5
10	8	2	4	6	2	2	2	6	2	6
11	7	8	2	6	7	8	6	5	6	6
12	7	8	7	1	7	4	2	5	7	1
13	2	7	3	6	8	2	2	7	5	2
14	7	5	7	5	1	3	8	6	4	7

This mathematical "model" provides the opportunity for students to experience a kind of improvised chance music. The ten squares indicated in red across the top of the model are ten blocks of sound controlled by the conductor. The conductor determines the time duration, the tempo, and the dynamics for the performance. The fourteen squares indicated in green down the lefthand side represent the performers.

Upon the signal of the conductor, the improvised piece starts. In the 10 seconds of the first block, performer No. 1 is responsible for improvising Sound 8 – clap hands in 4/4 meter in a crisp moderate tempo. Performer No. 2 is responsible for improvising Sound 7 – howling wind sound high pitch in cupped hands, etc.

This mathematical "model" was written in 15 seconds on a computer—the Randu Random Number Generator. "Randu" can issue 2,400,000 numbers before repeating a single line.

The model can be translated into sound with one conductor and fourteen performers. The conductor's guide, in red, is across the top of the model; each "time block" may be performed for 10 seconds or longer, and loudly or softly as the conductor indicates. Each performer, indicated in green, performs the sounds indicated by the number sequence in his horizontal blocks. Eight different sounds are required as basic musical materials.

RELATED ACTIVITIES 1. Discuss the role of the composer and the composer's relationship to "Systems." 2. Lead the class in a discussion on ways in which students might make their own models of random sounds.

PERFORMANCE SUGGESTIONS FOR "RANDU'S HOLIDAY."

These rhythm and vocal sounds may be used:

1. Silence
2. Sing "boom" at a low pitch. Repeat regularly.
3. Whispers
4. Snap fingers briskly in a habanera rhythm (♩. ♪ ♫)
5. Clacking tongue
6. Imitate a musical instrument as you play a favorite tune
7. Howling wind sound—high pitch in cupped hands
8. Clap hands in $\frac{4}{4}$ meter in a crisp moderate tempo

Experiment with other sounds and dynamics after recording "Randu's Holiday" to make the composition more effective.

Change the title and select percussion, vocal, or room sounds for your composition.

WHAT DO YOU THINK?

- Choose several compositions you like. What are the factors which make these compositions appealing to you? In later discussions, expect students to use musical terms in their evaluations and judgments.
- Think of the types of music you know—rock, opera, soul, etc., and list the kinds of composition on the chalkboard. Make three columns with the headings of **Like, Dislike,** and **Don't Know.** Make a check mark for each type of music listed and justify your choice.
- How would you define a folk song? Name your favorites. Are all folk songs written by known composers? No. The origins of many folk songs are unknown.

When comparing one or more compositions by listening, duplicate a chart for students' use with fairly large spaces in which they may write descriptive words or comments about the element(s) they hear or which are the focus of the comparative study.

This device may also be used to evaluate the limitations or depth of students' perceptions of music which is a part of the listening program.

ON AND OFF BROADWAY

The music of the American theater is built on a rich heritage—minstrel shows, variety shows, the operetta, and the Broadway musical. Such composers as Victor Herbert, Jerome Kern, Richard Rodgers, George Gershwin, and Cole Porter developed the Broadway musical into an important art form of the twentieth century.

Listen to three examples from famous Broadway musicals. How has each composer created a specific mood, feeling, or emotion in his work?

West Side Story

LISTENING . . .

Ol Man River (Show Boat)
Jerome Kern

Oh, What a Beautiful Mornin' (Oklahoma!)
Richard Rodgers

Tonight (West Side Story)
Leonard Bernstein

Scene from *Fiddler on the Roof*
starring Harry Goz
Courtesy of UPI

Scene from the original cast of *Oklahoma*
Courtesy of UPI

Key: C
Starting Tone: G (5-sol)

Meter: $\overset{2}{\text{𝅗𝅥}}$

Record 1, Side B, Band 5

FIDDLER ON THE ROOF

Words by Sheldon Harnick
Music by Jerry Bock

STUDENT INVOLVEMENT Sing the song (half the class sings while the other half listens) to permit one section of the class to chart the design of the song.

Piano
mf
Chorus
C
D♭
1. A - way a - bove my head I see the strang - est
2. (An) un - ex - pect - ed breeze could blow him to the

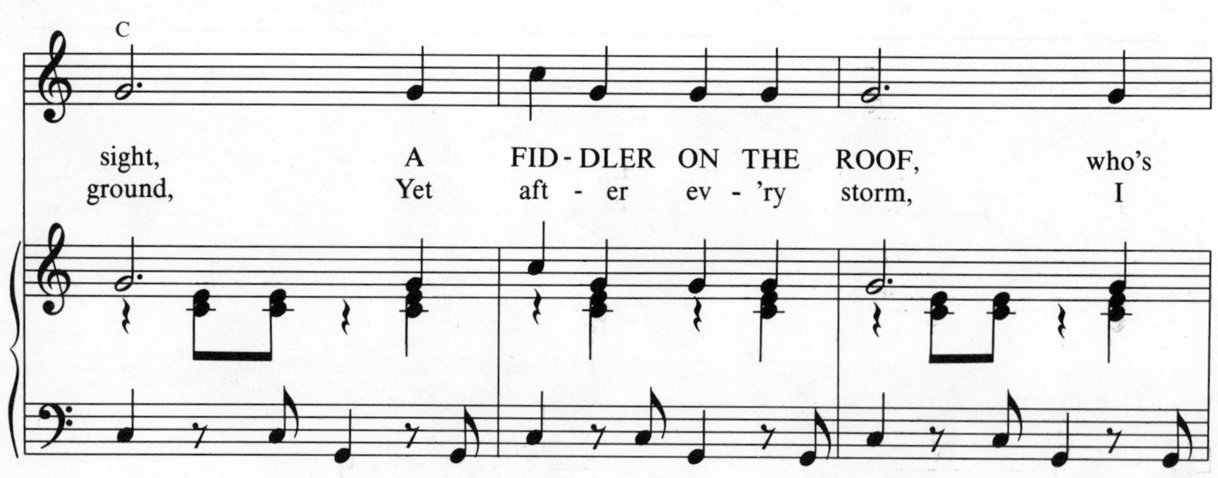
C
sight, A FID - DLER ON THE ROOF, who's
ground, Yet aft - er ev - 'ry storm, I

D♭
E♭
D♭
C
up there day and night; He fid - dles when it
see he's still a - round; What - ev - er each day
rains, He fid - dles when it snows, I've
brings This odd out - land - ish man; He
nev - er seen him rest, Yet on and on he
plays his sim - ple tune, As sweet - ly as he

goes.
can.
What does it mean, this FID-DLER ON THE ROOF, Who
D♭
C
fid-dles ev-'ry night and fid-dles ev-'ry noon? Why should he pick so
D♭
1. C
cu-ri-ous a place to plays his lit-tle fid-dler's tune? 2. An

2.
C
C
tune? A FID - DLER ON THE ROOF, A
D♭
C
most un - like - ly sight, It might not mean a
(Opt.)
D♭
E♭
D♭
C
thing, But then a - gain it might!

Key: Em
Starting Tone: E (6-la)
Meter: 4 ♩

Record 1, Side B, Band 6

ELEANOR RIGBY

Words and Music by John Lennon and Paul McCartney
Arranged by A.B.C.

the lonely people!
the lonely people!
the lonely people!
Unison
10
1. Eleanor Rigby, picks up the rice in the church where a wedding has been, lives in a dream
2. Father McKenzie, writing the words of a sermon that no one will hear no one comes near.
3. Eleanor Rigby, died in the church and was buried along with her name, nobody came.

15
Waits at the win - dow, wear-ing the face_ that she keeps_
Look at him work - ing, darn-ing his socks_ in the night_
Fa - ther Mc - Ken - zie, wip -ing the dirt_ from his hands_
_ in a jar_ by the door,_ who is it for?_
_ when there's no - bod - y there,_ what does he care?_
_ as he walks_ from the grave,_ no one was saved._
20
All the lone - ly peo - ple, where do_ they all_ come from?_

Soprano I
25
To Coda
All the lone - ly peo - ple, where do they all be- long?
Soprano II
All the lone - ly peo - ple, where do they all be- long?
Alto
All the lone - ly peo - ple, where do they all be- long?
25
1
2
D. C. al Coda
Coda

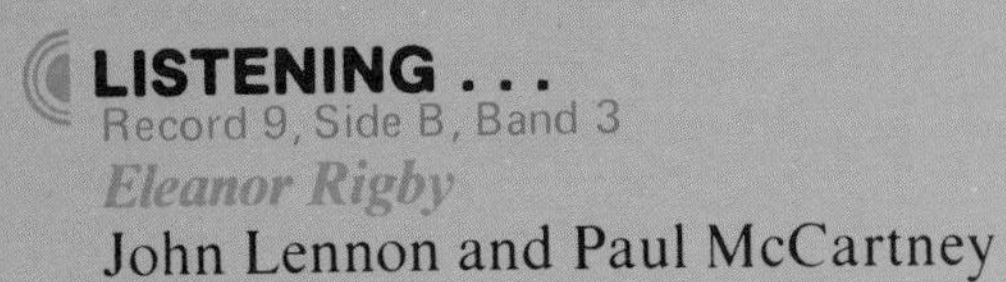

Record 9, Side B, Band 3

Eleanor Rigby

John Lennon and Paul McCartney

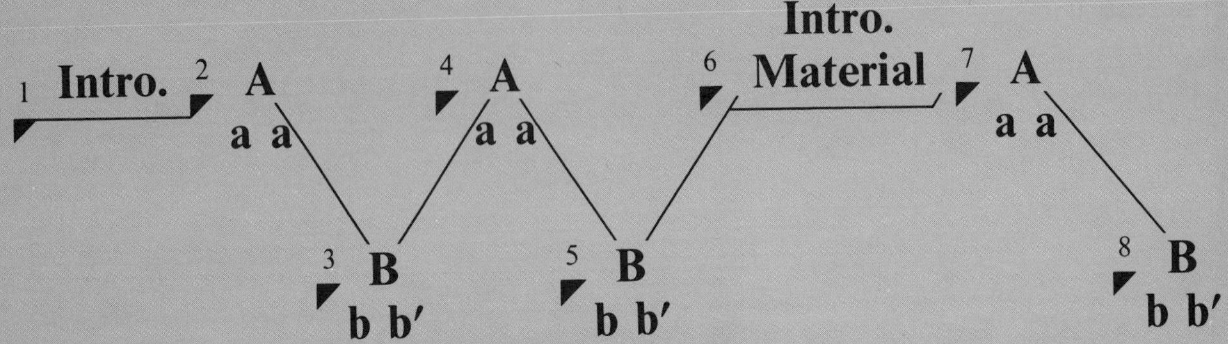

LEGEND:

1. **Intro. material:** (presented twice) Ah, look at all the lonely people
2. **Section A:** Eleanor Rigby . . . .
3. **Section B:** (presented twice) All the lonely people, where do they all come from . . . :||
4. **Section A:** (Repetition of (2) Father Mckenzie . . . . n
5. **Section B** Repetition of (3)
6. **Return of Intro. material** (1)
7. **Return of material from** (2) & (4) Now **first** "a" re: Eleanor Rigby; **Second** "a" re: Father Mckenzie
8. **Return of (3) & (5)—B material.**

Compare this version of "Eleanor Rigby" with those by Wes Montomery and Ray Charles.

John Lennon
Courtesy of CBS

Paul McCartney
Courtesy of CBS

Key: A
Starting Tone: E (5-sol)

Meter: 2 (quarter note)
Form: A A' B

Record 2, Side A, Band 1

NO OTHER MOON

Music by Catullo da Paixao Cearense
English Text by Georgina Castiglione

This song was written by Catullo Cearense, a popular composer in Brazil.

Help the students discover that it is possible to take a musical theme and through various alterations (melodic, rhythmic, metric, etc.) create an entire, self-contained melody.

1. Oh, how I'm lone - some for the moon - light in the
2. The moon - light speeds a - round the edg - es of the

still - ness of the hills, the moun - tain moon-light that I knew so long a -
hills, un - til it fills the night with sil - ver, light - ing all the lone - ly

go. The cit - y moon, so dark and lone - ly, leaves me
glen! Now folks are strum - ming their gui - tars and soft - ly

cold and brings me on - ly lone - some yearn - ings for the moon I used to know
hum-ming till the mu - sic blends with moon-light, and we're hap - py once a - gain

me; No oth - er moon can ev - er be my moon of mem - o - ry.

Rufino Tamayo, *Animals*—Museum of Modern Art, New York

Rufino Tamayo (b. 1899) is one of Mexico's most prolific painters. His subjects often reflect his interest of Aztec and Mayan art.

Moonlight

Then the moon blazed down
Upon the vast desolation of American coasts,
And on the glut and hiss of tides,
On all the surge and foaming slide
Of waters on lone beaches.
The moon blazed down on 18,000 miles of coast,
On the million sucks and scoops and hollows of the shore,
And on the great wink of the sea,
That ate the earth minutely and eternally.

The moon blazed down upon the wilderness,
It fell on sleeping woods,
It dripped through moving leaves,
It swarmed in weaving patterns on the earth,
And it filled the cat's still eye with blazing yellow.
The moon slept over mountains
And lay like silence in the desert,
And it carved shadows of great rocks like time.
The moon was mixed with flowing rivers,
And it was buried in the heart of lakes,
And it trembled on the water like bright fish.
The moon steeped all the earth
In its living and unearthly substance,
It had a thousand visages,
It painted continental space with ghostly light;
And its light was proper to the nature
Of all things it touched:
It came in with the sea,
It flowed with the rivers,
And it was still and living
On clear spaces in the forest
Where no men watched.

And in woodland darkness great birds fluttered to their sleep—
In sleeping woodlands, strange and secret birds,
the teal, the nightjar, and the flying rail
Went to their sleep with flutterings
Dark as hearts of men . . .

1. Have students try different ways to vary the color and mood of this text. Record and evaluate.

Thomas Wolfe,
A Stone, A Leaf, A Door
American author (1900-1938)

2. Create an accompaniment for readers. Use pentatonic (C-D-E-G-A) scale for a resource.

Help the students discover that much of today's music is the result of deliberate alterations caused mechanically and electronically.

When listening to music, you hear the composer's ideas as they are interpreted by the performer. He decides how to bring life to the musical score. Through the performer's sensitivity and imagination the composer's ideas are realized.

Compare several musical works in terms of performance. What portions of the music must be faithful to the composer's wishes? What parts are left to the performers? Why? (use any appropriate recordings)

Bob Dylan (above left), Concert hall (above right), School band (below)

 Initiate a discussion of the social roles of the various musicians on these pages. How do their life-styles differ? What does each contribute to society in his own way?

Band (above), Chinese opera, Taiwan (below, left and right)

Ask students to study this page very carefully. After they are familiar with the various techniques involved, proceed to the student involvement below.

BE A PERFORMER

Using the piano, try to interpret the following score. First study the score carefully to see that you understand all that is asked of you and get a "mental image" of the resultant sounds.

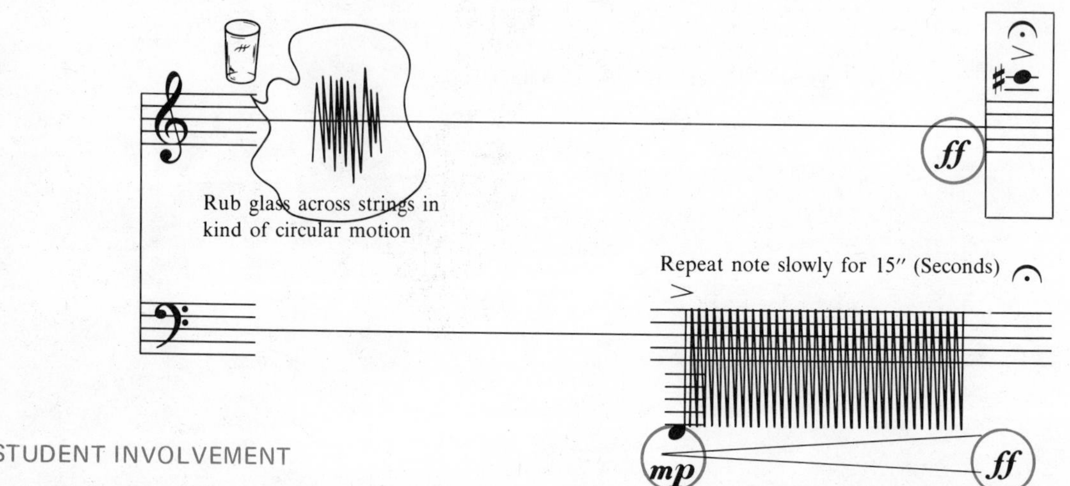

STUDENT INVOLVEMENT

1. Lead the class in discovering the myriad sonorities available on the piano, especially when it is "prepared."
2. Encourage the experimentation in sound on piano and any other instruments available.
3. Have students "score" their experimentations.

Place 12″ ruler (wood) on strings

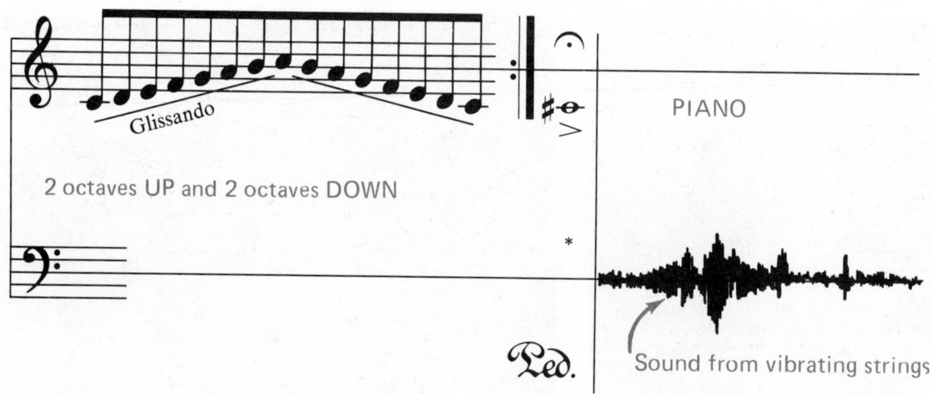

See page 144.

*Diagram represents strings of entire keyboard

1. Depress damper pedal. Hold while you . . .
2. Strum, scratch and pluck lower (thick bass) piano strings vigorously
3. Follow this action with glissandos on upper strings
4. Now gradually (*very slowly*) raise damper pedal
5. Listen for the unusual sonorities, sympathetic vibrations of strings

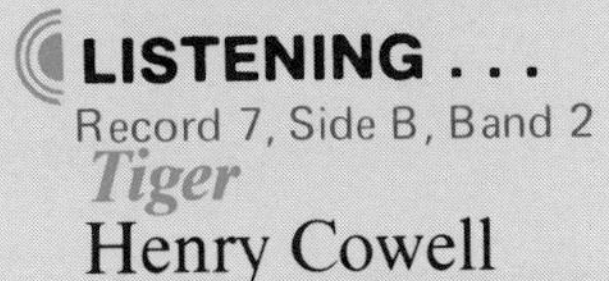

LISTENING . . .

Record 7, Side B, Band 2

Tiger

Henry Cowell

The following is an example of Henry Cowell's use of tone clusters in his compositions.

Allegro feroce

ff

Ped. *

Right Hand

Left Hand

Right

Left

mf *Play with flat of hand*

ff

Play with both forearms together

(*pp*)

Press without sounding

These are "tone clusters" or numerous adjacent tones played simultaneously. An overall impression of a texture results when tone clusters are performed. The sound is something between fixed pitch and noise.

Experiment with the classroom piano by plucking, strumming, or playing in a non-traditional way. Henry Cowell was a pioneer in developing new instrumental resources and performing techniques in America.

Listen to Cowell's composition. Describe the *sound* of this work in your own words.

Record 2, Side A, Band 2

AXIS

George Burt

1	2	3	4	5	6	7	8
5	1	6	2	7	3	8	4
2	4	1	3	6	8	5	7
6	4	7	1	8	2	5	3
3	5	2	8	1	7	4	6
7	5	8	6	3	1	4	2
4	8	3	7	2	6	1	5
8	7	6	5	4	3	2	1

LEARNINGS AND SKILLS The student should be able to: 1. Identify the fact that serial composers of the recent past have shown considerable interest in techniques illustrated in "Axis." 2. Identify the fact that the initial ordering of events in "Axis" exists as the primary musical idea, thus the basic unifying factor.

STUDENT INVOLVEMENT Examine the composition closely. Discuss the ordering of events (example: is 4 always preceded by 3 and followed by 5?) within each row. Are all numbers preceded and followed differently within all rows? How does row 1 compare with row 8? Does this comparison give a hint to why the title is "Axis"?

"Axis" is to be performed by eight groups of either singers or players. The score looks more like a bingo card than a music composition. The ordering of numerical values is critical; each number is to be given a sound. The loudness may correspond to the number itself if desired. In any case, all aspects of the sound—range, duration, attack, decay, color, etc.—are to be decided upon in advance. Any sounds are acceptable as long as they are memorable and have some appeal to the performers. It is crucial that the eight sounds contrast with one another. Once these decisions have been made, the conductor initiates attack points as the chorus produces the sounds. The score is to be read by rows from left to right.

SUGGESTED SOUNDS 1. hiss, 2. tongue click, 3. explosive "bah" sound, 4. whistle decay descending, 5. whistle ascending, 6. rattlesnake, 7. tom-tom beat one - two, 8. tone clusters on G-A-B. Tape results of each performance.

This painting of the original Fisk Jubilee Singers was completed in 1873 by Edmund Havel, Court Painter to Queen Victoria.

Fisk Jubilee Singers

The Fisk Jubilee Singers toured Europe in order to raise money for Fisk University. The tour was successful. Jubilee Hall, on the campus of Fisk, commemorates the original tour.

Leontyne Price, a native of Laurel, Miss. is one of the world's leading operatic stars. She sang the starring role in Samuel Barber's *Cleopatra* at the opening of the new Metropolitan Opera House, Lincoln Center, New York City.

Leontyne Price

Key: F
Starting Tone: F (1-do)
Meter: 4/♩
Record 2, Side A, Band 3

I COULDN'T HEAR NOBODY PRAY

Spiritual arranged by John W. Work

John Work was the director of the Fisk Singers.

The call-response style of singing is a characteristic of African and Afro-American choral music.

From American Negro Songs.
Used by permission.

(free)
On my knees!
In the Jor - dan!
could - n't hear no - bod - y pray
I
With my bur - den!
Cross - ing o - ver!
could - n't hear no - bod - y pray,
I
last time D.C. al fine
And my Sav - iour!
In - to Ca - naan!
O Lord!
O Lord!
could - n't hear no - bod - y pray,
I could - n't hear no - bod - y pray,

Record 7, Side B, Band 3

LISTENING . . .

Pop! Goes the Weasel

Lucien Caillet

Call Number

(1) Introduction: many repetitions of the first two notes of theme (*sol, do*); moves higher and higher in pitch.

(2) *THEME,* almost complete, moving in twos ($\frac{2}{\cdot}$), extended

(3) (*Mini-Call Chart: Tone Color*)

Variation I—Fugue (like a round), "pop" played in various ways.

Various tone colors bring in tune five times:

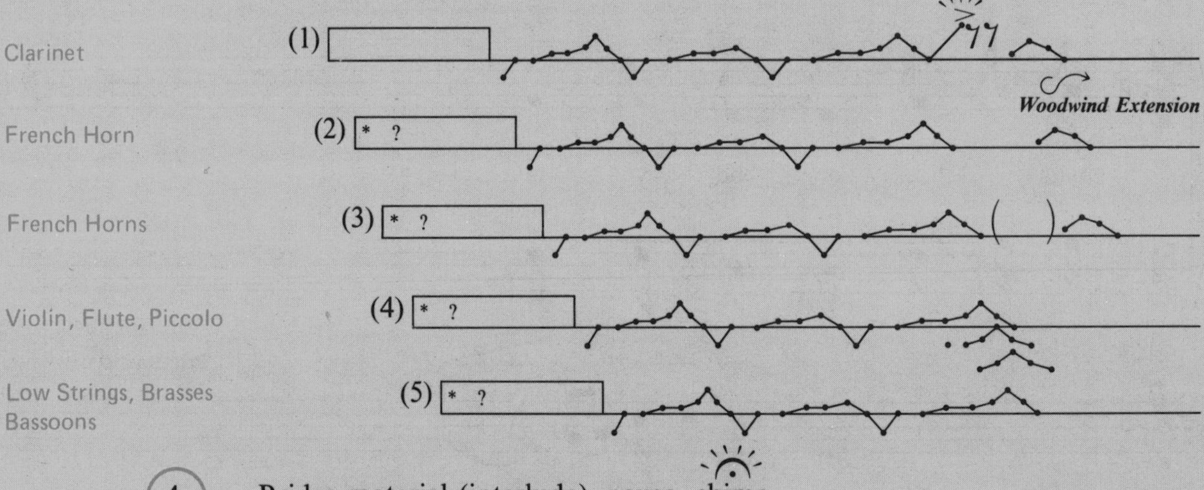

(4) Bridge material (interlude), pause, chime.

(5) Variation II—New minuet melody ($\frac{3}{4}$ time):

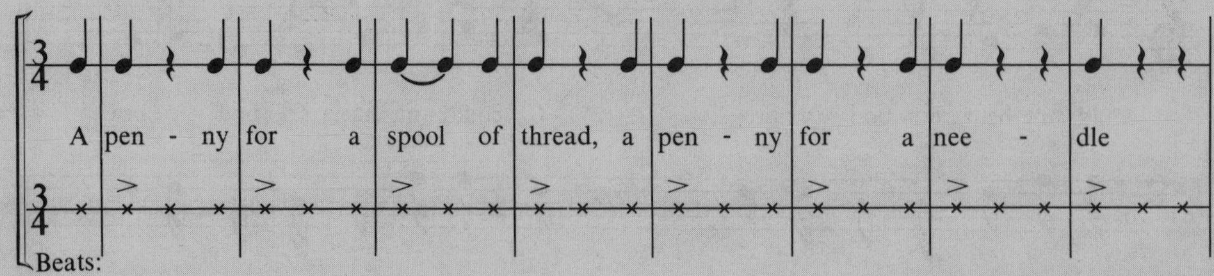

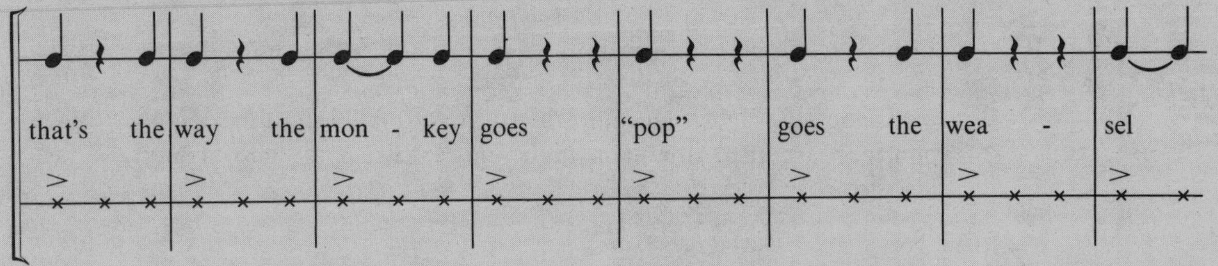
that's the way the mon - key goes "pop" goes the wea - sel

6 THEME enters in lower pitch and lengthened notes (augmentation) as new melody continues above it. Material extended.

7 Partial repeat of (6). New tune presented: "Bride and bridegroom Mazol tov:"

poco allargando
ff

8 Solo violin in virtuoso passage (cadenza) ending, leading to:

9 Variation III—Solo (*instrument?*), other instruments accompany, slow, $\frac{4}{8}$ time, very expressive;

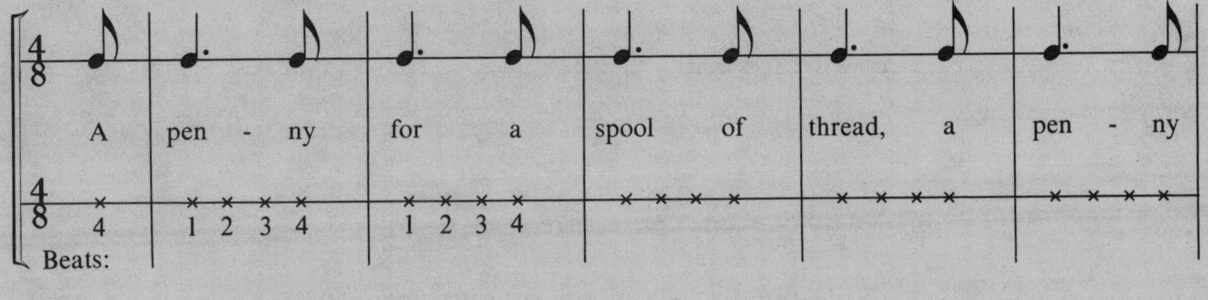
A pen - ny for a spool of thread, a pen - ny
4 1 2 3 4 1 2 3 4
Beats:

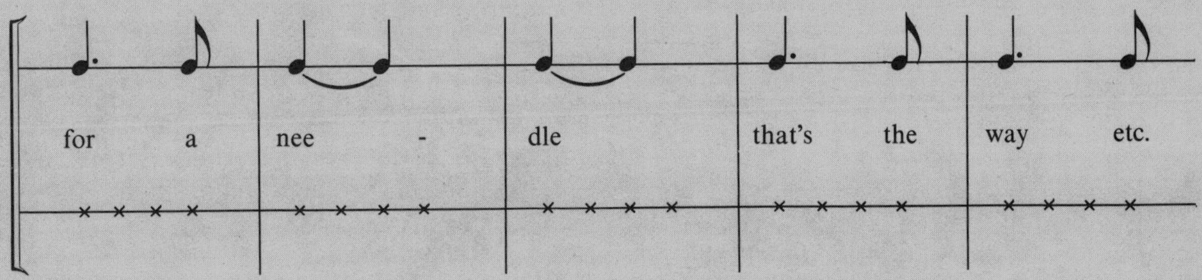
for a nee - dle that's the way etc.

Note return of "Bride and bridegroom Mazol tov" melody (wa wa mute used). Violin ascends scalewise in pitch.

(10) Muted trumpet on descending *wa wa wa wa wa wa wa* (*rit.* ⌒) introducing

Variation IV—light, staccato, jagged melody in waltz time. *Oom-pah, pah* accompaniment in high register. Brass in echo fashion lead to:

(11) Variation V—Whole orchestra *tr* (crescendo) syncopated; swing or jazz version of theme. Now moving in twos; incomplete; repetitious:

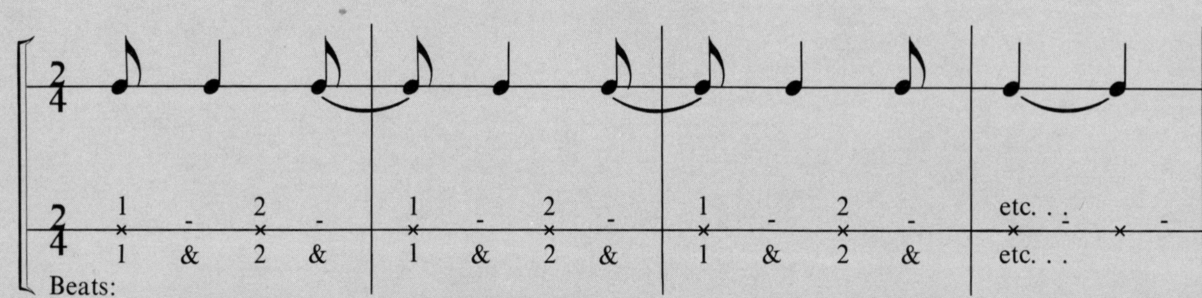

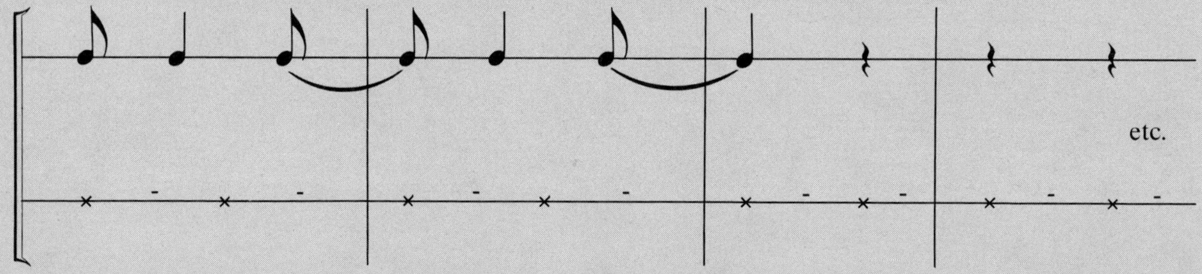

(12) Big Ritard & cymbal crash! (crescendo) Successive trills *tr tr tr*

(13) Summation: (On which part of tune?):

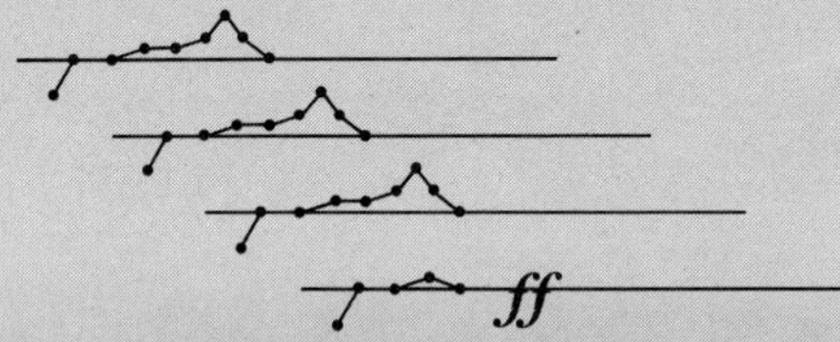

STUDENT INVOLVEMENT 1. Have the students raise their hands each time a new variation occurs. 2. After the first hearing, ask individuals to identify the 'character' (feeling) of the various sections. 3. Have the students graph the basic melody. 4. Have the class identify the cadenza. What instrument plays the cadenza? (violin).

UNIT 3

Frank Lloyd Wright, *Falling Water Terrace*—Bear Run, Pennsylvania

SEE GUIDE FOR UNIT LEARNING OBJECTIVES

Understanding Rhythm and Color

ABOUT THE ARTIST Frank Lloyd Wright (1869–1959) is recognized to be one of the major architects of the 20th century. He was largely self-taught. His Falling Water Terrace is a key monument of the 1930's. It is noteworthy for the use of cantilevered concrete planes that intersect horizontally. Frank Lloyd Wright's final project was the Solomon R. Guggenheim Museum (1959) in New York City.

The movement of music in time is called rhythm. Rhythm is a powerful element in music that echoes life itself. Primitive man made rhythm the basis of his first musical expression. Rhythm is organized into three basic elements: *tempo, pulse,* and *duration.* Tempo is the speed of a composition. Pulse is the organization of movement into beats. Duration is the relative length of tones. As you sing, play, and listen to music, discover how tempo, pulse, and duration are employed in the music. Tone color or timbre is the kind, or quality, of a sound.

ABOUT THE ARTIST Peter Paul Rubens (1577–1640) is considered to be one of the most dynamic artists of his day. He specialized in portraits and landscapes (historical, religious, and genre scenes).

Peter Paul Rubens, *Tiger and Lion Hunt*—Musée des Beaux-Arts, Rennes

STUDENT INVOLVEMENT Have the students experiment with changing the tempos of songs from their text. The tempo markings below will be sufficient. Discuss with the class the tempo which seems to "go" for each selection. Have various students read poems using the same technique.

TEMPO

Some terms follow which have been used by many composers to indicate tempo. Select one term and clap a rhythm pattern to illustrate it. It is up to you to decide exactly how fast or how slow your rhythm should be.

see additional terms in the glossary, p. 266.

Allegro	fast
Andante	moderately slow
Adagio	slow
Presto	very fast

Read a section of a letter written by Beethoven concerning the above terms. What was his opinion of the use of words indicating tempo? Do you agree or disagree with Beethoven? Why?

Have the class experiment with "Maelzel's Metronome" in order to determine if they agree or disagree with Beethoven's comments.

Vienna, 1817

Honourable Sir,

I am delighted to know that you share my opinion of those headings, inherited from times of musical barbarism, by which we describe the tempo of a movement. For example, what can be more absurd than allegro, which once and for all means cheerful, and how far removed we are often from the true meaning of this description, so that the piece of music itself expresses the very opposite of the heading!

For myself, I have often thought of giving up these absurd terms allegro, andante, adagio, presto. *Maelzel's metronome gives us an excellent opportunity to do so. I give you my word for it here, in my future compositions I shall not use those terms.*

Key: F
Starting Tone: C (5-sol)

Meter: 2 over quarter note

Record 2, Side A, Band 4

MAELZEL'S METRONOME

Words and Music by Ludwig van Beethoven

Tick, tick, tick, tick, tick, tick, tick, tick - i
tick, tick - i tick, tick - i ta, All hail to thee Mis-ter
Mael - zel, Tick, tick, tick, tick, tick, tick, tick, tick,
ta, Hail to thee, dear friend. Tick, tick, tick, tick,
tick, tick, tick, tick, ta, tick, tick - i ta, Hail to
thee, tick - i tick tick - i tick, tick, tick, tick, tick, tick, tick, tick,
Hail the migh - ty met - ro - nome, Hail the met - ro - nome.

Record 7, Side B, Band 4

LISTENING . . .

Symphony No. 8 in F Major
Second Movement
Ludwig van Beethoven

PROGRAMMED TAPE

Leslie Bell, *The Festival Song Book.*
Toronto: Canadian Music Sales Corporation Ltd., 1952.

METER

As you listen to music, you hear and feel a basic beat, a series of accents which mark the movement into strong and weak beats. Musical pulse is organized into groups or measures. This organized grouping of beats is called *meter*. When music is organized into sets of two or four in each measure it is called *duple* meter. When music is organized into sets of three in each measure it is called *triple* meter.

Champs Elysée, Paris

Can rhythm, pulse, and beat be seen? How?

Have the class analyze the above photograph which is a visual presentation of rhythm — the meter is illustrated by the movement of headlights and taillights.

Record 8, Side A, Band 1

LISTENING . . .

Waiting

Arr. by Albert Gianquinto

Some music has strong, driving rhythms that create the effect of excitement. How has the composer utilized this rhythmic effect in this composition?

Follow this chart in listening and reacting to the quality of the rhythm in this example. Describe the kind of movement you hear.

STUDENT INVOLVEMENT 1. Count the 1-2-3-4-5-6-7-8- patterns as a slow 1-2-3-4. This will aid in anticipating the entry of each numbered item on the chart. 2. Select a basic pattern; improvise on this pattern and then return to the original.

Call Number

(1) Bongo begins basic rhythmic pattern
/ 1 2 3 4 5 6 7 8 / 1 2 3 4 5 6 7 8 /

(2) Bass with abbreviated version of pattern / . . . . / . . . . /

(3) Drums with another variation / . . . . / . . . . /

(4) Timbale with variation III / . . . . / . . . . / . . . . /

(5) Organ and guitar build up to . . . .

(6) Melodic variation—organ solo (rhythmic accompaniment continues)

(7) Organ 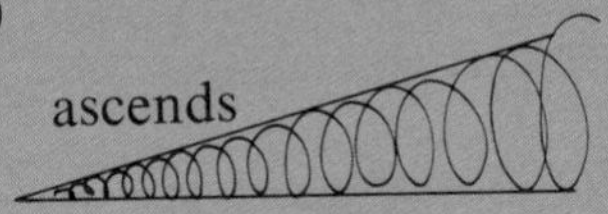 ascends leading to repeat in (6)

(8) Guitar and organ—conversation-like variation

(9) Rhythmic variation—timbale solo with rhythmic accompaniment

(10) Prominent guitar material introducing . . . . . .

(11) All instruments together—several rhythmic variations on basic rhythmic pattern

(12) Percussion return of (1) ends composition

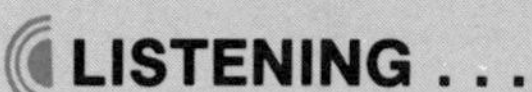

LISTENING . . .

Alleluia — Record 8, Side A, Band 2
Gregorian Chant

Piece for Tape Recorder — Record 8, Side A, Band 3
Vladimir Ussachevsky

Strange Meadowlark — Record 8, Side A, Band 4
Dave Brubeck

At times compositions are organized into free rhythmic systems with no discernible feeling of either downbeat or pulse. This is particularly true of early music and some contemporary music. Listen to three examples of this type of fluid rhythmic organization.

Write rows of quarter notes on the chalkboard. Insert various meter signatures and add appropriate bar lines. Place an accent on the first quarter note of each measure. Clap the resulting patterns with the class.

Write rows of quarter notes; place all accents on various weak and strong beats. Clap the resulting pattern with the class.

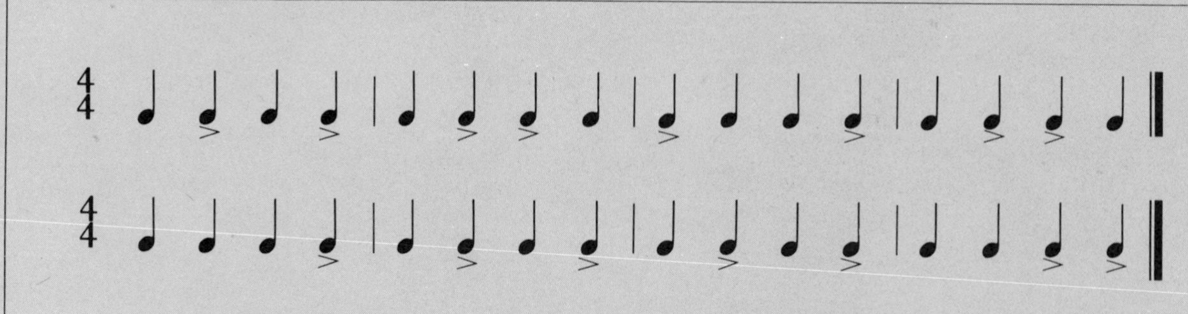

SOUNDS AROUND US

Substitute room sounds for strong beats and instrumental or vocal sounds for weak beats. Improvise percussion introductions and codas to extend the sound study.

Some contemporary music includes several different pulses at the same time. Practice clapping the following patterns, then divide the class into thirds and clap the three patterns simultaneously. Polyrhythms are created.

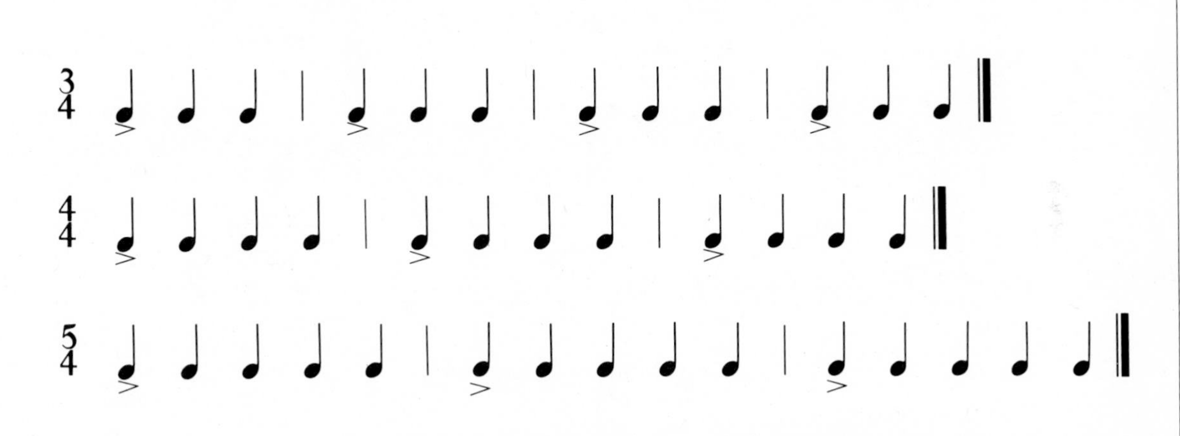

Experiment with additional patterns to create an extended sound composition. Use percussion instruments to add color, interest, and variety. When patterns are extended, use rests in your rhythm pattern for variety and points of silence.

A SOUND STORY

As a class project, decide on the events of some specific experience and relate the story with appropriate sound sources. Use devised notation; perform, record, and evaluate your work.

Enlist the help of a science teacher to show the class how to devise a kaleidophone. See Additional References Teachers Guide, page 20.

A SOUND EXPERIMENT

Make a *kaleidophone* to explore overtones, fundamentals, transverse and longitudinal vibrations of sound. Charles Wheatstone, an English physicist, devised this arrangement of vibrating rod, bead, and light, taking its name from three Greek words - *kalos* (beautiful), *lidos* (form), and *phone* (sound).

Key: F
Starting Tone: F (1-do)

Meter: $\overset{2}{\text{♩}}$

Record 2, Side A, Band 5

TONGO

Polynesian Folk Song

LEARNINGS AND SKILLS The student should be able to: 1. Identify the call-response technique as a characteristic of the music of Africa and Polynesia. 2. Identify the imitation patterns in the melody. 3. Interpret the song using the suggested dynamic markings.

f Leader
Group
Leader
Group
Tohn - goh Tohn - goh Jim nee bye bye oh Jim nee bye bye oh
Ton - go Ton - go Jim nee bye bye oh Jim nee bye bye oh

mf Leader
Group
f Leader
Group
Tohn - goh Tohn - goh Oom bah deh kim bye oh Oom bah deh kim bye oh
Ton - go Ton - go Oom ba de kim bye oh Oom ba de kim bye oh

mf Leader
Group
mp Leader
Group
Ooh - ah - lay Ooh - ah - lay Mah - leh - kah - ah low way Mah - leh - kay - ah low way.
Ooh - a - lay, Ooh - a - lay, Mah - le - ka - ah lo way. Mah - le - ka - ah lo way.

i thank You God for most this amazing
day: for the leaping greenly spirits of trees
and a blue true dream of sky; and for everything
which is natural which is infinite which is yes

(i who have died am alive again today,
and this is the sun's birthday; this is the birth
day of life and of love and wings: and of the gay
great happening illimitably earth)

how should tasting touching hearing seeing
breathing any—lifted from the no
of all nothing—human merely being
doubt unimaginable You?

(now the ears of my ears awake and
now the eyes of my eyes are opened)

e.e.cummings

Have the class experiment with the rhythm and color of this Cummings' poem. Vary both tempo and dynamics, accompany with melody (pentatonic) instruments and light percussion instruments. Tape and evaluate.

Key: C
Starting Tone: G (5-sol)

Meter: 3 ♩

Record 2, Side A, Band 6

MOON RIVER

Words by Johnny Mercer
Music by Henry Mancini

Locate and identify these symbols in the song:

p – (soft)		[cresc.]	– (get louder)
mp – (medium soft)		[decresc.]	– (get softer)
mf – (medium loud)			

Compare the quality of the rhythm in this song with "Waiting."

Slowly
MOON RIV - ER, wid - er than a
p
p
mp
mile: I'm cross - in' you in style some day. Old
dream - mak - er, you heart - break - er, wher-
p

Evaluate the recording on: interpretation of tempo and dynamics, vocal and instrumental color. "What changes would you make? Why?"

er the same rain - bow's end wait - in' 'round the
f
mp
bend, my Huck-le-ber-ry friend, MOON RIV - ER
p
and me. me.
1.
2.
rall.
pp

Record 8, Side A, Band 5

LISTENING...

Trilogy

Music by Don Shirley

Arr. by Archie Bleyer

Pulse in gospel music is generally very strong. How would you describe the pulse in this composition?

Call Number

(*Slow Tempo*)

(1) Piano: recitative-like; single line on "Glory, glory, hallelujah—when I lays my burden down."

(2) Strings join piano: low register, ascending. Piano has hymn tune "Where He leads Me I will Follow."

(3) Bridge—piano ascends, strings tremolo.

(4) Varied and abbreviated repetition of (2) in higher register. Much < > < > and rubato.

(5) Mock, Gregorian chant-like melody in high register of piano over a continuous chord roll in left hand.

(6) Tune "No Mo Auction Block for Me!" Emphatic presentation; insistent trill on "for." Repetitions, strong cadence.

(7) Piano, bass hammers out: da da da da da da da da da da da da da on single note introducing:

(*Faster Tempo*)

(8) Tune "If I Had a Hammer." Full ensemble; strong pulse; much contrast between high and low registers. Piano bass patterns play important role. Much < > and accents. Typical gospel style.

Listen to this last section again. How many times was the tune repeated? How is each repetition varied? Discuss other performance and compositional techniques heard.

Key: G
Starting Tone: D (5-sol)
Meter: 2/𝅗𝅥

Record 2, Side A, Band 7

DONA NOBIS PACEM

GRANT US PEACE

Two-Part Round
Music by Clemens non papa

Sing "Dona Nobis Pacem," accenting the primary beat. Sing the song as a round. What is the underlying pulse of this song?

1
2
3
Doh - nah noh - bees pah - chem
Do - na no - bis pa - cem,
pah - - chem doh - - nah
pa - - cem, do - - na
noh - bees pah - - - - chem.
no - bis pa - - - - cem.

Mexican National Tourist Council

THE HUMAN VOICE

The human voice is undoubtedly the most versatile and expressive of all musical instruments. The expressive use of the voice can be traced in primitive cultures in our world today. It has provided inspiration for composers down through the centuries.

Voices are classified types according to vocal range—highs and lows. The primary classifications of the adult female voice are soprano, mezzo-soprano, and alto. The primary classifications of the adult male voice are tenor, baritone, and bass.

LISTENING . . .

Requiem Mass Number 3, Tuba Mirum Record 8, Side A, Band 6
Wolfgang Amadeus Mozart

Call Number	Melody	Accompaniment	Use of Medium
1	Trombone		
2	Bass solo	Trombone duet with voice over chords in strings	Thin; soft
3	Tenor solo	Strings in repeated notes; trombone enters to continue duet	fp > cresc. <
4	Alto solo	Strings punctuated by rests	p < sf. >
5	Soprano solo	Strings punctuated by rests	p, short phrases and with rising interval of 4th give a slowing up effect
6	Bass, tenor, alto and soprano	Strings, bassoon and horn	Softly; voices rest one measure; texture thickens; p-f-p < f > soft ending

INSTRUMENTS

Traditionally, the four instrumental colors of the orchestra include strings, winds, brass, and percussion. Keyboard instruments such as the piano, organ, and harpsichord are considered as solo, rather than orchestral instruments. Today, electronic instruments and sounds, along with new and experimental uses of traditional instruments, have created totally new tone colors—colors undreamed of only thirty years ago. The wide interest in non-western music has increased the degree of expressive qualities in much of our new music.

Musicians of all cultures have explored human feeling through rhythms, tones, and tonal relationships. Listening to traditional, experimental, or non-western music, focus your attention on the most important element: the expressive uses of sound.

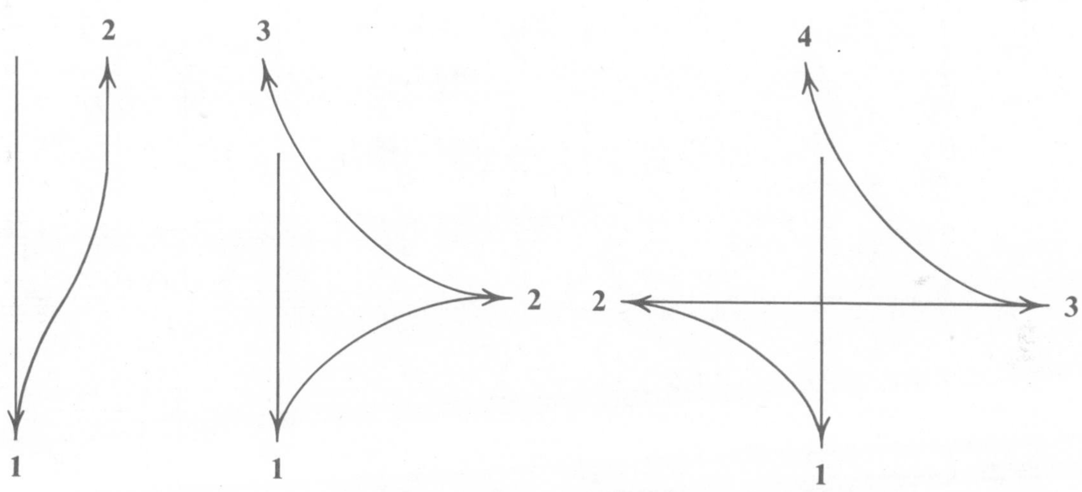

Basic Conducting Patterns

Practice the "down-up" conducting pattern with the students standing. Use the right arm, moving it from the shoulder rather than the elbow or wrist. Have the students chant "down-up" and, later, "one-two" as they conduct. Emphasize flowing and relaxed arm movements.

After the students have mastered the first pattern, move to the next – "down-right-up" "one-two-three." Follow this by the third pattern, "down-left-right-up" or "one-two-three-four."

Give students ample opportunities to practice conducting with the rest of the class performing. Let the class as a whole conduct some of the song recordings. Include a variety of meters in each session.

OPENING PAGES FROM MOZART SYMPHONY NO. 41 IN C, THE *JUPITER*

Encourage the class to study the score and follow one of the melody lines as they listen to the recording. Have the class identify both tempo and dynamic markings in the score. Are these markings followed on the recording? Explain the organization of a traditional orchestral score: Woodwinds at top
Brass below
Percussion
Strings

Record 9, Side A, Band 2

LISTENING . . .

PROGRAMMED TAPE

Symphony No. 41 in C major, the Jupiter

W. A. Mozart

LISTENING . . .

Quintet in C Major *(Excerpt)*
Franz Schubert

Record 8, Side B, Band 2

Listen to an example of string color.

Record 8, Side B, Band 3

LISTENING . . .

Toccata for Percussion *(Excerpt)*
Carlos Chávez

Listen to an example of percussion color.

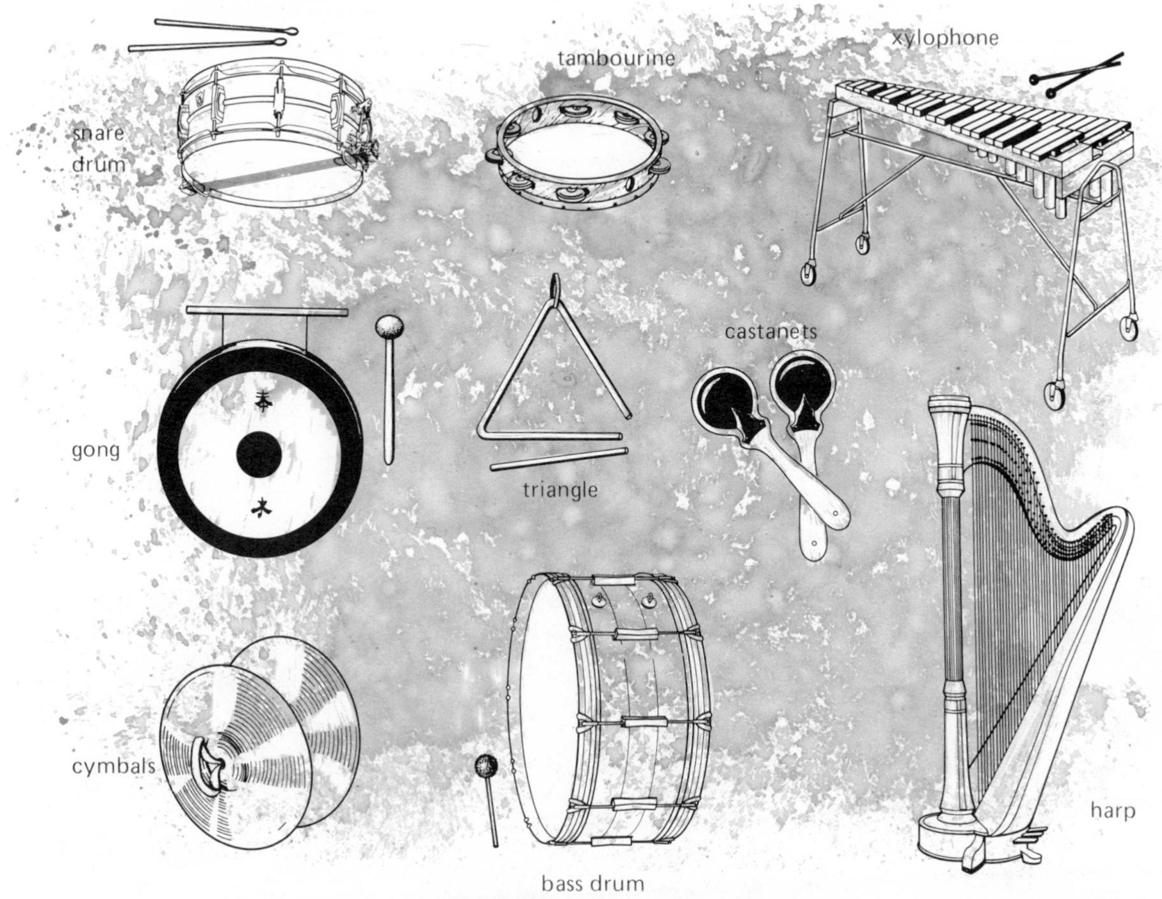

snare drum

tambourine

xylophone

gong

triangle

castanets

cymbals

bass drum

harp

Record 8, Side B, Band 4

LISTENING . . .

Canzona Per Sonare No. 28 *(Excerpt)*
Giovanni Gabrieli

Listen to an example of brass color.

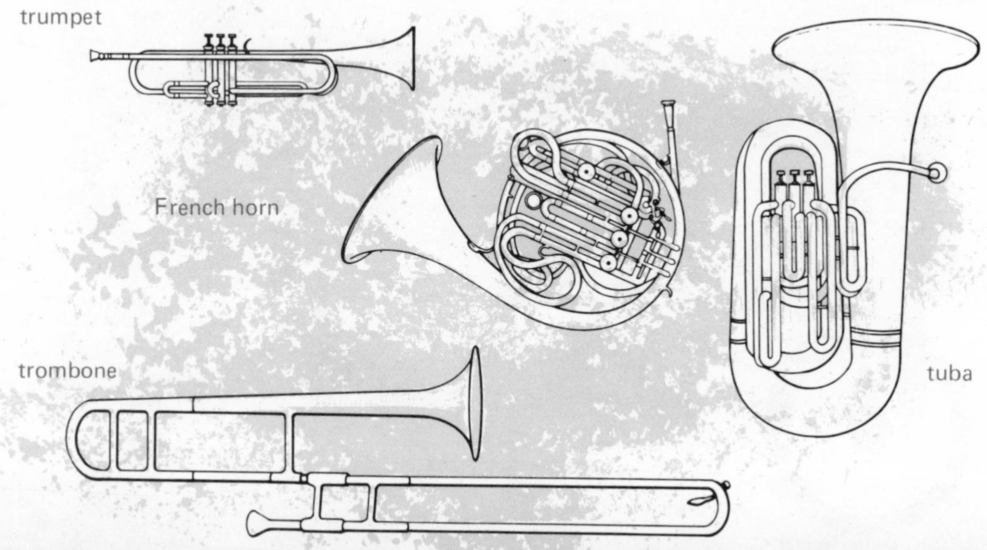

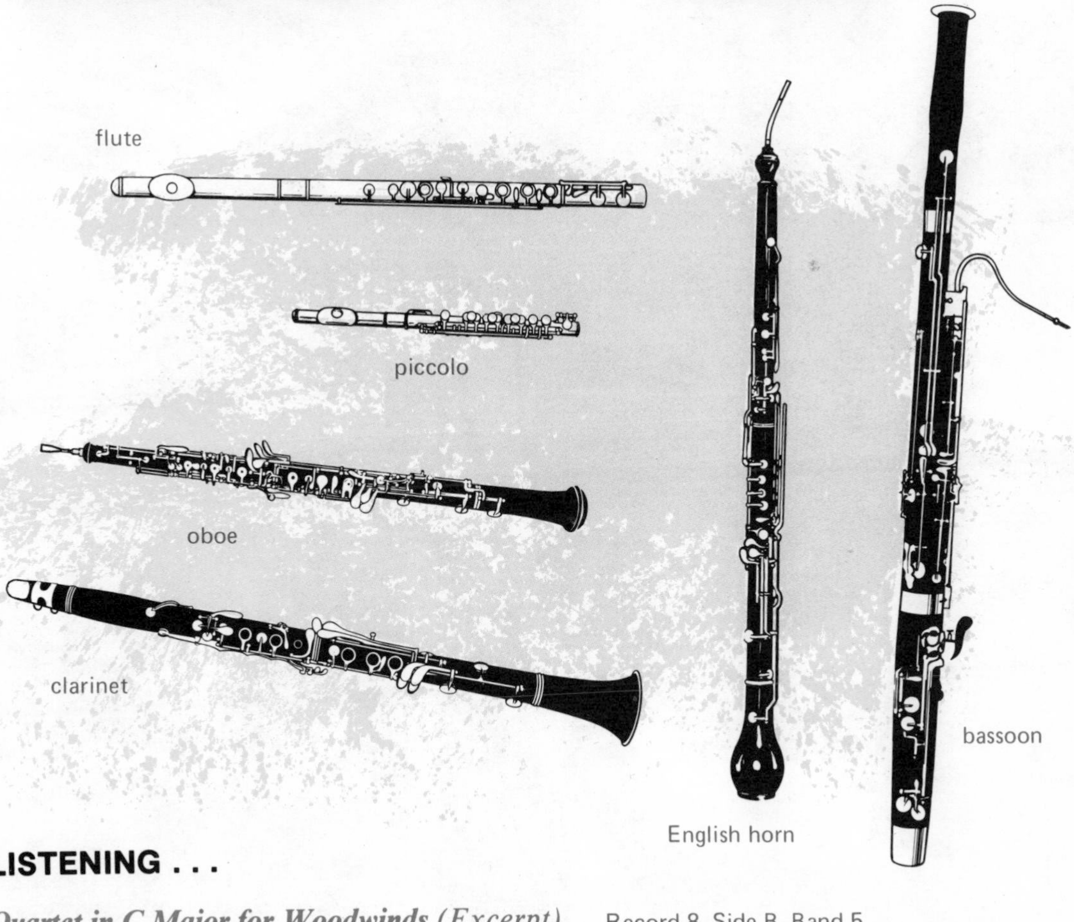

flute

piccolo

oboe

clarinet

English horn

bassoon

LISTENING . . .

Quartet in C Major for Woodwinds (Excerpt) Record 8, Side B, Band 5
Jean Berger

Listen to an example of woodwind color.

Electronic music synthesizers

LISTENING . . .

Piece for Tape Recorder
Vladimir Ussachevsky
and Otto Luening

Record 8, Side A, Band 3

Record 7, Side B, Band 1

LISTENING . . .

Reconnaissance
Donald Erb

The basic tone colors used in the recording include: Moog synthesizer, violin, double bass, and percussion.

Call Number

1 piano
a. percussion, electronic sounds, prominent accents
b. pizzicato string bass
c. violin pizzicato

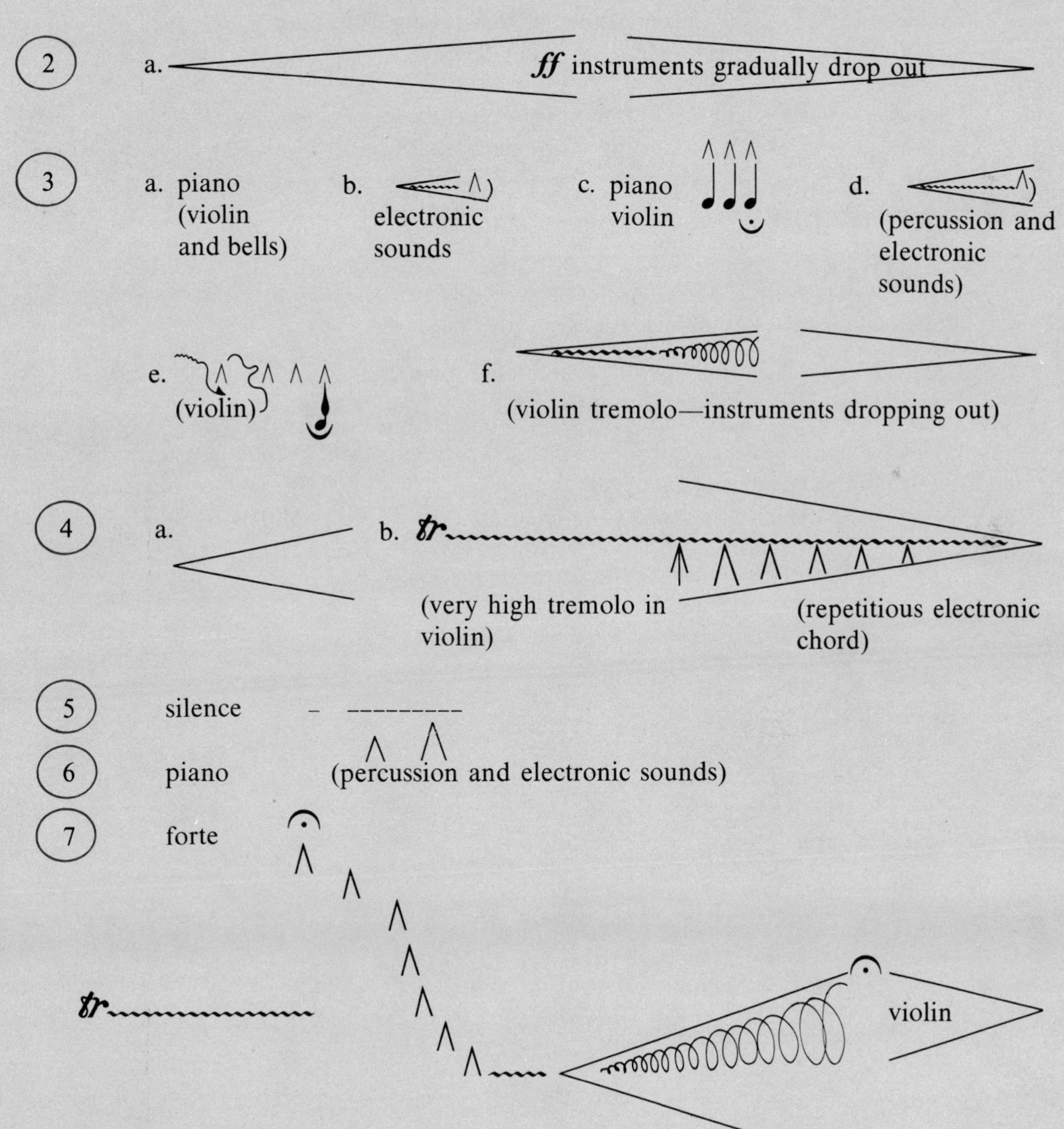

MAKING YOUR OWN MUSIC

Many composers have turned to electronic music in their search for new sounds and structures. Two basic sound-sources exist—electronic, including oscillators and generators, and non-electronic, *musique concrète,* which uses sounds which already exist (instrumental, mechanical, nature sounds). Sounds are recorded on tape, treated with many transformations, edited skillfully, and a composition is created!

Experimentation with tape recorders will help you better understand the three common speeds—$7\frac{1}{2}$, $3\frac{3}{4}$, and $1\frac{7}{8}$ inches per second (i.p.s.). With two tape recorders, you may lower or raise the pitch of sounds many times over. By using tape loops, changing tape speed, varying the volume and microphone distance, a wide range of musical structures may be created.

1. Begin with recording only one vocal or instrumental tone. Make alterations of the tone, experimenting with the transformations, and eventually create a short sound structure. Use additional sounds, make alterations, edit, and play your work.

2. Build a library of sound resources that are different and exciting. Include nature sounds, city sounds, and environmental sounds. Use these sounds as bases for transformation and development.

3. Select a poem from this text and create an appropriate sound setting. Tape with readers and your sound setting as a background.

4. Develop an abstract film and create and tape a score and a suitable text for it. If appropriate, dancers may perform as part of this multimedia project. Some projects which have been completed are "Earth, Sky, and Sea," "Spacescape," "Improvisation," and "City Rhythms," What other titles might suggest an exciting film?

LISTENING . . .

Record 8, Side B, Bands 7 and 8

Listen to: "Gesang der Jünglinge" (Song of the Youths) by Karlheinz Stockhausen and "Sonata in G Major" by Scarlatti from the "Well-Tempered Synthesizer."

Karlheinz Stockhausen (1928–) is one of the most controversial composers of our time. After works in many styles, he turned to electronic music. "Song of the Youths" (1956) was one of Stockhausen's first major electronic works and is a classic in this field. The Biblical hymn of praise was sung and spoken by a twelve-year old boy using his normal voice, the tape manipulated in many ways and electronically-produced sound added. Designed for five loudspeakers, the work used their direction of sound and movement in space as aspects of the form.

The Scarlatti "Sonata in G Major" is performed by Walter Carlos on a custom-built Moog Synthesizer which is twice the size of the Moog Mark III. Numerous synthesizers and other electronic instruments are being developed and afford excellent opportunities for experimentation by students.

In all composition projects, the problems related to form become critical for the student. The composer gives shape and structure to music by his use of repetition and contrast. As the remaining projects necessitate both structured as well as free forms, suggestions are presented below which can assist students in their uses of repetition and contrast. Students should be given opportunity to suggest or discover these possibilities by examining or listening to many music examples.

Further understanding of repetition and contrast as "form-givers" may be gained from study of paintings, architecture, and poetry in this text. Let the student discover these means by encountering these works – not once, but many times.

USING RHYTHM AND TONE COLOR

Rhythm and tone color afford infinite opportunities for experiments in composition. The following group projects are suggestions. Use your own imagination and creativity to develop a composition!

CHAMELEON

Write a four-measure phrase of rhythm patterns using any rhythm set. After performing the phrase, combine four phrases for Part A of "Chameleon." This may then be followed by four other phrases in a different rhythm set for Part B. For Part C, repeat Part A as a round. Incorporate every compositional device you know to create change and variety. How can you extend the composition?

COMICS

Each composition group may select a favorite comic strip and characterize the comic in a short sound composition—a composition without words.

WORLD OF WORDS

Music and poetry use rhythm patterns and tone color. Write or select a poem which has interesting meter and words that have unusual sounds. Create a sound background for a reading of the poem.

YOUR 2500th BIRTHDAY

Did you know that you are almost 2500 years old—and really much older? You look and think much as people did in the days of ancient civilizations. The rhythm of life now is similar, at times, to the rhythms of thousands of years ago. As you look at the paintings and listen to or sing the music, visualize or feel an appropriate rhythm to accompany them. Write some poetry or music—something that might reflect a feeling or rhythm of past time. For contrast, write some music that might reflect a rhythm of the future.

If an assignment were a sound piece for five percussion sounds (low and high drums, cymbal, wood block, and triangle), by limiting the piece to 20-30 seconds, the following concepts could be learned within several class periods:

EXACT REPETITION

All instruments repeat. An ostinato, or two-measure rhythm pattern, is repeated constantly on low drum while others improvise above the ostinato. In immediate succession, instruments repeat a four-measure pattern; others improvise when not playing pattern. A four-measure pattern is performed as a four-part round. The cymbal sustains an even beat throughout.

VARIED REPETITION

The sound piece is repeated with varied dynamics, tempo, or color. The piece may be repeated three times: I variation in dynamics, II variation in tempo, III variation in color.

CONTRAST

The sound piece in two contrasting sections: fast-slow, loud-soft, high-low, etc. (two-part form)
The sound piece in three sections: fast-slow-fast, loud-soft-loud, etc. (three-part form)

Piano and Drums

When at break of day at a riverside
I hear jungle drums telegraphing
the mystic rhythm, urgent, raw
like bleeding flesh, speaking of
primal youth and the beginning,
I see the panther ready to pounce,
the leopard snarling about to leap
and the hunters crouch with spears poised;

And my blood ripples, turns torrent,
topples the years and at once I'm
in my mother's lap a suckling;
at once I'm walking simple
paths with no innovations,
rugged, fashioned with the naked
warmth of hurrying feet and groping hearts
in green leaves and wild flowers pulsing.

Then I hear a wailing piano
solo speaking of complex ways
in tear-furrowed concerto;
of far-away lands
and new horizons with
coaxing diminuendo, counterpoint,
crescendo. But lost in the labyrinth
of its complexities, it ends in the middle
of a phrase at a daggerpoint.

And I lost in the morning mist
of an age at a riverside keep
wandering in the mystic rhythm
of jungle drums and the concerto.

Gabriel Okara

MUSIC PROJECT

Compose a short work which has no reference to any specific subject. Make your composition as colorful, expressive, and imaginative as possible. The design of your work may be in any form you wish—A-B, A-B-A, theme and variations, rondo, or free form. Develop your composition in such a way that contrast, variety, and impact are highlighted!

Van Gogh: *Cypresses*
The Brooklyn Museum

SEEING SOUNDS

Study the works of art on these pages. Select one example that appeals to you because of a particular element in the work—rhythm, line, color, texture, or design. Create a sound collage using a single element. Vary it with other sound sources.

Encourage complete freedom in creating the sound collage.

ABOUT THE ARTIST Wassily Kandinsky (1866-1944). Although he started the study of law, Kandinsky left the university in Moscow at the age of eighteen to study painting in Germany. In 1902 he opened his own school of painting. His early works were characterized by long, flowing strokes of color applied with a palette knife. Many of his later works were characterized by disordered, violent lines and vivid, pure colors. In 1921 Kandinsky founded the Academy of Arts and Sciences in Moscow. The artist is recognized especially by his later compositions in which he virtually abandoned all reference to the real world and created a world of fantasy, humor, and mysticism.

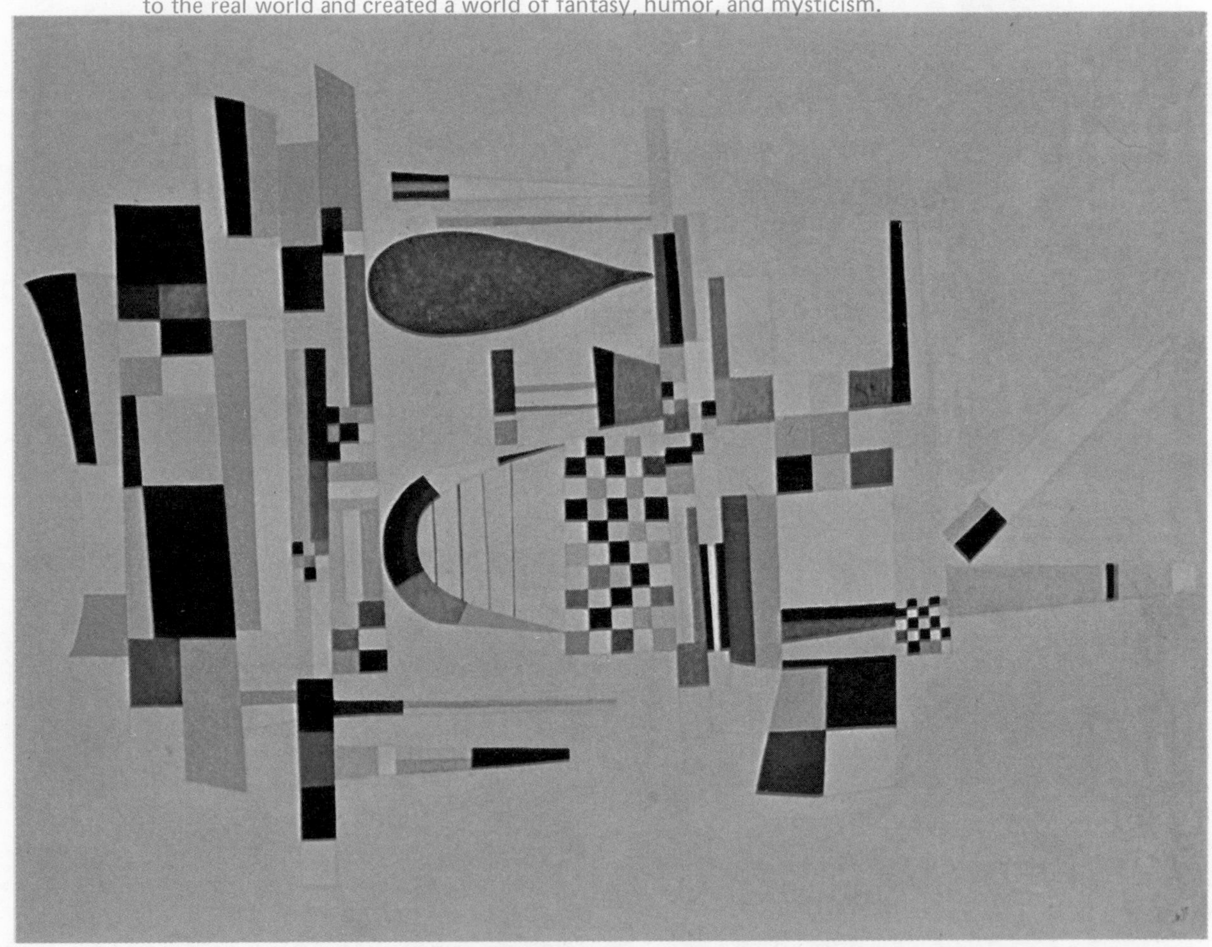

Wassily Kandinsky, *Yellow Painting*—Solomon R. Guggenheim Museum, New York

ABOUT THE ARTIST Alberto Giacometti (1901–1966). A swiss surrealist painter and sculptor, Giacometti is associated with both human isolation and disembodiment.

Lynbov Popova, *Architecture Painting* (above left), Alberto Giacometti, *Woman with her Throat Cut* (above right)—Museum of Modern Art, N. Y.

Jackson Pollock, *Autumn Rhythm*—Metropolitan Museum of Art, New York

ABOUT THE ARTIST Jackson Pollock (1912–1956) was the leader of the action painters in the United States and founded the school of abstract expressionism. He was a pupil of Thomas Hart Benton. Pollock's method of dripping paint over his canvas has attracted worldwide attention.

From Christus Apollo

. . . We seek new Gardens there to know ourselves.
We seek new Wilderness,
And send us forth in wandering search.
Apollo's missions move, and Christus seek,

And wonder as we look among the stars
Did He know these?

. . . You must go there.
In the long winter of space
And lie you down in grateful innocence
At last to sleep . . .

Ray Bradbury American writer (1920-)

Stopping by Woods on a Snowy Evening

Whose woods these are I think I know.
His house is in the village though;
He will not see me stopping here
To watch his woods fill up with snow.

My little horse must think it queer
To stop without a farmhouse near
Between the woods and frozen lake
The darkest evening of the year.

He gives his harness bells a shake
To ask if there is some mistake.
The only other sound's the sweep
Of easy wind and downy flake.

The woods are lovely, dark and deep,
But I have promises to keep,
And miles to go before I sleep,
And miles to go before I sleep.

Robert Frost American poet (1874-1963)

I Wandered Lonely as a Cloud

I wandered lonely as a cloud
That floats on high o'er vales and hills,
When all at once I saw a crowd,
A host, of golden daffodils,
Beside the lake, beneath the trees,
Fluttering and dancing in the breeze.

Continuous as the stars that shine
And twinkle on the milky way,
They stretched in never-ending line
Along the margin of a bay;
Ten thousand saw I at a glance,
Tossing their heads in a sprightly dance.

The waves beside them danced, but they
Outdid the sparkling waves in glee;
A poet could not but be gay,
In such a jocund company;
I gazed—and gazed—but little thought
What wealth the show to me had brought:

For oft, when on my couch I lie
In vacant or in pensive mood,
They flash upon that inward eye
Which is the bliss of solitude;
And then my heart with pleasure fills,
And dances with the daffodils.

William Wordsworth English poet (1770–1850)

Fog

The fog comes
on little cat feet.

It sits looking
over harbor and city
on silent haunches
and then moves on.

Carl Sandburg American poet, historian,
and biographer (1878–1967)

UNIT
4

SEE GUIDE FOR UNIT LEARNING OBJECTIVES

Exploring Line, Texture, and Design

ABOUT THE ARTIST Paul Klee (1879-1940), a Swiss artist, is acknowledged to be one of the most influential and imaginative painters of the 20th century. His works, that number over a thousand, capture the craftsman's keen sense of the basic ingredients in the arts: rhythm, line, texture, color, and design. The almost childlike qualities found in many of Klee's works appeal to the young student. He was an accomplished musician, as well as an artist.

Understanding music requires a knowledge of its various elements—

rhythm—duration

melody—line

harmony—texture

tone color—timbre

form—design

In music there are sounds—**tone color,** which move—**rhythm.** These sounds in traditional music have **pitch** and are related to one another—**melody.** The sounding of tones together creates a **texture—harmony.** Every composition in this book has its own combination of these elements, from the very simple to the extremely complex.

Explore line, texture, and design in the painting opposite—Klee's tribute to his friend, the violinist Adolf Busch. Here, sea monsters are transformed into musical notes and the peg, bridge, and scroll of a violin.

GRAPHING A MELODY

An interesting way to see a melody in a new perspective is to plot it out on a graph. The graph below illustrates the first two phrases of "The Saints Go Marching In."

Make a graph of one of the melodies in this book. Make a second graph of a melody which you know. But do not look at the notation of the melody– use your ear!

Experiment further in graphing music by including symbols which represent additional elements in music–rhythm, harmony, tone color, and form. Illustrate ways in which the music on the graph can be extended and altered. Introduce symbols into the graph which will indicate a change in the mood or feeling of the composition. Prepare a graph for a composition to be performed by the class.

As you study various melodies, identify their characteristics by–

direction

length

structure

key

range

design

cadences

A melody consists of a series of related or unrelated tones ordered in time. When tones change in a melody, they give the melody direction. Some melodies move primarily upward. When they reach a crest, they usually taper downward. Other melodies start on a high tone and move downward. Most melodies move both up and down, giving a sense of rise and fall. The upward and downward motion of a melody, the ease or tension with which it follows or changes direction, the rate of change in its direction, all are effective in making a melody expressive.

The effect of a melody differs when the register is changed. Sometimes the same melody is sounded in different registers – the effect is changed. The shape of a melody contributes to its expressiveness also . . . some are smooth, some are jagged. The pitch range of a melody adds to its expressiveness. Melodies are usually divided into sections, phrases. These phrases are separated by cadences, or places of rest.

Key: G
Meter: $\overset{3}{\text{♩}}$
Record 2, Side B, Band 2
Starting Tone: G (1-do)

I NEVER WILL MARRY

Words and music by Mrs. Texas Gladden

Have the students chant the rhythm of the melody and improvise a clapping ostinato to accompany the chant.

Is the melody of this song easy to sing? How many phrases does it have?

Texture in music may be varied as in a painting or a tapestry. Texture is described as *thick* or *thin*—the combinations of sounds, chords, instruments, or voices.

Sing this song first without an accompaniment, then with a chordal accompaniment. How does the texture change?

G
D
1. One day as I ram - bled, Down
I spied a fair dam - sel, Make a
G
C
by the sea - shore, The wind it did
pi - ti - ful cry, It sound - ed so
G
D7
G
whis - tle, And the wa - ters did roar.
lone - some. In the wa - ters near by.

Chorus:

I never will marry, I'll be no man's
   wife,
I expect to live single, all the days of
   my life.
The shells in the ocean will be my
   death bed,
The fish in deep water swim over my
   head.

2. My love's gone and left me, he's the
   one I adore,
He's gone where I never shall see him
   any more. (*Chorus*)

3. She plunged her dear body, in the water so deep,
She closed her pretty blue eyes, in the
   waters to sleep. (*Chorus*)

STUDENT INVOLVEMENT 1. Identify important melodic and rhythm patterns.
2. Experiment with the chords for the accompaniment by changing the sound – G to Gm, D to Dm, C to Cm.

Key: Em
Starting Tone: B (3-mi)

Meter: 4/♩

Record 2, Side B, Band 3

A HUNDRED YEARS FROM NOW

Words by Paul Field
Music by Nancy Fletcher

Is the melody strongly accented? How? Is the range wide or narrow? Are the phrases of this song long or short? Have the students analyze the melody line – upward motion, long melody line, minor mode, wide range.

Em A7
1. A pure white cloud a - bove me. A
2. A coun - try - side of pave - ment. A
Em D Em
beach that's bright and clean. An o - cean wave that
moun - tain range of trash. A lake that foams with
A C D E
spar - kles. A mea - dow lush and green. These
phos - phate. A breeze that's gray with ash. The
G Em G
things are worth pro - tect - ing. They must be saved some -
earth may soon be si - lent. For man's dis - cov - ered
B7 Em A
how. Or else they'll just be mem-o - ries, a
how, to make him - self a mem-o - ry, a

Have the class discuss the implications of the text. Encourage the students to bring in other songs and recordings related to the general theme of ecology.

"A HUNDRED YEARS FROM NOW."
Music by Nancy Fletcher Lyrics by Paul Field
(From Infovision film "It's Our Choice")

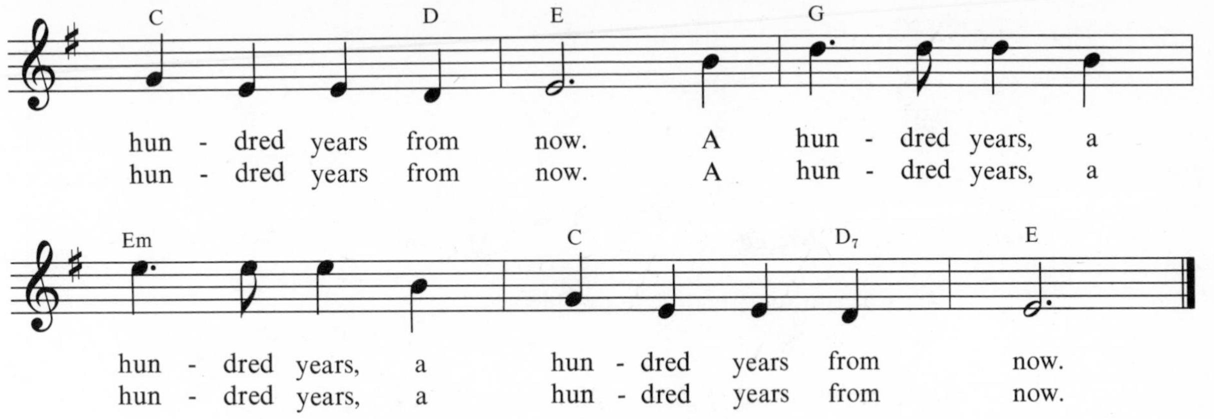
C D E G
hun - dred years from now. A hun - dred years, a
hun - dred years from now. A hun - dred years, a
Em C D7 E
hun - dred years, a hun - dred years from now.
hun - dred years, a hun - dred years from now.

3. The choice is very simple,
It's smog, or air that's clear.
It's water fish can swim in,
Or rivers worse each year.
We've got to make our minds up,
And save our land somehow,
Or we might all be memories
A hundred years from now.
A hundred years, a hundred years,
A hundred years from now.

Montauk Point Lighthouse

Record 8, Side B, Band 1

LISTENING . . .

El Salón México
Aaron Copland

Be certain to allow all interested students to identify the events during the recording.

Call Number	Melody	Harmony
1	Upward motion; skips; major; jagged	High register
2	Sudden downward shift	Becomes thicker
3	Generally upward; jagged	Dissonant; leaps
4	Smooth; short	Low register; static
5	Staccato; short; strong cadences	Pace quickens; thin, strong cadences
6	High register; smooth; short	Thicker; high register; smooth
7	Repeated notes	Rapid increase in thickness; pace slows momentarily
8	High register; jagged theme heard in several different voices	Thin texture, gradually becoming more dense; pace increases; some dissonance
9	Texture thins out; jagged; dissonant	Moving toward a modulation
10	Upward; jagged theme in several voices	New key; becomes thick again; moves quickly toward another modulation
11	Middle register; short	New key; thick block chords; prominent strong cadences
12	Middle register; upward motion; some dissonances	Thick; staccato chords; more active
13	High register; jagged; major	Thicker; more active; toward a modulation
14	Upward; high register	New key; thin texture

FORMS BASED ON REPETITION WITH CONTRAST

A very simple form based on contrast is a musical idea **A** followed by a contrasting idea **B.** This form consists of two sections, **A-B,** called **binary.** Sometimes either the A section or the B section is repeated; sometimes both are repeated. The repetitions do not affect the overall form.

Record 9, Side A, Band 3

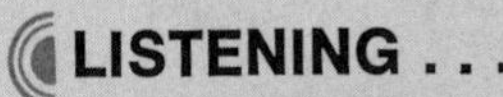

LISTENING . . .

Die Schöne Mullerin No. 1
Franz Schubert

Form: unity and variety.
Form or design in music is based on —
1. repetition (AAA)
2. repetition and contrast (ABA)
3. repetition with variation
(A A1 A2 A3)
4. repetition with development
(sonata allegro form)
5. free form (toccata, etude, etc.)
6. combination of the above.

Number

Number		
1	A	A
1		A repeated
2	B	B

Record 9, Side B, Band 4

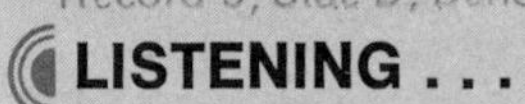

LISTENING . . .

Suite No. 2, B Minor for Orchestra
Johann Sebastian Bach

1	A	A
1		A repeated
2	B	B
2		B repeated

Record 7, Side A, Band 3

LISTENING . . .

Cantata 80., No. 8 "Chorale"
Johann Sebastian Bach

1	A	A
1		A repeated (different words)
2	B	B

FORM IN THE ARTS

Music is based on an organized relationship of sounds. The unifying principles in art are repetition and contrast. Compose and notate a short melody. Experiment with various ways to create repetition. How can you create contrast in this melody? How are repetition and contrast illustrated on these pages?

Variation

Color

Texture

RELATED ACTIVITIES: See Filmstrip "Making Hopi Cachina Dolls", Indian Crafts of the Southwest Series. Educational Development Corporation. #606-3 (Record or cassette).

ABOUT THE ARTIST

Mark Rothko (1903–1970), a Russian-American abstract/expressionist painter, was educated at Yale University. His later works are limited to rich units of form and color.

Mark Rothko, *Green on Blue*—University of Arizona Art Gallery

Two principles are identified in a work of art. First, the work must have unity. It must give a sense of wholeness and relatedness. Second, the work must have variety. It must contain enough interesting elements to grasp and hold one's attention. We hear the expression, "that grabs me." Among the important reasons for a work of art "grabbing" a student are its unity and variety.

Art uses form to express a unique idea. For the Hopis, the *kachina* (opposite left) brings the promise of rain. *Chephren* (opposite right) embodied divine kingship in Egypt 3,000 years ago. The Cathedral of Chartres (opposite top) shadows forth a vision of God in Medieval France. In *Green on Blue* Rothko reveals the inner harmony we all seek.

Key: Dm
Starting Tone: D (6-la)

Meter: 4 over half note

Record 2, Side B, Band 4

ONE GRAIN OF SAND

Words and Music by Pete Seeger

Have the students listen to the recording. Is the texture of the song constant or does it change from verse to verse? (changes.)

Experiment with various ways to change the texture of this song in a performance. How would you describe the general shape of this melody?

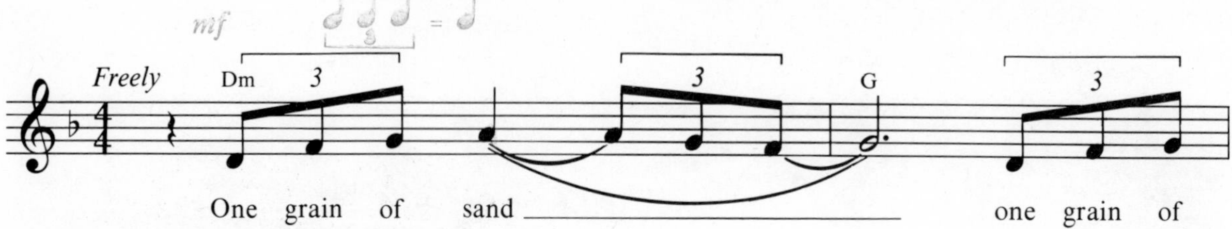

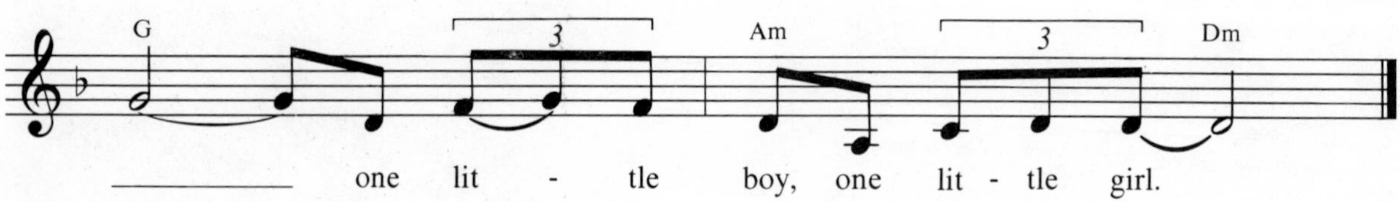

One grain of sand—
One little star up in the sky
One grain of sand
One little you, one little I

One grain of sand—
One drop of water in the sea
One grain of sand
One little you, one little me

One grain of sand—
One leaf of grass—on a windy plain
One grain of sand
We come and go again and again,
again, and again, again and again

I love you so—
I love you so—I love you so
I love you so—
More than you will ever,
Ever know

One grain of sand—
One little snowflake lost in the swirling
storm
One grain of sand
I'll hold you close and keep you warm

One grain of sand
One grain of sand on an endless shore
One grain of sand
One little life, who'd ask for more?

One grain of sand—
One grain of sand, one grain of sand
One grain of sand
One grain of sand, one grain of sand

M-m-m-m-m-m-
One little star—up in the blue
M-m-m-m-m-m-
One little me, one little you

Key: Gm
Starting Tone: G (6-la)

Meter: 2 (quarter note)

Record 2, Side B, Band 5

KOL DODI

Help the class to discover the relatively small range of the melody.

Song of Songs

Yemenite Folk Song

Follow the repeat signs carefully. How would you describe the design of this song? Use letter names for your description. (AABBAA or ABA)

Joyously (a dance)
Gm Cm Gm Cm Gm Cm Gm
Fine
Kohl doh - dĕ, kohl do - dé, kohl do - dĕ, hē - néh sch bah
Kol do - di, kol do - di, kol do - di, hi - në ze ba.
D. C. al Fine
Gm Cm Gm 1. Gm 2. Gm Gm
M' dah - lehg ahl heh - hah - rĕm - m' kah-péhts ahl hah - g'vah - óht hah - g'vah - óht.
M'-da - lëg al he - ha - rim, m' ka-pëts ah ha-g'va - ot. ha-g'va - ot.

Kol Dodi from the New Jewish Song Book by Harry Coopersmith. Published by Behrman House, N.Y.

The Grasshopper's Song

Have the class explore a variety of ways to read this poem – one reader, two readers, seven readers. Encourage students to improvise percussion and melody accompaniments as the poem is read. Tape the performance and evaluate.

A scraping sound: The grasshopper
In the field does purr and whir-r-r.

"Come forth, grasshoppers, come to dance,
And chant to God your lovely chants.

"Let all who can, be heard and seen
With pirouette and tambourine.

"For none shall hide where grass is deep,"
But if you've legs, arise and leap!

"All that are here, respond, proclaim:
Blessed is He and blessed His name!

"Blessed be God who for our sake
This happy summertime did make.

"A plenteous feast in field and fen,
Enough for all.—Amen, amen!"

H.N. Bialik

(translated from the Hebrew by Jessie Sampter)

Key: C

Starting Tone: C (1-do)

Meter: $\overset{2}{\text{𝅗𝅥}}$

Record 2, Side B, Band 6

MATILDA

Trinidad Folk Song

Help the students to discover how the bass line provides a sharp contrast to the highly syncopated right-hand accompaniment.

Arr. by William Attaway. Used by permission.

Verse
C
G
C
thou - sand dol - lars friend I lost
mon - ey was to buy me house and land, The
F
G7
Wo - man ev - en take me cart and hoss; —
Ma - til - da she
Wo - man she got a seri - ous plan; —
Ma - til - da she
C
F6
C
G7
C
D.S. al Fine
take me mon - ey and, Run Ven - e - zue - la.
take me mon - ey and, Run Ven - e - zue - la.
D.S. al Fine

3. Now the money was safe in me bed
Stuck in the pillow beneath me head
But Matilda she find me money
And run Venezuela.
(*Repeat Chorus*)

4. Never will I love again
All me money gone in vain
'Cause Matilda she take me money
And run Venezuela.
(*Repeat Chorus*)

Add an accompaniment based on rhythm patterns in the song, such as

Key: D Meter: 3 (quarter note) Record 2, Side B, Band 7

Starting Tone: A (5-sol)

EL DIA DE TU SANTO

New Mexico Folk Song

This song may be accompanied by two chords. Experiment with other chords for an accompaniment. How does this affect the texture?

♩=96
The theme of this birthday song is "May God bless this day of fortune and bless the prize I adore."
f
D
dióhs behn - dē̈ - gah éhs - teh dē̈ - ah behn - tu - róh - soh,
Dios ben - di - ga es - te di - a ven - tu - ro - so,
A7
D
ē behn - dē̈ - gah lah préhn - dah keh-ah - dóh - roh; yah lohs
y ben - di - ga la pren - da que a - do - ro; ya los
G
D
áhn - wheh - lehs káhn - tahn ehn - kóh - roh pohr lohs áh - nyohs keh
an - gel - es can - tan en - co - ro por los a - nos que
A7
D
A7
kúm - plehs me biéhn. lahs ehs - tréh - yahs seh bē̈s - tehn deh
cum - ples mi bien. Las es - tre - llas se vis - ten de
D
A7
D
gáh - lah, ē lah lu - nah seh yéh - nah deh ehn-káhn - toh
ga - la, y la lu - na se lle - na de en-can - to,
G
ahl sah - béhr keh teh dē̈ - ah deh tu sáhn - toh pohr lohs
al sa - ber que te di - a de - tu san - to por los

D
A7
D
áh - nyohs keh kúm - plehs me biéhn.
a - nos que cum - ples mi bien.

Key: D
Starting Tone: A (5-sol)

Meter: 3

Record 3, Side A, Band 1

HEY, MOTSWALA

South African Folk Song

Improvise a percussion accompaniment for this Bantu melody.

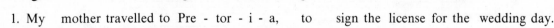

Compare the texture and design of "Hey, Motswala" with that of "El Dia De Tu Santo." How are the melodies similar? How are they different?

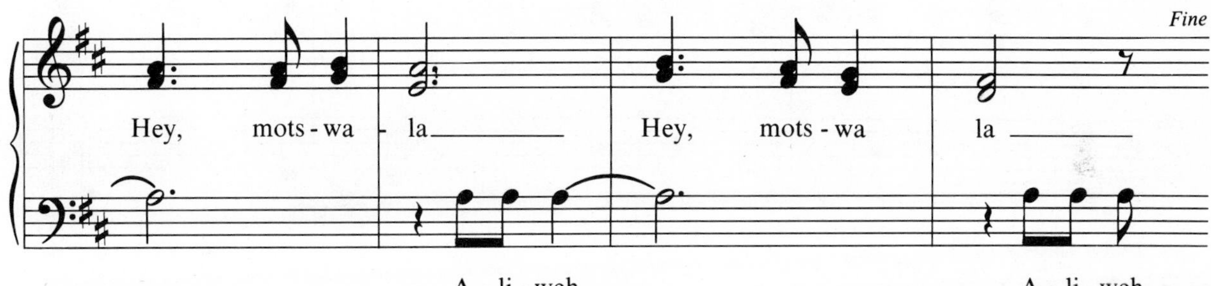

1. My mother travelled to Pre - tor - i - a, to sign the license for the wedding day.

My mother travelled to Pre - tor - i - a, to sign the license for the wedding day.

2. Her father wants to give the bride away
I think he's waiting for the dowry. (twice)

3. And now the time has come I have to go
I wish perhaps I hadn't hurried so.

Key: C
Starting Tone: C (1-do)

Meter: $\overset{2}{\text{𝅗𝅥}}$

Record 3, Side A, Band 2

FISHERMAN'S SONG

Have the class echo clap the syncopated beats.

Calypso Tune

What chords are needed to accompany this song? What is the basic design of this song? Compare the melody of "Fisherman's Song" with "Matilda."

Calypso-Moderately
C G7 C G7 C G7 C G7 C G7 C G7
Verse
C G7 C F C
1. Fish-er-men sleep when the fish don't bite,— Weigh - up Sus - i - an - na, Salt
2. Fish-er-men's la - dy don't use no comb,— Weigh - up Sus - i - an - na, She
F C G7 C G G7 C
fish in the hold and we two ton light,— 'Round the Bay of Mont-ser - ray.
comb her— hair with— cod-fish bone,— 'Round the Bay of Mont-ser - ray.

Arr. by William Attaway. Used by permission.

3. Fisherman's lady got a dimple knee
Weigh up—Susianna
She boil her porgy with rice and peas
'Round the Bay of Montserray.

Chorus:
Weigh up—Susianna
'Round the Bay of Montserray.
Fish all night and we sleep all day
'Round the Bay of Montserray.

Key: Dm
Starting Tone: A (3-mi)

Meter: 2

Record 3, Side A, Band 3

When you combine two or more melodies, interweaving them in various ways, *polyphony* is created. Another name for polyphony is *counterpoint.*

SHALOM HAVËRIM (ROUND)

Composer Unknown
Edited by Harry Coopersmith

Sing "Shalom Haverim" to illustrate monophony — one melody line, then as a round illustrating polyphony.

①
②
Shah - lóhm whah - beh - rēm, shah - lóhm whah - beh - rēm shah - lóhm, shah - lóhm.
Sha - lom ḥa - vë - rim, sha - lom ḥa - vë - rim, sha - lom, sha - lom.
③
④
leh - hé - trah - óht, leh - hé - trah - óht, shah - lóhm, shah - lóhm.
L' - hit - ra - ot, l' - hit - ra - ot, sha - lom, sha - lom.

DUNDAI

Composer Unknown

Key: Dm
Starting Tone: D (6-la)

Meter:

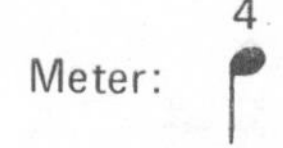

4

Record 3, Side A, Band 4

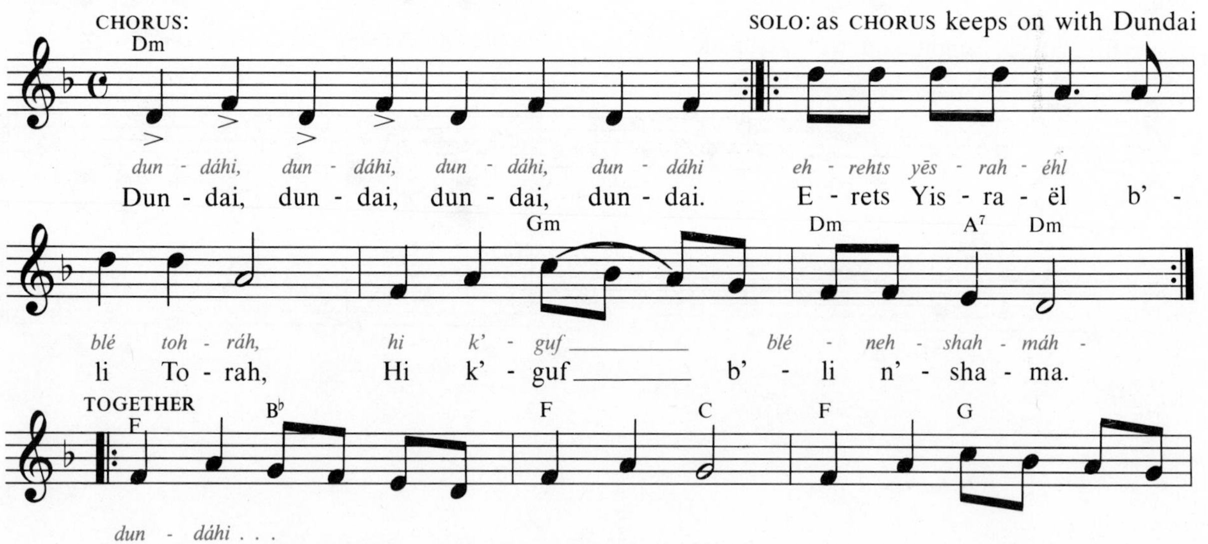

CHORUS:
SOLO: as CHORUS keeps on with Dundai
Dm
dun - dáhi, dun - dáhi, dun - dáhi, dun - dáhi eh - rehts yēs - rah - éhl
Dun - dai, dun - dai, dun - dai, dun - dai. E - rets Yis - ra - ël b' -
Gm Dm A7 Dm
blé toh - ráh, hi k' - guf ___ blé - neh - shah - máh -
li To - rah, Hi k' - guf ___ b' - li n' - sha - ma.
TOGETHER
F B♭ F C F G
dun - dáhi . . .
Dun - dai, dun - dai, dun - dai, dun - dai - dai, dun - dai, dun - dai, dun - dai,

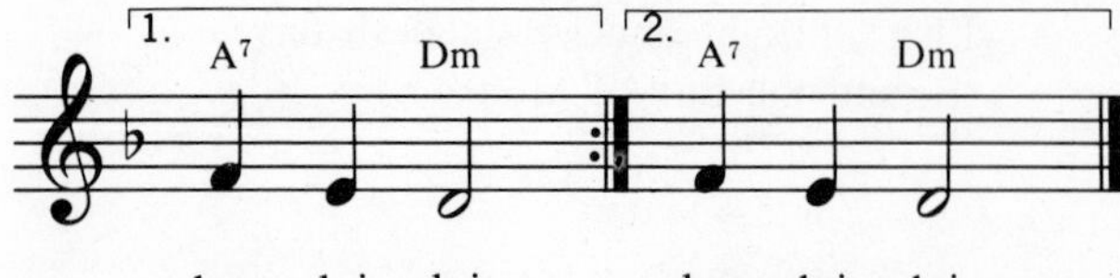

1.
A7 Dm
2.
A7 Dm
dun - dai - dai. dun - dai - dai.

Shalom Havërim and Dundai from the New Jewish Song Book by Harry Coopersmith.
Published by Behrman House, N.Y.

Key: G Meter: 4 (quarter note) Record 3, Side A, Band 5

Starting Tone: G (1-do)

THE SPACIOUS FIRMAMENT

Words by Joseph Addison

Music by Thomas Tallis

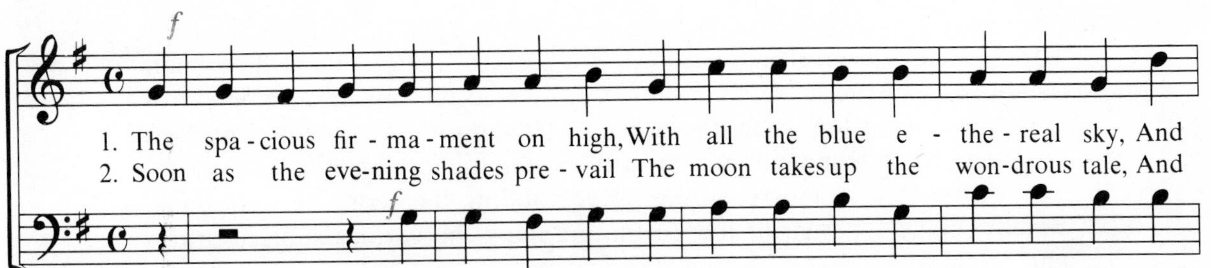

f
1. The spa - cious fir - ma - ment on high, With all the blue e - the - real sky, And
2. Soon as the eve-ning shades pre - vail The moon takes up the won-drous tale, And
f

1. The spa - cious fir - ma - ment on high, With all the blue e -
2. Soon as the eve-ning shades pre - vail The moon takes up the

mf

span - gled heav'ns, a shin - ing frame, Their great O - rig - i - nal pro - claim. The un -
night - ly to the list' - ning earth Re - peats the sto - ry of her birth: While

the - real sky, And span - gled heav'ns, a shin - ing frame, Their great O - rig - i - nal pro - claim.
won - drous tale, And night - ly to the list' - ning earth Re - peats the sto - ry of her birth.

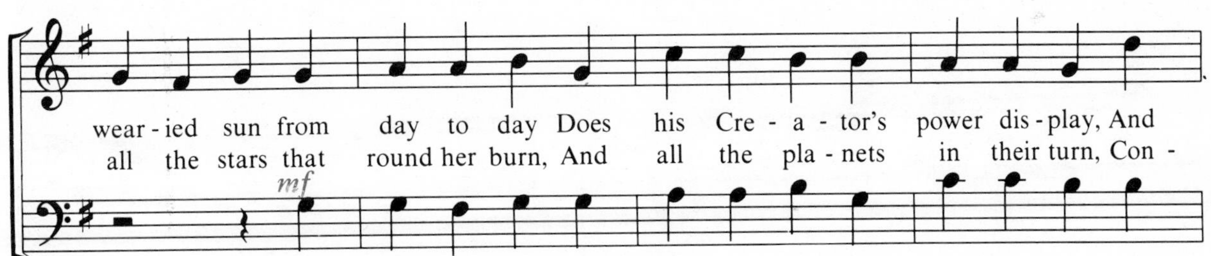

wear - ied sun from day to day Does his Cre - a - tor's power dis - play, And
all the stars that round her burn, And all the pla - nets in their turn, Con -
mf

The un - wear - ied sun from day to day Does his Cre - a - tor's
While all the stars that round her burn, And all the pla - nets

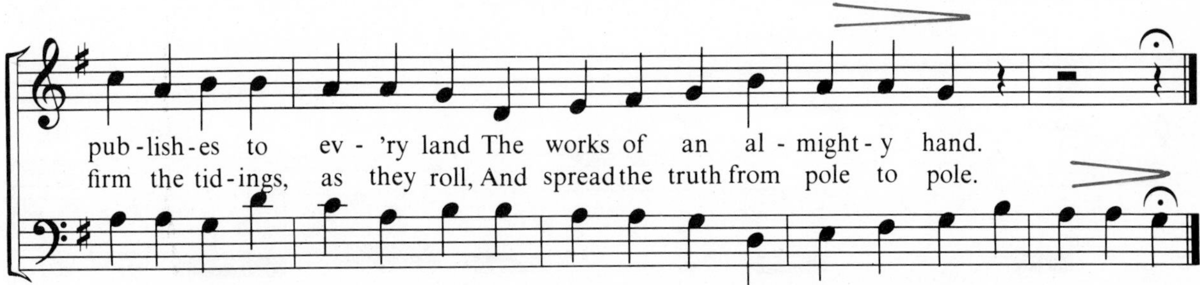

pub - lish - es to ev - 'ry land The works of an al - might - y hand.
firm the tid - ings, as they roll, And spread the truth from pole to pole.

power dis - play, And pub - lish - es to ev - 'ry land The works of an al - might - y hand.
in their turn, con - firm the tid - ings as they roll, And spread the truth from pole to pole.

Record 9, Side A, Band 5

LISTENING . . .

Fugue in C Major for Organ From Toccata, Adagio, and Fugue in C for Organ S-564
(The Fanfare Fugue)
Johann Sebastian Bach

The fugue is the most highly developed form of counterpoint. The main melody of a fugue is called a subject. Listen to the opening statement of the fugue by the top voice, the soprano. How do the alto, tenor, and bass voices enter? How many times do you hear the fugue subject in its entirety? Listen carefully to the recording as you follow the score in your book. Finally, make a design of this fugue, graphing the various subject entries and bridge sections.

On the second playing of the fugue, have the class raise their hands each time the fugue subject is introduced. Have them sing the fugue subject on "la" each time it appears.

③ I
(subject)

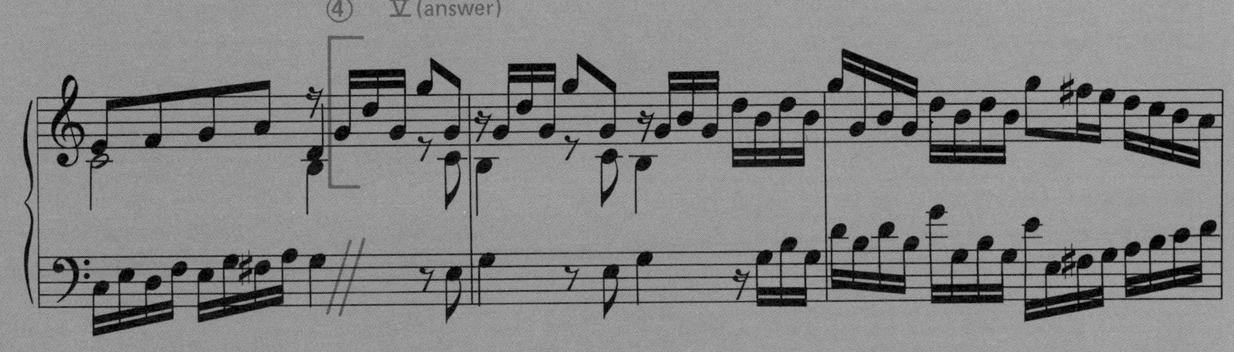

④ V (answer)

⑤ I (subject)

⑥ V (answ
⑦ I (subject)

⑧ I (subject)

Coda
tr
tr
tr
tr
tr

Record 9, Side B, Band 1

LISTENING . . .

Messiah, "Hallelujah Chorus"
George Frederic Handel

Compare this work with Bach's "Fanfare Fugue." Discuss differences and similarities between the two.

Call Number	
1	Polyphonic: orchestra imitates voices; thick sonority
2	Polyphonic: imitative; contrasting colors; thick sonority
3	Homophonic: melody and blending accompaniment; thick sonority
4	Polyphonic: (fugal) imitative; contrasting colors and registers; thick sonority
5	Polyphonic: nonimitative; two basic melodies; contrasting colors (women—men, instruments—voices); all are ascending with sopranos prominent
6	Polyphonic: imitative; contrasting color; thick sonority
7	Polyphonic: nonimitative; two basic melodies; contrasting color
8	Mixed texture in voices and countermelodies in brasses; orchestral accompaniment; thick sonority

Messiah remains (and probably always will) Handel's best-loved work. In its massive choruses, beautiful solos, and fine orchestral background, it embodies an affectionate and intimate portrayal of the Christ story through its three phases — birth, death, and resurrection.

Surpassing all in majestic dignity is the great "Hallelujah," about which Handel himself said: "Whether I was in my body or out of my body when I wrote it, I know not. God knows."

Though some of his music may have been in his mind before he began to write it, he composed Messiah in three weeks, utilizing here and there pieces he had written for other purposes. His orchestration did not take that long, for this art was not yet thought to be of equal importance to choral and vocal writing.

Howard D. McKinney

Key: G
Starting Tone: G (1-do)

Meter: 3 (quarter note)

Record 3, Side A, Band 6

MY FRIENDS, DO NOT WORRY

English by Florence Hudson Botsford
Arr. by Anna von Wohlfarth-Grille

Homophonic texture is based on a main melody with accompanying harmony. Sometimes this harmony is a series of chords. At other times the harmony is divided into several parts which move in a note-to-note fashion. The music remains homophonic as long as the accompaniment does not consist of melodies which rival the main melody in primary importance.

mf I*
Fine*
Do not wor - ry, do not wor - ry, My friends, do not wor - ry!
mf
II*
Do not wor - ry, do not wor - ry, My friends, do not wor - ry!
III*
D.C.*
Wait till to - mor - row, your troub - les to bor - row. Then

*Without the accompaniment, this song may be sung as a round, the voices entering as indicated by the Roman numerals.

Key: Ab
Starting Tone: Eb (5-sol)

Meter: 4 over a quarter note

Record 3, Side A, Band 7

PAUL SAID TO THE CORINTHIANS

Translated by James Moffatt
Music by Florence Hudson Botsford

Improvise a jazz or rock accompaniment to this text. Experiment with various techniques to change the character of the texture.

The text is written above the staff to denote that it is to be read, not sung, with music accompaniment.

Love is very patient, ver - y kind; Love knows no jeal - ous - y;
Love makes no pa - rade, Gives it - self no airs;

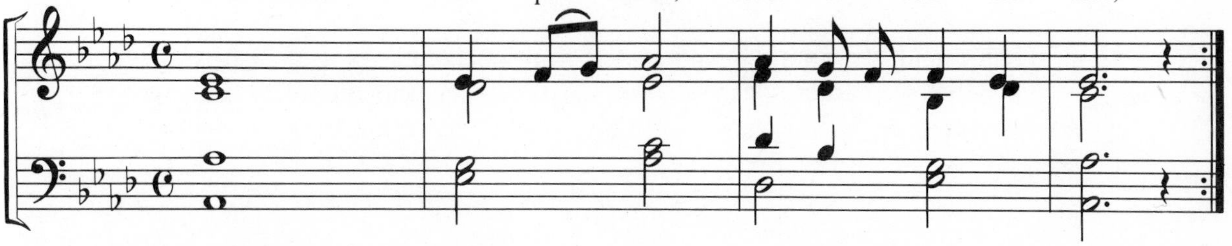

Is never rude, never selfish, nev - er irritated, never re - sent - ful;

Love is never glad when others go wrong; Love is gladdened by goodness, always

slow to ex - pose, al - ways ea - ger to be - lieve the best, al - ways

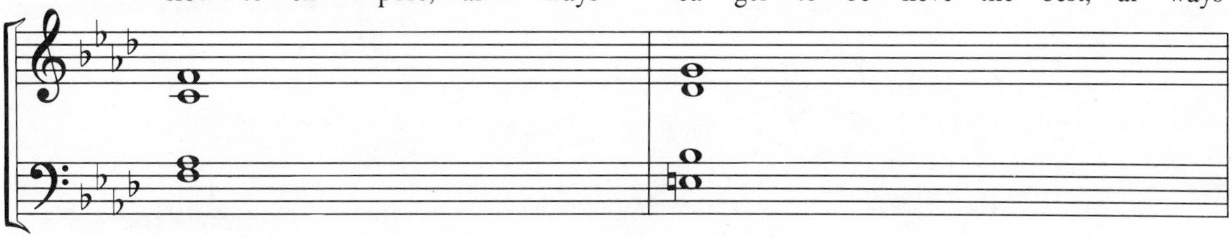

help - ful, al - ways pa - tient; Love nev - er fails!

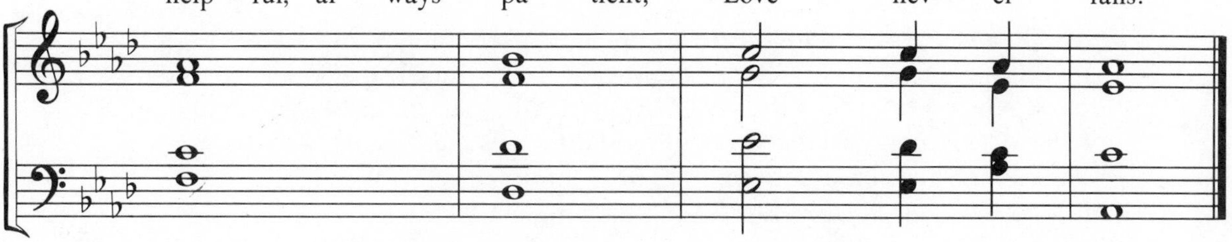

Record 9, Side B, Band 2

LISTENING . . .

Ah, vous dirai-je, Maman

Wolfgang Amadeus Mozart

THEME:

In Theme and Variations, a musical theme is stated in a straightforward way, so that the listener can hear it clearly. Then the theme is restated several times, each time varied in some way. Each variation, in this form, is a separate section of the piece.

Call Number			Call Number		
THEME			VARIATION II		
(1)	A		(1)	A	
(2)	A	Repetition	(2)	A	Repetition
(3)	B	Contrast	(3)	B	Contrast
(4)	A		(4)	A	
VARIATION I			VARIATION III		
(1)	A		(1)	A	
(2)	A	Repetition	(2)	A	Repetition
(3)	B	Contrast	(3)	B	Contrast
(4)	A		(4)	A	

Continue this lesson by giving brief descriptions of each variation while you listen.

Compose and notate your own theme. Experiment with the melody, the rhythm, and the harmony to create variations on your original theme.

This theme and variations on an old French nursery tune was written in Paris during the summer of 1778, a low point in Mozart's life. He disliked Paris and the separation from his wife, found his patron difficult to please, then had to write to his father about the death of his mother who had accompanied him to Paris. Was his mood reflected in this composition? Do you think the composition helped free Mozart from his problems? How?

MAKING YOUR OWN MUSIC

1. Demonstrate, by singing or playing, your understanding of these terms: motive, phrase, sequence, repetition, imitation, contrast.
2. "FOLLOW THE LEADER." Students select an event to describe, such as an opera, rock or symphony concert, or a trip to the zoo or beach. All clap hands and snap fingers on alternate beats. Two or three leaders alternate, describing activities during the trip. Improvise a melodic motive which the class repeats, while all maintain a steady clapping and snapping pattern. As the story continues, motives should become increasingly longer. Variants: Assign each student a number; change dynamics and tempos. Each student calls out a number and plays a rhythm pattern which must be repeated by another student with the number who in turn repeats the process, using the same or a different motive.
3. "IMAGINATION." How do composers get inspiration for their melodies? The following are some suggestions: A fine melody of your own; a city skyline; a country scene; an angry or peaceful tune; design of buildings (AB, ABA, skyscraper); snake, grasshopper, sea gulls; bicycles, sports cars. Can you use several for your music? Graph your melody, determine rhythm, set sound sources, and tape.
4. Explore the possibilities of vocal and instrumental improvisation and composition, using pentatonic, major and minor scales, whole tone, 12-tone, or twelve-tone "row." These pitch organizations afford challenges for advanced composition.
5. Textures are often described as thin or thick, light or heavy. Sing "Michael, Row the Boat Ashore," or the round "Hey, Ho Nobody Home." Using as many vocal and instrumental devices as possible, develop an increasingly thicker texture. At the same time maintain the style of the songs.
6. "THE MORNING PAPER." Bring a small section of the morning newspaper which you should be prepared to sing. How could you vary the performances to portray textures as well as the design of a composition?
7. You have learned to harmonize these chords: I (Tonic), IV (Subdominant), and V (Dominant). Write these three chords for three voice-parts on the chalkboard.

Record 10, Side A, Band 7

LISTENING . . .

West End Blues

Louis Armstrong

PROGRAMMED TAPE

Listen to hear when the above chords are used and what changes are made. Hum with the recording. Later, use drums for accompaniment, hum, and make chord changes. Have a vocalist or instrumentalist improvise with the class. Play other recordings to utilize the "blues" pattern or form of chord progressions.

Sixty-Six Highway Blues — Record 4, Side A, Band 5
John Henry — Record 5, Side B, Band 3
The 3-Way Canon Blues — Record 5, Side B, Band 5

WOMEN IN MUSIC

This picture essay may generate a special interest in the many roles women play in music — Sarah Caldwell, as an operatic conductor; Antonia Brico, as a symphonic conductor; Beverly Sills, as one of the world's leading operatic stars, Kyumg Wha Chung, an international concert violinist; and Mahalia Jackson, the great American gospel singer.

Top: Sarah Caldwell, conductor
Bottom: Beverly Sills, soprano; director, New York City Opera

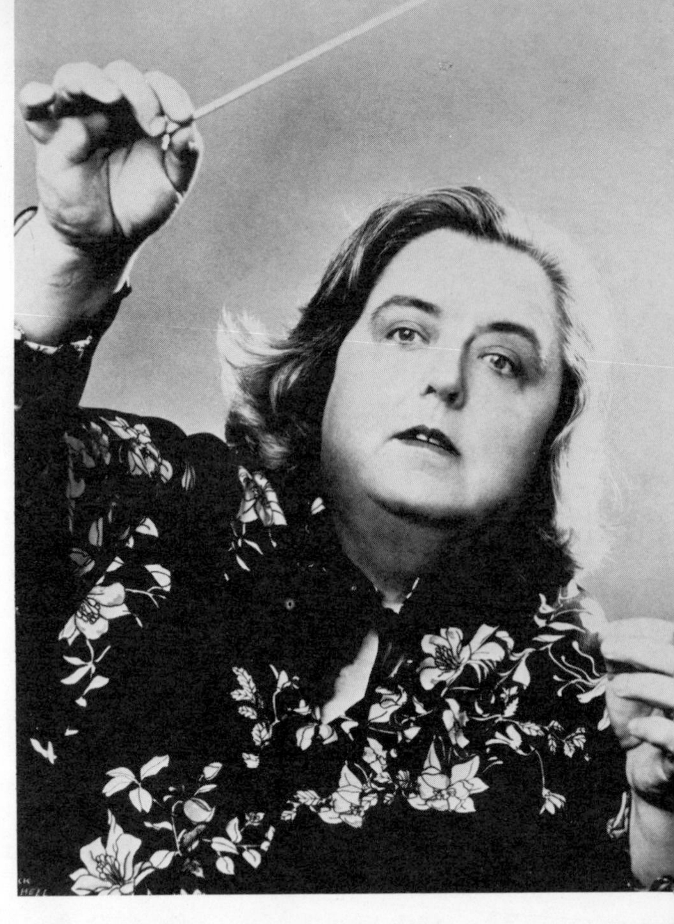

Antonia Brico, Conductor
Kazuko Hillyer International, Inc.

Kyumg Wha Chung, violinist
Courtesy of CBS

Diana Ross, pop singer
Courtesy of United Press International

Andres Segovia (b. 1893) is an internationally famous Spanish guitar virtuoso. His playing has had much influence in recognizing the guitar as a concert instrument.

UNIT 5

Theodore Bikel

Theodore Bikel (b. 1924, Vienna, Austria) is known as an actor, singer, guitarist, and folk music authority. He became an American citizen in 1961. Bikel has appeared in both motion pictures and on the stage. He is especially remembered for his performances in Sound of Music and Fiddler on the Roof.

Josh White

Josh White (b. 19 has appeared on Broadway and ha made concert appearances as a fol singer and guitari He has recorded both spirituals ar blues songs.

José Feliciano, composer, singer, and guitarist is a popular performer with wide audience appeal.

Andres Segovia

José Feliciano

Playing Instruments

The guitar and the piano are both favorite instruments of young people in many parts of the world. In this unit you will be introduced to the basic fundamentals of playing these instruments.

Many of the folk songs in this book include chord indications. After studying this unit, you should be able to accompany these songs on the guitar or the piano.

Study the diagram below to learn the important parts of the guitar.

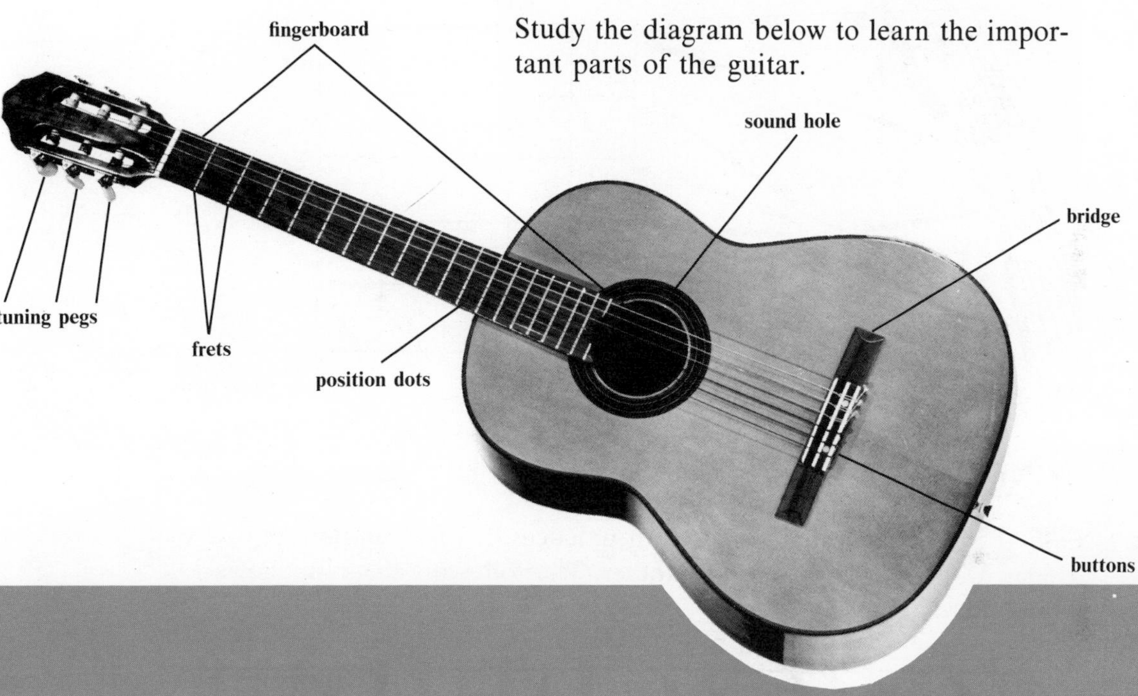

THE FINGERBOARD

The diagram below illustrates the fingerboard of the guitar. The vertical lines represent six strings. Reading from left to right the strings are numbered 6, 5, 4, 3, 2, and 1. The thickest string is number 6. The thin string is number 1. The horizontal lines are frets. The black dots indicate the finger placement.

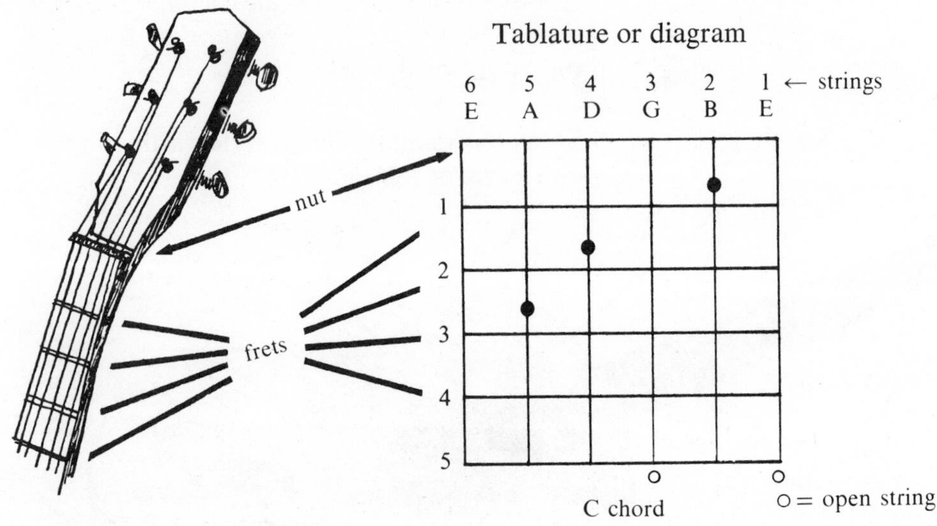

TUNING THE GUITAR

Ease of tuning the guitar comes with practice. It is very important for you to match one pitch sound with another. The following diagram shows you how to tune to a piano.

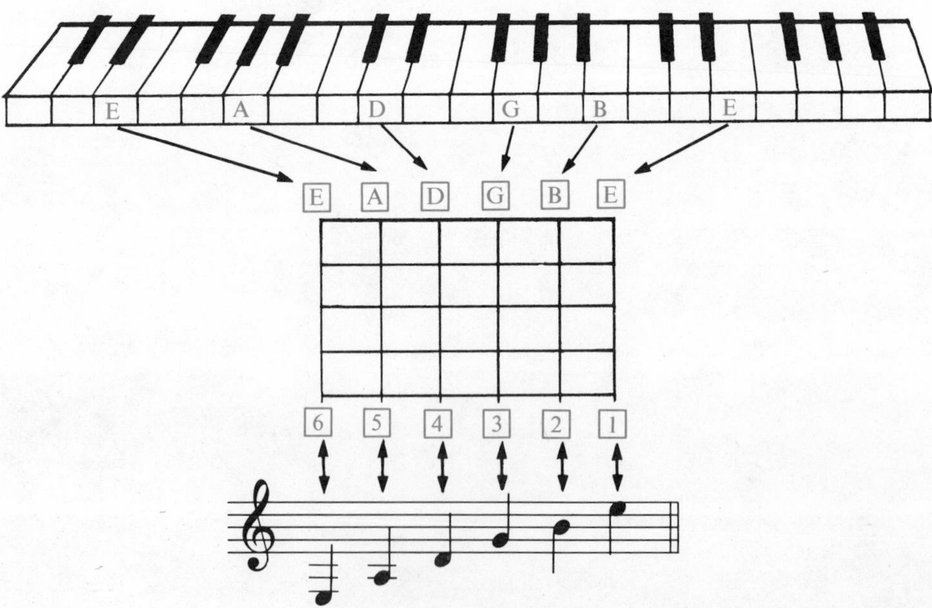

In hammering the desired string, make certain that the finger comes down firmly directly behind the appropriate fret. If the resulting sound is poor or inaccurate in pitch, check to see that the finger is close enough to the fret and/or not holding the string down firmly enough.

PLAYING THE GUITAR

To play the guitar, place your finger firmly on a string behind the fret. The fingers of the left hand hammer the strings on the fingerboard. The right hand is used to strum, pluck, and scratch the strings in the sound hole area. The illustration below shows the left hand in playing position.

The ball of the left thumb is placed firmly at the back of the neck of the guitar. Never hook or loop the thumb around the neck of the guitar.

READING THE CHORD DIAGRAMS

In the chord diagram chart on page 132 the vertical lines represent the six strings of the guitar. The horizontal lines represent frets. The dots indicate finger placement. The numbers above the chord diagram indicate the fingers of the left hand to be used. The fingers are numbered 1, 2, 3, 4, as shown in the picture below.

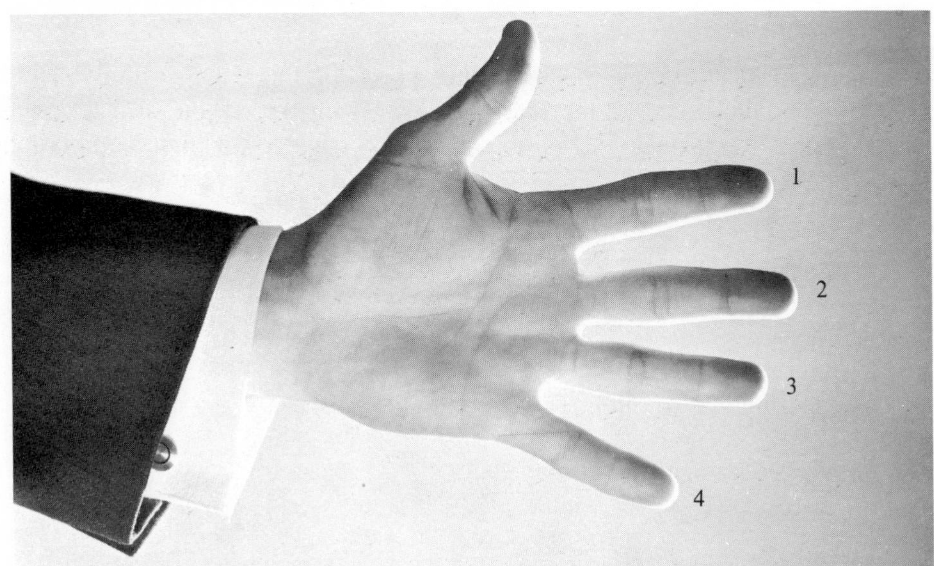

During practice you will find that other fingering is possible. Use alternate fingering or invent original fingering to suit individual circumstances.

A chord diagram using numbers and letters instead of music notation is known as a *tablature*.

CHORD DIAGRAM CHART

The following chart is provided to help you play the chords in this unit. Memorize as many of these chords as possible. Each fret represents one half step in pitch. Numbers refer to fingers. Short lines in the diagrams indicate that these strings are not to be played.

MAJOR KEYS

A	0 0 2 1 3 0 A(I)	0 2 0 1 0 0 $E_7(V_7)$	0 1 3 2 D(IV)
E	0 2 3 1 0 0 E(I)	2 1 3 0 4 $B_7(V_7)$	0 0 2 1 3 0 A(IV)
G	2 1 0 0 0 3 G(I)	0 2 1 3 $D_7(V_7)$	3 2 0 1 0 C(IV)
D	0 1 3 2 D(I)	0 0 2 0 1 0 $A_7(V_7)$	2 1 0 0 0 3 G(IV)

MINOR KEYS

A	0 0 2 3 1 0 Am(I)	0 2 0 1 0 0 $E_7(V_7)$	0 2 3 1 Dm(IV)
D	0 0 2 3 1 Dm(I)	0 0 2 0 1 0 $A_7(V_7)$	0 1 Gm(IV)
E	0 2 3 0 0 0 Em(I)	2 1 3 0 4 $B_7(V_7)$	0 0 2 3 1 0 Am(IV)
B	3 4 2 1 Bm(I)	3 2 1 0 $F\sharp_7(V_7)$	0 2 3 0 0 0 Em(IV)

Study the illustrations on the preceding pages of this unit carefully. Hold the guitar as illustrated in the photographs. Strum the strings with a downward motion. Remember, the guitar sounds an octave lower than the notation on the staff.

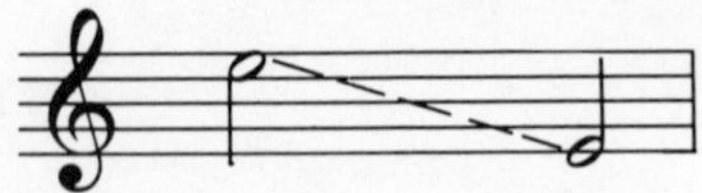

0 = open string played but not fingered

unmarked strings are not played

Strums may be executed by lightly brushing all strings with fingers of the right hand or by using only the right thumb to brush the strings. As an aid in learning the above chord patterns, use songs suggested on page 143 – "Improvising Accompaniments on the Guitar."

Key: D
Starting Tone: D (1-do)

Meter: 3 (quarter note)

Record 3, Side B, Band 1

KUM BA YAH

(koom bah yah)

Afro-American Song "kum ba yah" means "come by here."

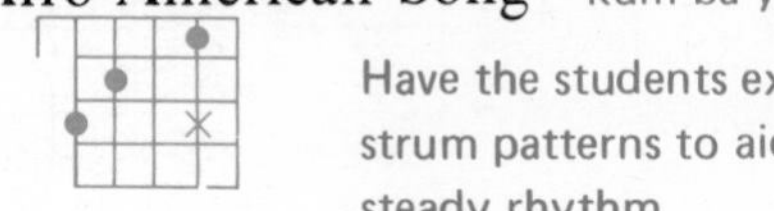

Starting Note (×)

Have the students experiment with various strum patterns to aid them in keeping a steady rhythm.

Chords used in these songs:

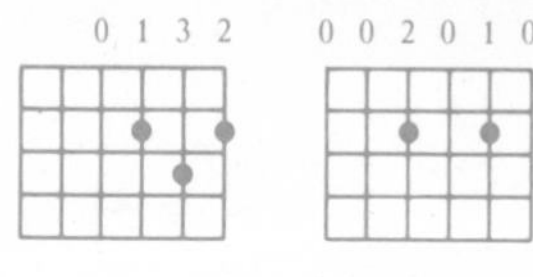

Remember, place your finger firmly on the string behind the fret.

1. Kum ba yah, my Lord, kum ba yah! Kum ba yah, my Lord, kum ba yah!

Kum ba yah, my Lord, kum ba yah! Oh, Lord,_ kum ba yah!

2. Someone's sleeping Lord, kum ba yah! . . .
3. Someone's praying, Lord, kum ba yah! . . .
4. Someone's shouting, Lord, kum ba yah! . . .
5. Someone's singing, Lord, kum ba yah! . . .

THE COLORADO TRAIL

American Folk Song

Key: D
Starting Tone: F# (3-mi)

Meter: 4 (quarter note)

Record 3, Side B, Band 2

1. Eyes like the morn-ing star, cheeks like a rose. Lau-ra was a pret-ty girl
2. She was a laugh-ing girl, joy - ful all day, Lau-ra was the sweet-est girl

ev - 'ry - bod - y knows;
now she's gone a - way,
Weep, all ye lit - tle rains, wail, winds,_ wail,

all a - long, a - long, a - long the Col - o - ra - do trail.

Key: D | Meter: 2/♩ | Record 3, Side B, Band 3

Starting Tone: D (1-do)

BUFFALO GALS

Folk Song

Chords used in these songs:

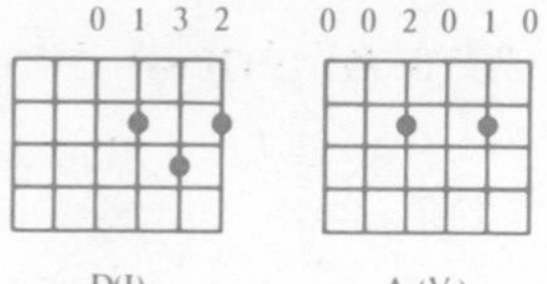
0 1 3 2
0 0 2 0 1 0
D(I)
A7(V7)

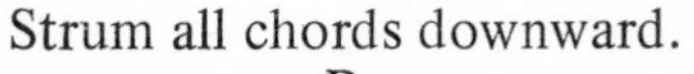
Strum all chords downward.

D D A7 D
1. As I was walk - ing down the street, down the street, down the street,
2. I asked her if she'd stop and talk stop and talk, stop and talk,

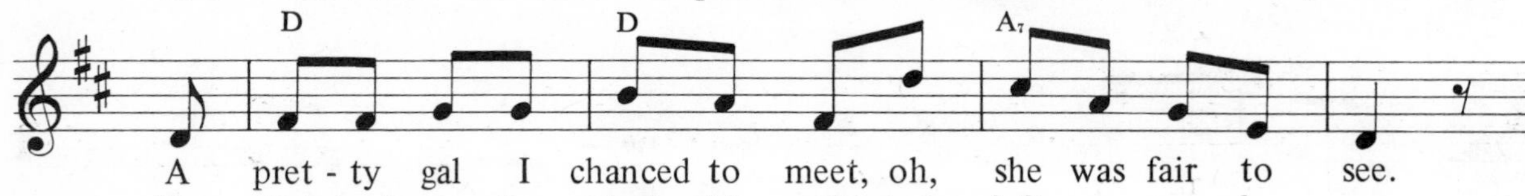
D D A7
A pret - ty gal I chanced to meet, oh, she was fair to see.
Her feet took up the whole side - walk, and left no room for me.

D D A7
Oh, Buf - fa - lo Gals, won't you come out to - night, come out to - night,

D D D
Come out to - night? Oh, Buf - fa - lo Gals, won't you come out to - night,

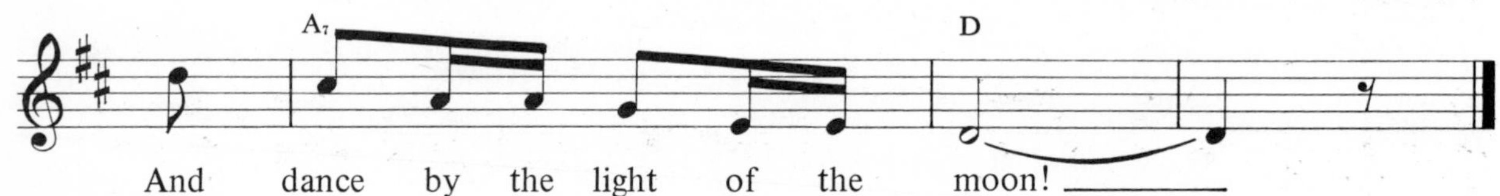
A7 D
And dance by the light of the moon!

3. I asked her if she'd be my wife, be my wife, be my wife,
Then I'd be happy all my life, if she'd marry me.
Oh, Buffalo Gals, won't you come out tonight, come out tonight, come out tonight?
Oh, Buffalo Gals, won't you come out tonight, and dance by the light of the moon?

Key: G
Starting Tone: D (5-sol)

Meter: $\frac{2}{♩}$

Record 3, Side B, Band 5

HUSH, LITTLE BABY

Southern Folk Song

Listen to the recording of the song before playing the G and D7 chords. Point out to the class how these two chords form the harmonic structure of this song.

Chords used in these songs:

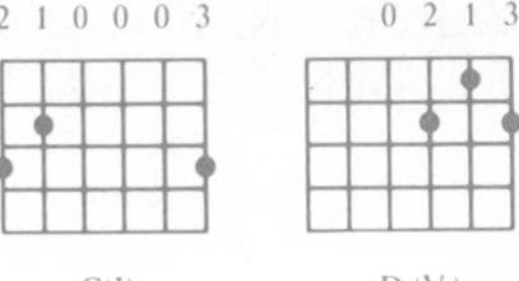
2 1 0 0 0 3
0 2 1 3

G(I) D7(V7)

Slowly
G
D7
D7
G

1. Hush, lit-tle ba-by, don't say a word, Pa-pa's gon-na buy you a mock-ing bird.
2. If that dia-mond ring turns to brass, Pa-pa's gon-na buy you a look-ing glass.

G
D7
D7
G

If that mock-ing-bird won't sing, Pa-pa's gon-na buy you a dia-mond ring.
If that look-ing glass gets broke, Pa-pa's gon-na buy you a bil-ly goat.

3. If that billy goat won't pull,
Papa's gonna buy you a cart and bull.
If that cart and bull turn over,
Papa's gonna buy you a dog named Rover.

4. If that dog named Rover won't bark,
Papa's gonna buy you a horse and cart.
If that horse and cart fall down,
You'll be the sweetest little one in town.

Key: G
Starting Tone: G (1-do)

Meter: $\frac{4}{♩}$

Record 3, Side B, Band 5

FRÈRE JACQUES

French Folk Song

Experiment with various tempos and dynamics in performing this song.

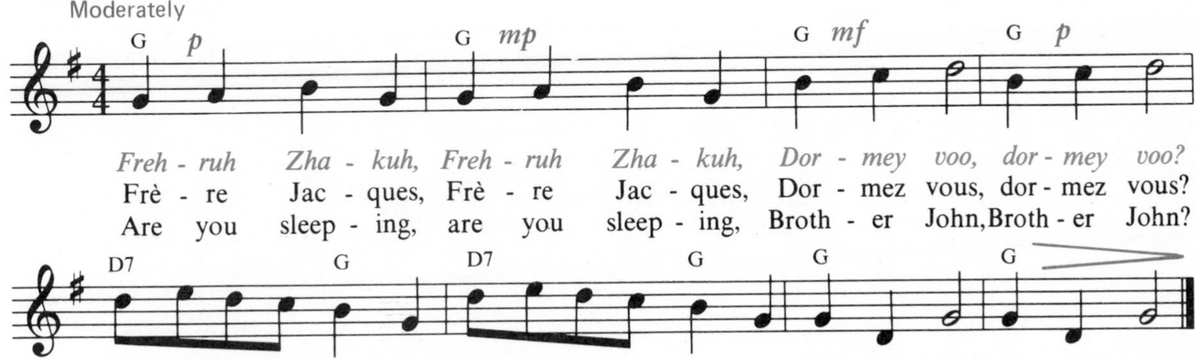
Moderately
G p
G mp
G mf
G p
Freh - ruh Zha - kuh, Freh - ruh Zha - kuh, Dor - mey voo, dor - mey voo?
Frè - re Jac - ques, Frè - re Jac - ques, Dor - mez vous, dor - mez vous?
Are you sleep - ing, are you sleep - ing, Broth - er John, Broth - er John?
D7
G
D7
G
G
G

Soh - ney leh ma - tee - nuh, Soh - ney leh ma - tee - nuh, Din, don, din, din, don, din.
Son - nez les ma - ti - nes, Son - nez les ma - ti - nes, Din, don, din, din, don, din.
Morn - ing bells are ring - ing, Morn - ing bells are ring - ing, Ding, dong, ding, ding, dong, ding.

Key: G
Starting Tone: G (1-do)

Meter: 3 (quarter note)

Record 3, Side B, Band 6

GOODNIGHT, IRENE

Words and Music by Huddie Ledbetter and John Lomax

Chords used in this song:

Encourage the students to "harmonize" on the chorus. Does this change the texture of the song? How? (The texture is thicker when a harmony part is added.)

2 1 0 0 0 3
0 2 1 3
3 2 0 1 0
G(I)
D7(V7)
C(IV)
Starting Note
Chorus
G D7 G
I - rene, good - night: I - rene, good - night.
G C D7
Good - night, I - rene, good - night, I - rene; I'll see you
G Fine G D7
in my dreams.
1. Sat - ur - day night I got mar - ried,
2. Some-time I live in the coun - try,
G
Me and my wife set - tled down. Now me and my
Some-time I live in town; Some - time I
C D7 G D.C. al Fine
wife are part - ed I'm gon-na take an-oth-er stroll down - town.
have a great no - tion To jump in the ri - ver and drown.

3. Stop ramblin', stop your gamblin',
Stop staying out late at night.
Go home to your wife and your fam'ly,
Sit down by the fireside bright. (Chorus)

Key: D   Meter: 4   Record 3, Side B, Band 7

Starting Tone: D (1-do)

MICHAEL, ROW THE BOAT ASHORE

Work Song and Spiritual

Chords used in this song:

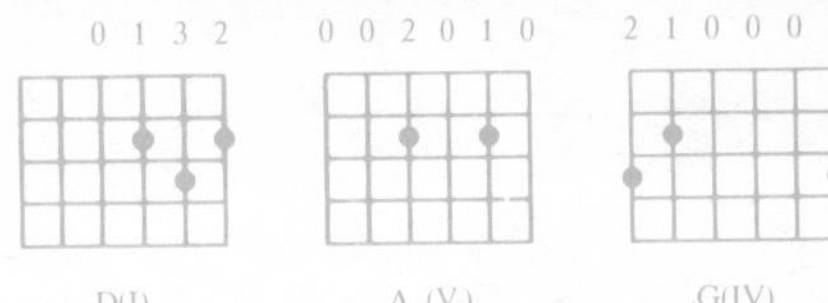

What chord is outlined by the first three notes? (D major, D – F# – A)

Slowly
1. Mi - chael, row the boat a - shore, Hal - le - lu - jah!
D
A7
D
D
Mi - chael, row the boat a - shore, Hal - le - lu - jah!

2. Michael boat a gospel boat . . .
3. Michael boat a music boat . . .
4. Gabriel, blow the trumpet horn . . .
5. Brother, lend a helpin' hand . . .
6. Jordan stream is wide and deep . . .
7. Michael, row the boat ashore . . .

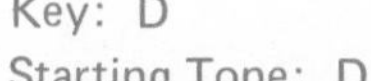

Key: D   Meter: 3 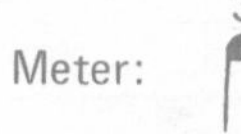   Record 4, Side A, Band 1

Starting Tone: D (1-do)

ON TOP OF OLD SMOKY

Kentucky Folk Song

What chord is outlined in the first full measure of this song? (D major chord, or D major triad)

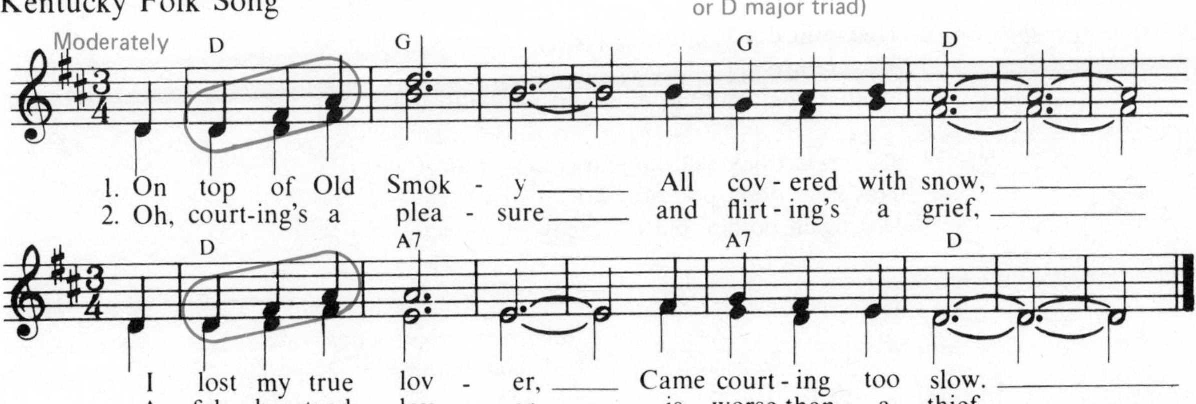

Test the students' memory of the D Major chord patterns. Have the class sing "On Top of Old Smoky" and add the appropriate chord when their ears tell them to. As an aid, decide that only three chords (D, G, and A_7) will be used.

Key: D
Starting Tone: D (1-do)

Meter: 2/♩

Record 4, Side A, Band 2

THIS TRAIN

Congregational Spiritual

Chords used in this song:

0 1 3 2
0 0 2 0 1 0
2 1 0 0 0 3
D(I)
A7(V7)
G(IV)

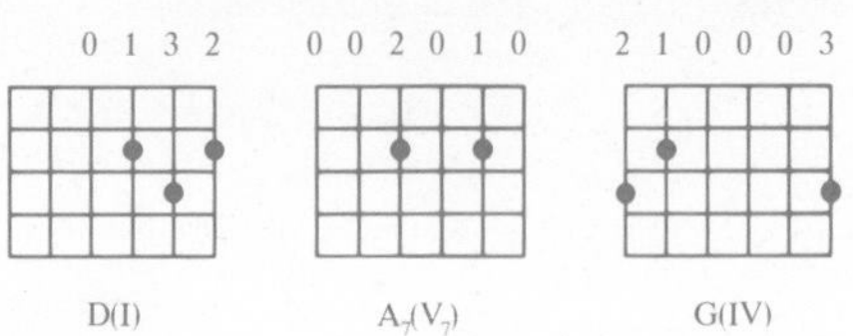

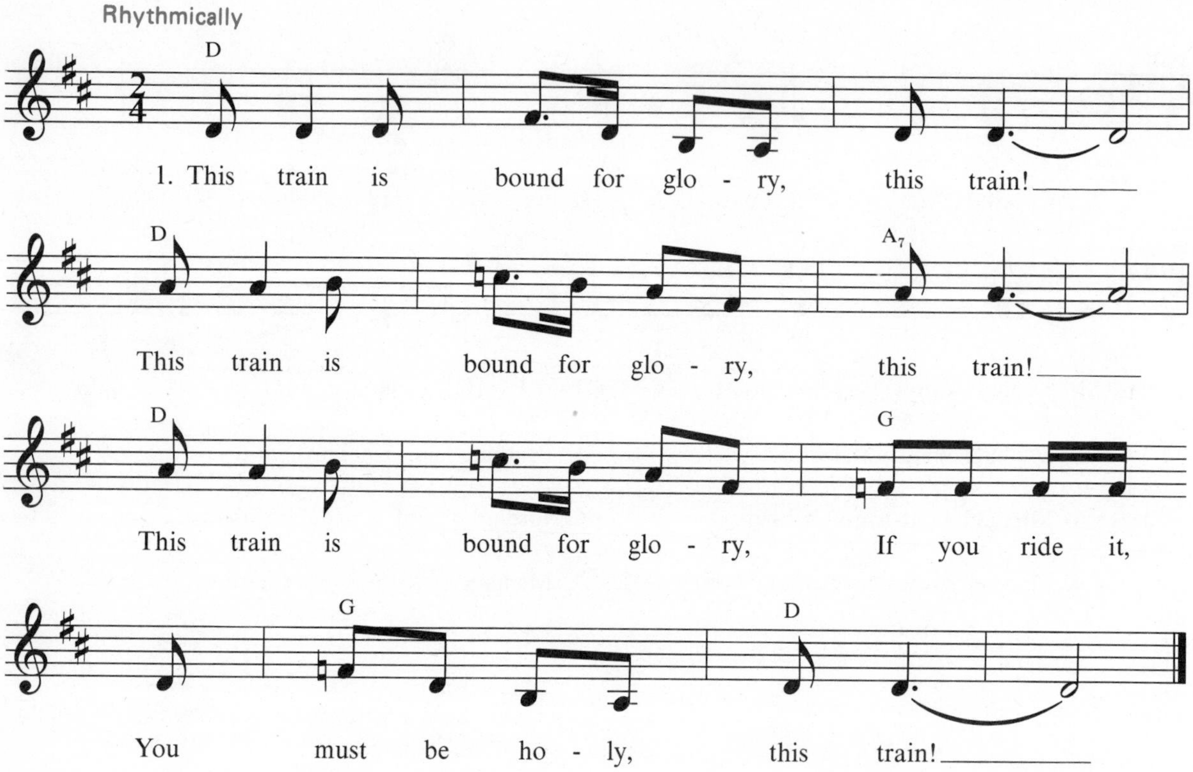

Rhythmically
D
1. This train is bound for glo - ry, this train!
D
A7
This train is bound for glo - ry, this train!
D
G
This train is bound for glo - ry, If you ride it,
G
D
You must be ho - ly, this train!

2. This train don't pull no gamblers, this train! (*twice*)
This train don't pull no gamblers,
Neither don't pull no midnight ramblers, this train!

3. This train don't pull no extras, this train! (*twice*)
This train don't pull no extras,
Don't pull nothin' but the Heavenly Special, this train!

Have the students experiment in various ways to change the sound, beat, and feeling of this song; first verse — loud and fast; second verse — slower and medium loud; third verse — fast and soft.

Key: Am Meter: 2 (dotted quarter) Record 4, Side A, Band 3
Starting Tone: E (3-mi)

I WONDER AS I WANDER

Chords used in this song:

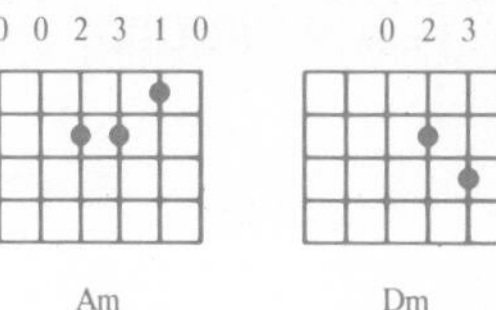
0 0 2 3 1 0
0 2 3 1
Am
Dm

Words and Music by John Jacob Niles

Have students hum the melody as they strum the chords.

mp
Am
1. I won - der as I wan - der out un - der the sky
How Je - sus our Sav - ior did come for to die;
For poor on - 'ry peo - ple like you and like I.
I won - der as I wan - der out un - der the sky.
Dm
p

2. When Mary birthed Jesus 'twas in a cow's stall,
With wise men and farmers and shepherds and all,
But high from God's heaven a star's light did fall,
And the promise of ages it then did recall.

3. If Jesus had wanted for any wee thing,
A star in the sky or a bird on the wing,
Or all of God's angels in heaven to sing,
He surely could have it, 'cause He was the King.

STUDENT INVOLVEMENT 1. Ask a student to read the text aloud and comment on how the text should affect the interpretation of the song (dynamics and tempo). 2. Rehearse the song over a period of time. Discuss the type of things that one expects to hear in both ensemble singing and playing: blend between individual voices and instruments; balance between voices and instruments; the overall sound, beat, and feeling of the composition.

Key: G Meter: 2 (quarter note) Record 4, Side A, Band 4
Starting Tone: D (5-sol)

BONSOIR, MES AMIS

French Canadian Folk Song

Have the students harmonize the chorus section (mainly in thirds) after they have mastered the I and V7 chords for this song.

Chords used in this song:

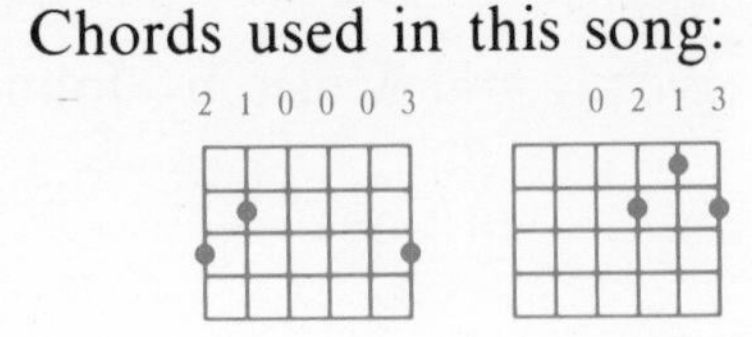

Brightly

Bohn - swahr, meh za - mee, bohn - swahr! Bohn - swahr, meh za - mee, bohn -
Bon - soir, mes a - mis, bon - soir! Bon - soir, mes a - mis, bon -
Good - night, my ___ friends, good - night! Good - night, my ___ friends, good -

swahr! Bohn - swahr, meh za - mee, bohn - swahr, meh za - mee, bohn -
soir! Bon - soir, mes a - mis, bon - soir, mes a - mis, bon -
night! Good - night, my ___ friends, good - night, my ___ friends, good -

swahr meh za - mee, bohn - swahr! O ruh - vwahr! ___
soir, mes a - mis, bon - soir! Au re - voir! ___
night, my ___ friends, good - night. Now, good - bye! ___

Fine

Marchlike

Kahn ohn eh see byehn ahn - sahm - bluh poor - kwah
Quand on est si bien en - sem - ble, pour - quoi
When we're so hap - py to - geth - er It's too

dohnk suh sey - pa - rey? ___ Poor - kwah
donc se sé - pa - rer? ___ Pour - quoi
bad that we must part ___ It's too

dohnk; poor - kwah dohnk, poor - kwah dohnk suh sey - pa - rey? ___
donc, pour - quoi donc, pour - quoi donc se sé - pa - rer? ___
bad, it's too bad, it's too bad that we must part. ___

D. C. al Fine

Experiment with various tempi and dynamics for this song before playing the recording.
Have students test their ability to identify the Key, Starting Tone, and Meter of songs in their books.

Key: G
Meter: 2
Record 4, Side A, Band 5
Starting Tone: D (5-sol)

SIXTY-SIX HIGHWAY BLUES

Words of first verse by Woody Guthrie
Additional verses by Jerry Silverman
Music by Pete Seeger

Chords used in this song:

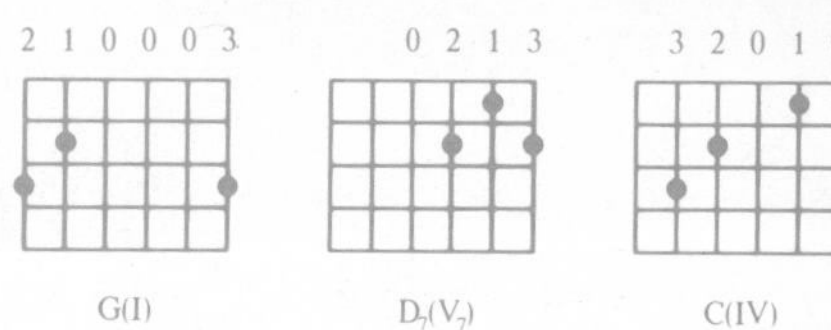

Listen to the recording. Experiment with other chords to add variety and interest to the accompaniment.

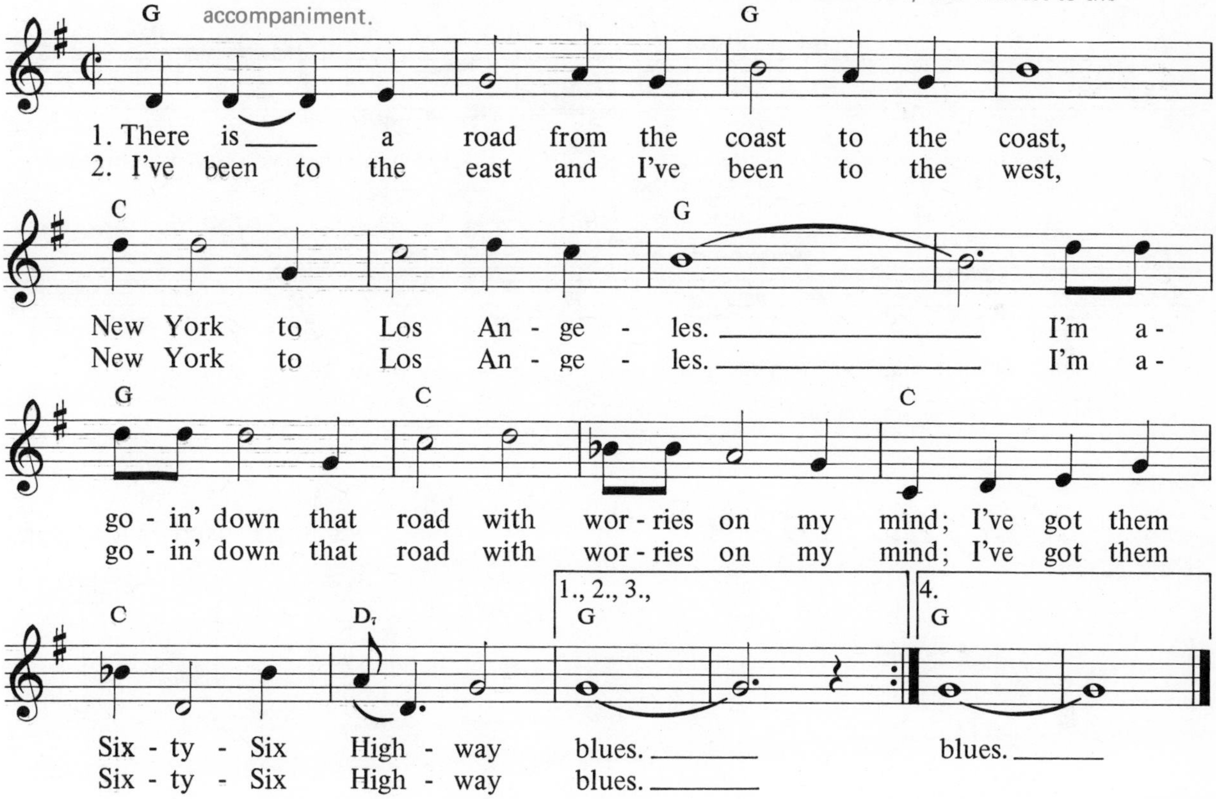

G G C G G C C C D_7 G G

1. There is a road from the coast to the coast,
New York to Los An - ge - les. I'm a-
go - in' down that road with wor - ries on my mind; I've got them
Six - ty - Six High - way blues.

2. I've been to the east and I've been to the west,
New York to Los An - ge - les. I'm a-
go - in' down that road with wor - ries on my mind; I've got them
Six - ty - Six High - way blues.

1., 2., 3., 4. blues.

3. Been tryin' to make an honest dollar a day,
New York to Los Angeles.
I'm a-goin' down that road with worries on my mind;
I've got them Sixty-Six Highway blues.

4. I ain't got no home in this world any more,
New York to Los Angeles.
I'm a-goin' down that road with worries on my mind;
I've got them Sixty-Six Highway blues.

Key: D Minor
Starting Tone: A (5-mi) Meter: 2 𝅗𝅥 Record 4, Side A, Band 6

OH, SINNER MAN

Spiritual

Chords used in this song:

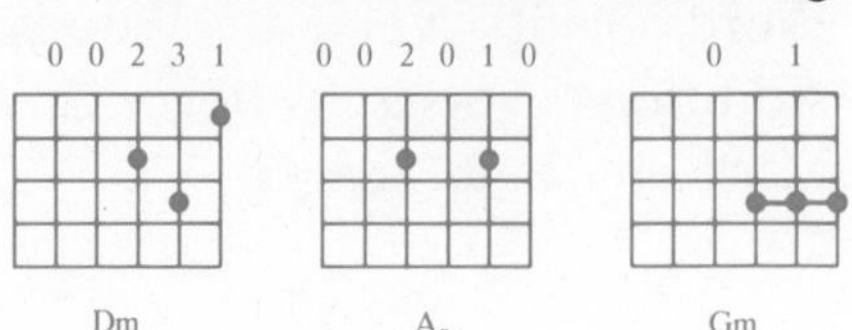

Oh, sin-ner man, where you gon-na run to? Oh, sin-ner man, where you gon-na run to?

Oh, sin-ner man, where you gon-na run to? All on that day?_____

Record 4, Side A, Band 7

BLACK IS THE COLOR

Folk Song

Chords used in this song:

0 2 3 0 0 0 — Em
3 4 2 1 — Bm
0 0 2 3 1 0 — Am

Key: Modal, Aeolian Meter: 2 𝅗𝅥
Starting Tone: B

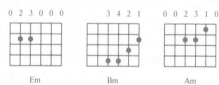

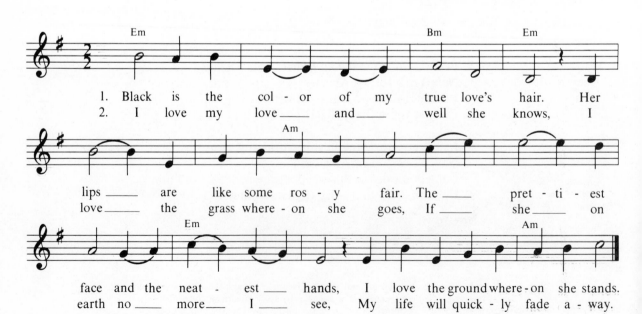

Em Bm Em

1. Black is the col - or of my true love's hair. Her
2. I love my love____ and____ well she knows, I

lips____ are like some ros - y fair. The____ pret - ti - est
love____ the grass where - on she goes, If____ she____ on

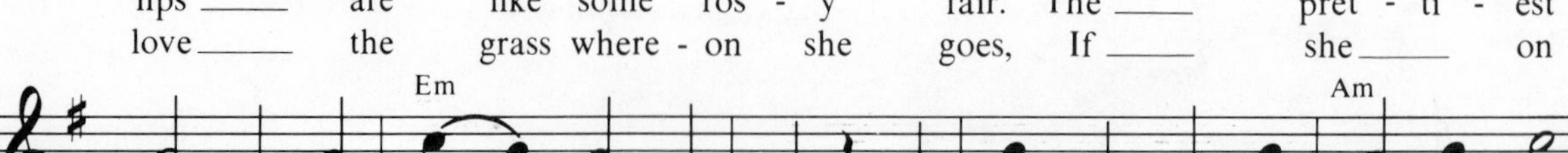

face and the neat - est___ hands, I love the ground where - on she stands.
earth no____ more___ I____ see, My life will quick - ly fade a - way.

IMPROVISING ACCOMPANIMENTS ON THE GUITAR

After you have mastered a few basic chords on the guitar, you can improvise your own accompaniments for many songs. Review the chords you learned in this unit and improvise your own accompaniments.

Key of G (Chords used: G, D7, C)

"I've Been Working on the Railroad"
"All Night, All Day"
"Clementine"
"Sylvie"
"This Land Is Your Land"
"Aunt Rhody"
"When the Saints Go Marching In"
"Sing Your Way Home"
"Little David, Play on Your Harp"
"Home on the Range"
"The Roving Kind"

Key of D (Chords used: D, A7, G)

"Down by the Riverside"
"He Knows"
"If I Had a Hammer"
"A-Roving"
"Sweet Betsy from Pike"
"Wait for the Wagon"
"Sourwood Mountain"
"He's Got the Whole World in His Hands"
"Row, Row, Row Your Boat"
"Bell Bottom Trousers"
"So Long"

Try playing the Key of G major list above in A major. Try playing the songs listed in the Key of D major in E major. Notice that you have changed keys to a number of songs. This is called *transposing*.

LEARNINGS AND SKILLS The history and structure of the piano.

THE STORY OF THE PIANO

Delos Smith

STUDENT INVOLVEMENT 1. Make sympathetic vibration experiments striking a fundamental tone, using damper pedal, and then pressing the same note several octaves higher without sounding the note. The result should be a faint sounding of the higher note because of the sympathetic phenomena. 2. Experiment with the effects produced by other pedals.

More than 200 Strings

The piano has 88 keys and 88 actions, but many more strings. Only the lowest notes are produced by 1 string. Others, directly above them in scale, are sounded by 2 strings, tuned in unison and struck by 1 hammer. All remaining notes require 3 strings. This gives equal strength to all notes.

What the Pedals do

Left pedal, by shifting all keys and actions a bit to the right, causes hammers to strike only 1 string of 2-string notes and only 2 of 3-string notes. Result-same pressures on keys produce softer sounds. Middle pedal holds 1 note or chord. Right pedal lifts dampers from all strings, so that all the sounds produced while this pedal is down are held.

The Piano Keyboard

The piano has 88 keys (52 white and 36 black). This is the arrangement used today. Many other keyboards have been devised (a famous one with six rows of keys, recommended by Liszt and Rubinstein) but the "C Major Keyboard" as we know it has become standard. The white keys struck in succession (c d e f g a b c, for example, play the notes of the C Major scale. There are whole-tone intervals between adjoining notes except from each e to f and b to c, which are semitone intervals or "half-steps." The black keys are placed between those adjoining white keys which are separated by whole-tone intervals. Black keys play the semitones between the white keys. The full keyboard, black and white keys together, plays 88 notes, each separated by a semitone interval. Thus the piano keyboard is the closest visual representation of musical notation and is the most versatile of all instruments.

Octaves are the tones at each end of a scale (C-C; D-D; E-E, etc.) This is the most perfect consonance–the two played together even sound like the same

two-manual harpsichord

concert grand

note, perhaps because the higher one vibrates exactly twice as fast as its lower counterpart. (Thus, **a** vibrates 440 times per second, and its octave **a′** above, exactly 880 times.) Chords are combinations of tones played simultaneously.

One-piece Frame supports 17 Tons

Because strings are of superstrong steel wire stretched to a tension of 165 pounds to the square inch, the piano requires a massive braced one-piece cast metal frame. This frame supports a total pull of about 35,000 pounds, more than 17 tons.

Longest Strings produce Lowest Notes

They are slightly bigger in diameter and weighted with coiled copper wire to slow their vibrations when struck. In this way, they give off correct sound values. They get the additional length they need by being overstrung above the other strings.

The Glory of the Pianoforte

This familiar instrument could be called The Soft-Loud, because pianoforte means that in Italian. Nothing else musical which can whisper so softly can also thunder so loudly.

Its range is over all the sounds from low to high that the ear hears with comfort. These sounds can be freely mixed, projected in layers, and held while new sounds are built upon or mingled with them.

The piano can equal the orchestra in breadth and approximate it in depth, and it can accompany itself. Furthermore, it is the easiest of all instruments to draw music from. Yet its complexities are as enormous as those of music. Great performers have devoted lifetimes to it without exhausting its potentials. Almost every composer has created music for it.

The piano is the most useful and used of music-makers except the voice. Its sound come from vibrating strings, really steel wires. The strings vibrate by being struck; thus the piano is both a string and a percussion instrument.

RELATED ACTIVITIES 1. See 16mm. color film, The Piano, Film Associates. 2. Read Percy Young's Masters of the Piano. 3. Do additional research on keyboard instruments.

STRUCTURE OF THE KEYBOARD

The piano keyboard has eighty-eight keys. Of these, there are fifty-two white keys. The remaining thirty-six black keys are divided into groups of two black keys and three black keys. At the keyboard, sit in front of the group of two black keys in the middle of the keyboard. This will be the fourth group of two black keys from your left as you face the keyboard.

As you move to your left, the sound is lower. As you move to the right, the sound is higher. Strike some keys at random to experiment with the sound.

Each note of the keyboard has a letter name. The only letters used, as on the staff, are: A, B, C, D, E, F, G.

Find all the A's, the B's, the C's, and so on.

The black keys also are given letter names.

Since the first black key is located to the *right* of white key A, it sounds half a step (half a tone) *higher.*

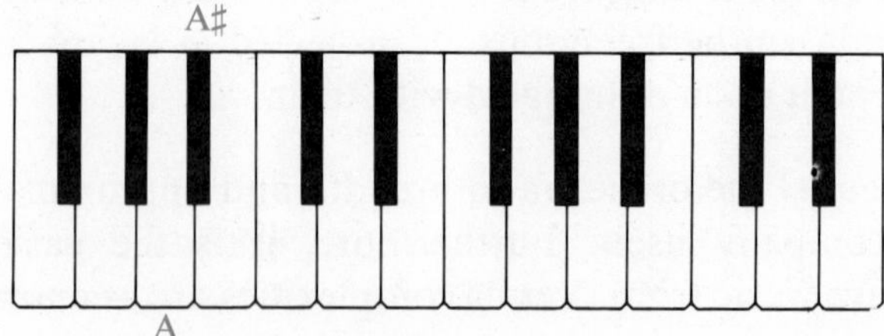

Every black key to the right of a white key thus has a name which shows that it is half a step higher than that white key.

However, it is also located half a step to the left of its white neighbor on the right, so it may have another (lower) name also:

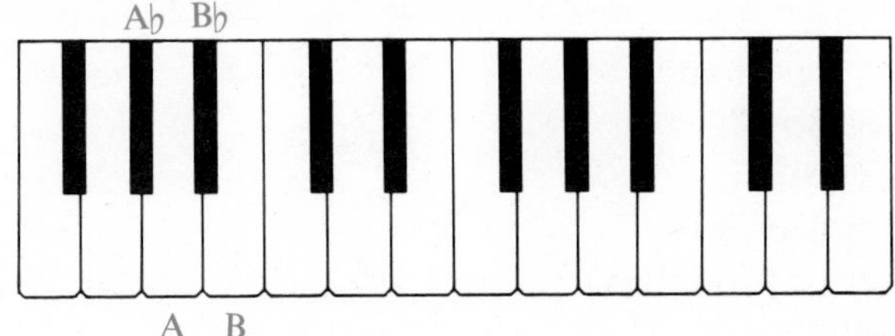

A# and B♭ are the same black key. On the piano they sound alike, but they may have different names or "spellings." Which spelling the note is given depends upon how it is used. This is the range of possible key names:

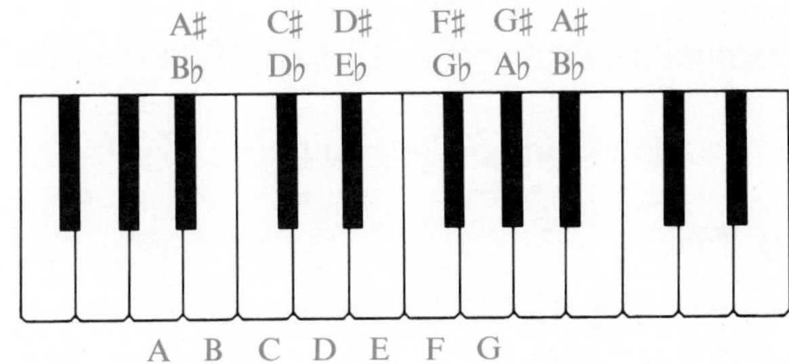

Is your next question "What do you do if you need to play E♯ or F♭ or B♯ or C♭, where there are no black keys?"

What would you do? Experiment with the sound and see if your ears will tell you. When you have found an answer, ask your teacher if your solution is correct.

LEARNINGS AND SKILLS 1. Help the student discover that E# is enharmonic to F and played on a white key; that Cb is enharmonic to B and played accordingly.

2. Devise a "find-the-note game" that will be a self-teaching help to the student. Using 19 cards, write the name of a note (C, A, D#, etc.) on one side; diagram the note position on the back. The student shuffles the cards, draws one, plays the note, turns the card over to check the note he has played. Students may work in teams of two to check each other.

For students who are working on both guitar and keyboard, call attention to the differences in finger numbering.

MYSTERY TUNES

Before we see how the keyboard relates to the staff, try playing the mystery tunes below. The titles of the tunes (not in the order that you will see them) are:

"Give Peace a Chance"
"Row Your Boat"
"Hot Cross Buns"
"Are You Sleeping?"
"In the Silv'ry Moonlight"
"Born Free"

If you are not familiar with them, ask your teacher for the recording which will help you recognize and play them.

Each letter is a beat if it is followed by a space.
If a letter has a dash following, hold it an extra beat.
If a letter has three dashes, hold it for three extra beats.
If there are two letters without a space between, play them both within the same beat (twice as fast).
If there are three letters, unspaced, play all three in the length of one beat.
Letters are grouped to form melody patterns.

1. First Mystery Tune HOT CROSS BUNS

E D C–	E D C–
/ / / /	/ / / /
CCCCDDDD	E D C–
/ / / /	/ / / /

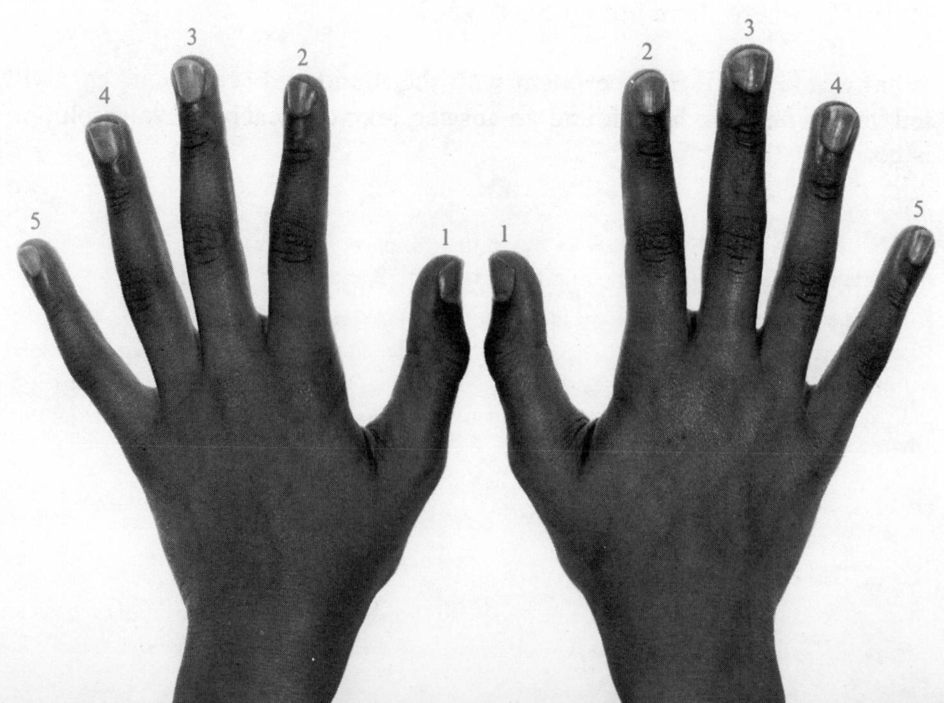

Put your right hand on the keyboard so that your fingers fall on the notes C D E F G.

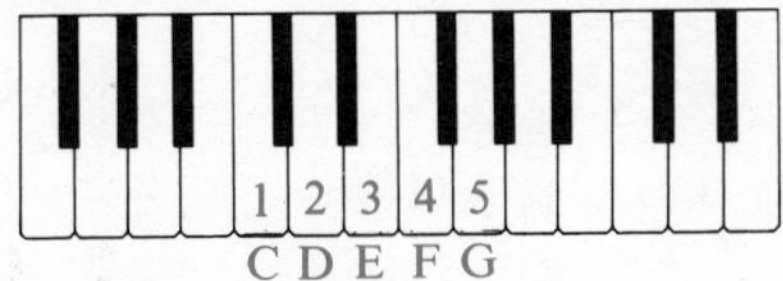

Start the melody with your third finger on E. Let the other fingers follow naturally. After you are sure of the melody, try it with your left hand. Start with finger 3 again, but use 3, 4, 5 of the left hand instead of 3, 2, 1. This may take a little more action for those weaker fingers.

2. Second Mystery Tune

IN THE SILV'RY MOONLIGHT
(Au clair de la lune)

Left hand

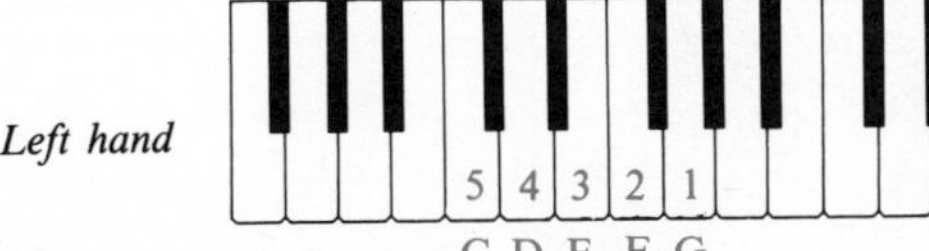

C C C D	E - D -	C E D D	C - - -
/ / / /	/ / / /	/ / / /	/ / / /
C C C D	E - D -	C E D D	C - - -
/ / / /	/ / / /	/ / / /	/ / / /
D D D D	A - A -	D C B A	G - - -
/ / / /	/ / / /	/ / / /	/ / / /
C C C D	E - D -	C E D D	C - - -
/ / / /	/ / / /	/ / / /	/ / / /

If you play it with your right hand, put your finger number 1 on the starting note C.

If you play it with your left hand, try starting with finger number 3 on the note C.

Here is the same tune, but it starts on a different note. *Find a letter that needs a chromatic sign.* (Let your ears help you as you play.)

G G G A	B — A —	G B A A	G — — —
G G G A	B — A —	G B A A	G — — —
A A A A	E — E —	A G F E	D — — —
G G G A	B — A —	G B A A	G — — —

F is the letter which needs a chromatic sign. It should be F #.

3. Third Mystery Tune ROW, ROW YOUR BOAT

Start with finger number 1

C--C--	C-DE--	E-DE-F	G-----
//////	//////	//////	//////
CCCGGG	EEECCC	G-FE-D	C-----
//////	//////	//////	//////

Start on a different pitch.

Do you need chromatic signs? Yes. F should be F#.

D--D--	D-EF--	F-EF-G	A-----
//////	//////	//////	//////
DDDAAA	FFFDDD	A-GF-E	D-----
//////	//////	//////	//////

4. Fourth Mystery Tune ARE YOU SLEEPING (Frère Jacques)

CDEC	CDEC
////	////
EFG-	EFG-
////	////
GAGFEC	GAGFEC
/ / //	/ / //
CGC-	CGC-
////	////

Start on a different pitch.

What chromatic sign do you need?

FGAF	FGAF
////	////
AB♭C-	AB♭C-
////	////
CDCBAF	CDCBAF
/ / //	/ / //
FCF-	FCF-
////	////

B needs a chromatic sign. It should be written Bb.

5. Fifth Mystery Tune: BORN FREE

C - G -	--G A GF
////	// / /
E - C -	--G A GF
////	/// / //

B - G -E F -F FE D

/// // / / / /

C - - -

////

6. Sixth Mystery Tune GIVE PEACE A CHA

E -D- C	D - - -	G---G
////	////	////
F -E- D	C---	
////	////	

Choose a note value for the beat and write these tunes on a staff.

Have the students notate the letter melodies on a staff following the suggestion in the student's book. Encourage the students to think of other comparatively simple tunes to notate in letters or on the staff and then to try the "Mystery Tunes" out on their classmates.

KEYBOARD AND STAFF

C D E F G A B C D E F G A B C D E F G A B C D E F G A B C

Great C
C

Small C
Small C
c

Middle C
or C¹

C²

C³

Notes above Great C and below small c are Great D, Great E, Great F, etc.
Notes above c′ are d′, e′, f′, etc.
The terminology is included for easy and accurate reference to specific notes.

Play this mystery tune from the notation below. Use the above keyboard and staff chart for help.

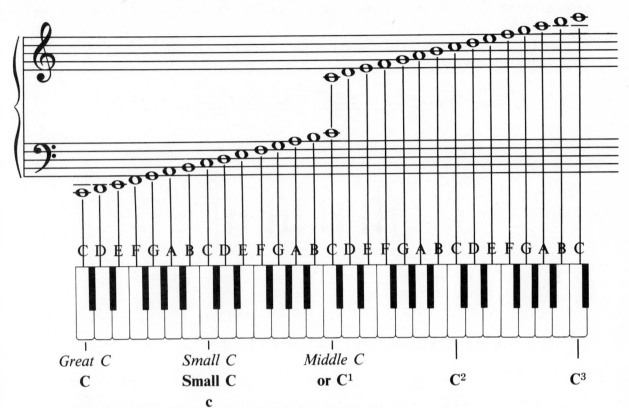

LEARNINGS AND SKILLS 1. Primary chords in the key of C. Learn the chord spellings for triad and the major minor sevenths:

I	–	C	E	G	
IV	–	F	A	C	
V	–	G	B	D	
V7	–	G	B	D	F

MELODIES IN C MAJOR

Some songs, particularly rounds, may be accompanied with one chord in the left hand.

Left Hand Pattern:

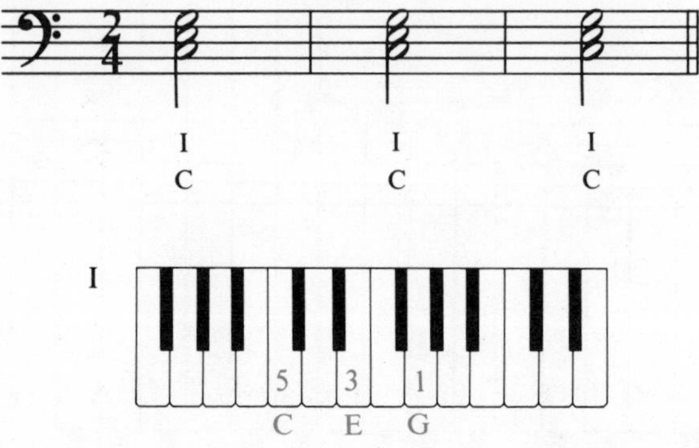

Try this chord accompaniment with a melody on page 150.

TWO CHORD MELODY IN C MAJOR

"Spanish Guitar" needs two chords: tonic (I) and dominant (V). Use this left hand pattern.

Left Hand Pattern:

STUDENT INVOLVEMENT 1. Help students achieve a firm touch and complete sounding of the chord. 2. Help students with melodic fingerings which make playing easier, e.g.: in "Spanish Guitar"

Meas.	Note	Fingering
1	C2	4
9	C2	5
21	B1	3

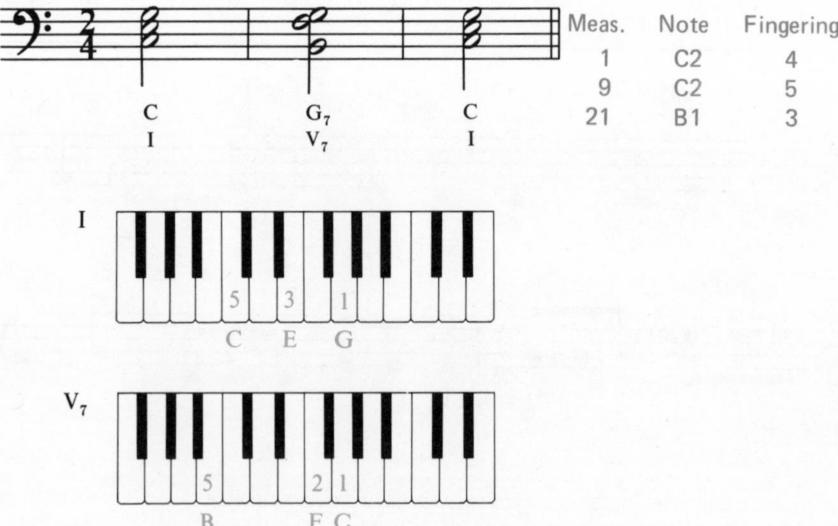

You may use the music in the keyboard section for playing some of the chords that you have learned on the guitar, also.

You may use the music of the keyboard unit for playing the chords which you have learned on guitar, also.

Key: C
Starting Tone: G (5-sol)

Meter: 3/♪

Record 4, Side B, Band 1

SPANISH GUITAR

Folk Song

mf
When I was a stu - dent at Ca - diz I played on my
used to make eyes at the la - dies I think of them
C
G7
Span - ish gui - tar Ching, ching I Ring, ching, ching, ring, ching, ching, Ring out ye
still from a - far Ching, ching
C
C
G7
bells! Oh, ring out ye bells! Oh, ring out ye bells Ring, ching, ching,
C
C
ring, ching, ching, ring out ye bells! As I played on my Spanish guitar. Ching, ching!
C
G7
C

In order to vary the accompaniment, the chords may be broken — e.g. the first measure: play C the first beat, E the second, and G the third.

THREE CHORD MELODY IN C MAJOR

The most frequently used chords for harmonization are the Tonic (I), the Dominant (V), or the richer Dominant Seventh (V_7), and the Subdominant (IV). Here is the left hand pattern. Practice it until you can do it very easily, for you can transfer this same pattern to many other keys.

Left Hand Pattern:

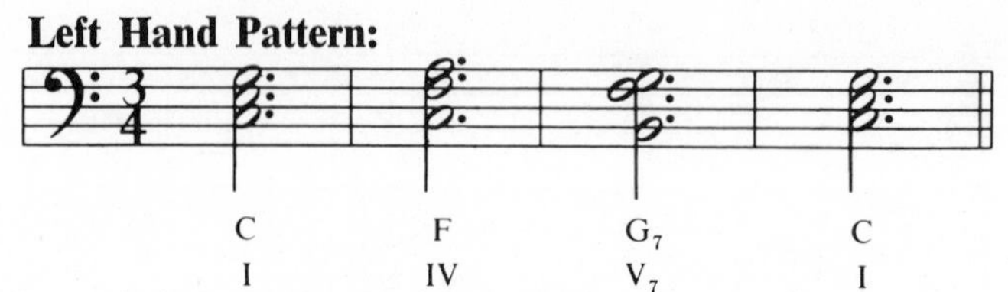

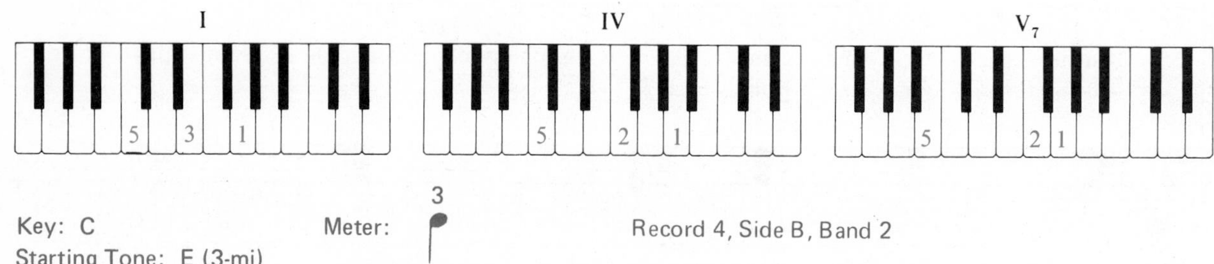

Key: C
Starting Tone: E (3-mi)

Meter: 3 (quarter note)

Record 4, Side B, Band 2

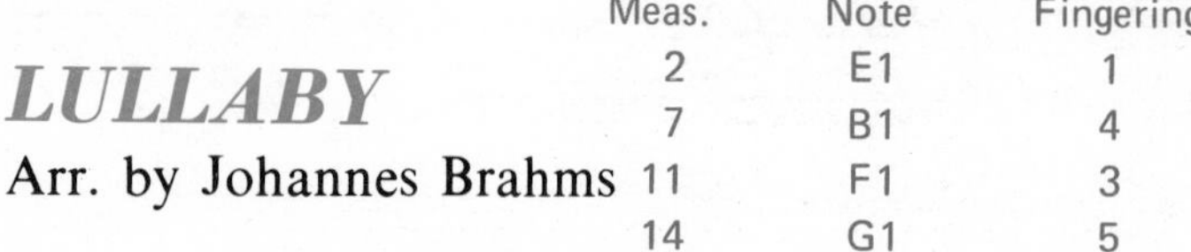

LULLABY

Arr. by Johannes Brahms

Help students with melodic fingerings:

Meas.	Note	Fingering
2	E1	1
7	B1	4
11	F1	3
14	G1	5

Use the same left hand pattern, but a different rhythm. Where there is no chord marked, continue playing the last chord named.

Lul - la - by and good night! With ro - ses be - dight, With li - lies o'er -
spread is ba - by's wee bed. Lay thee down now and rest, May thy slum - ber be
blest, Lay thee down now and rest, May thy slum - ber be blest.

STUDENT INVOLVEMENT 1. Find other compositions in this book in the key of C. Try chord patterns with new materials. 2. Play these songs with chords learned for guitar.

TWO CHORD MELODY IN G MAJOR

Left Hand Pattern:

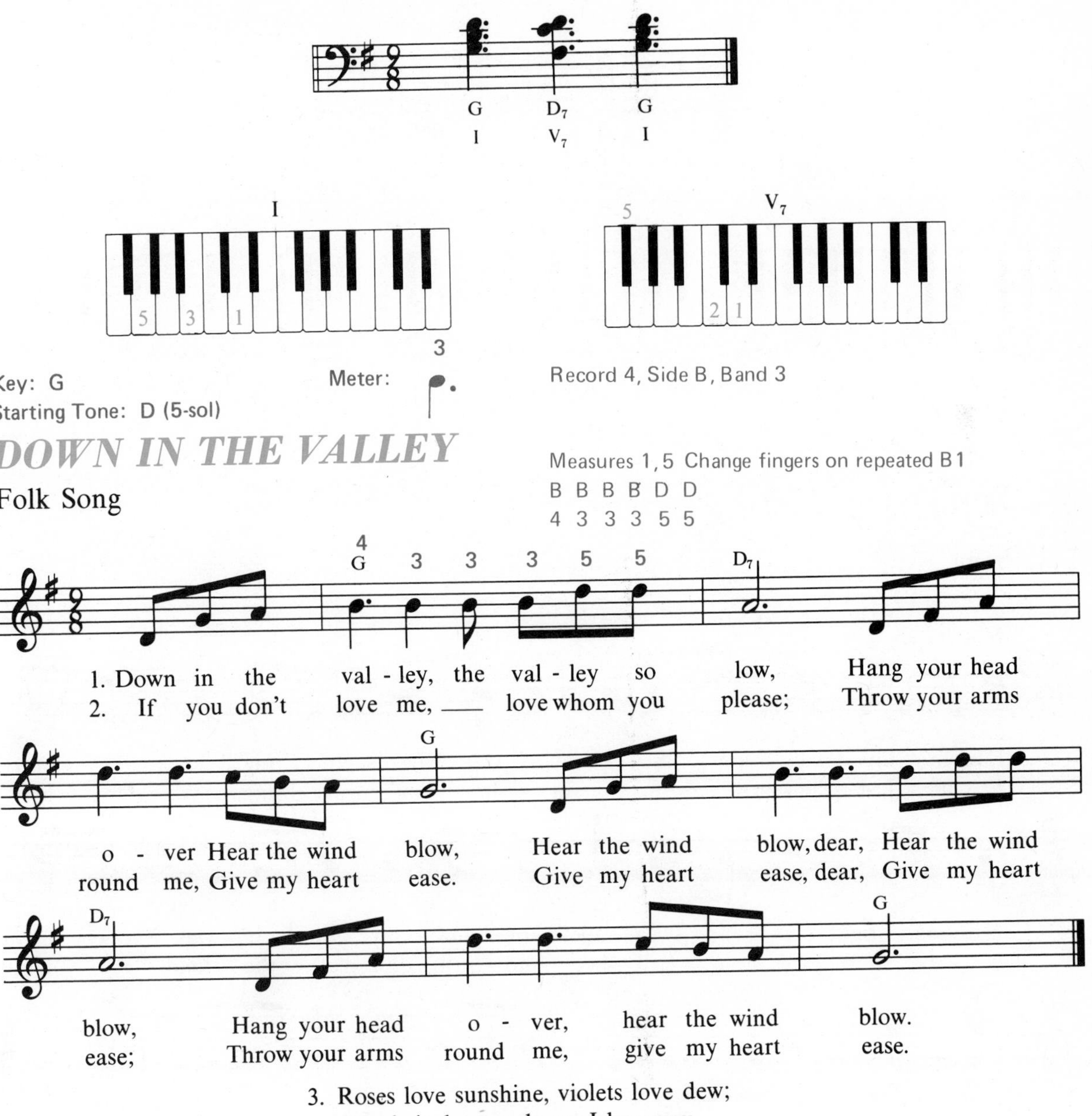

G D7 G
I V7 I
I
5 3 1
V7
5
2 1
Key: G
Starting Tone: D (5-sol)
Meter: 3
Record 4, Side B, Band 3
DOWN IN THE VALLEY
Folk Song
Measures 1,5 Change fingers on repeated B1
B B B B D D
4 3 3 3 5 5
1. Down in the valley, the valley so low, Hang your head over Hear the wind blow, Hear the wind blow, dear, Hear the wind blow, Hang your head over, hear the wind blow.
2. If you don't love me, — love whom you please; Throw your arms round me, Give my heart ease. Give my heart ease, dear, Give my heart ease; Throw your arms round me, give my heart ease.

3. Roses love sunshine, violets love dew;
Angels in heaven know I love you,
Know I love you, dear, know I love you,
Angels in heaven know I love you.

4. Writing this letter, only three lines,
Answer my question, "Will you be mine?
Will you be mine, dear, will you be mine?"
Answer my question, "Will you be mine?"

Look for other compositions in the key of G.

THREE CHORD MELODY IN G MAJOR

Left Hand Pattern:

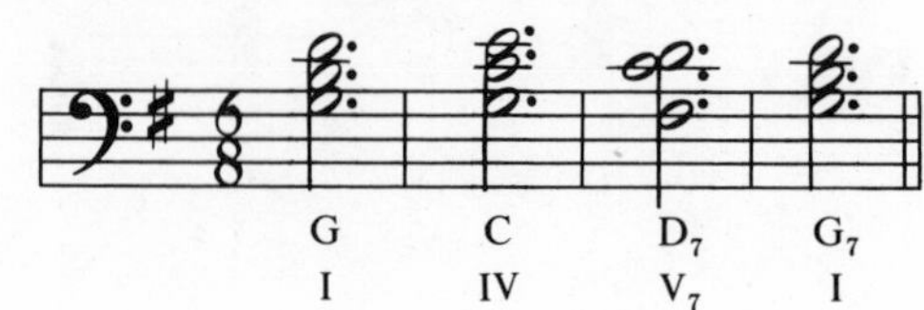

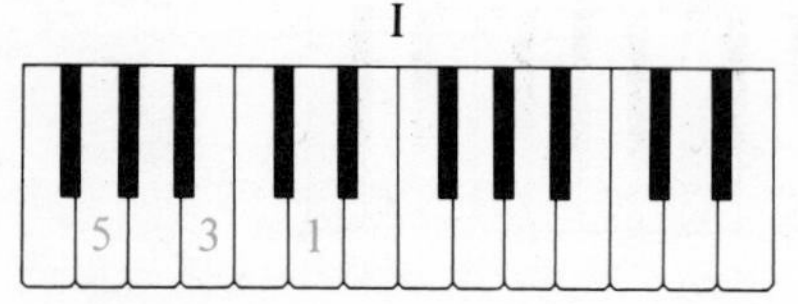

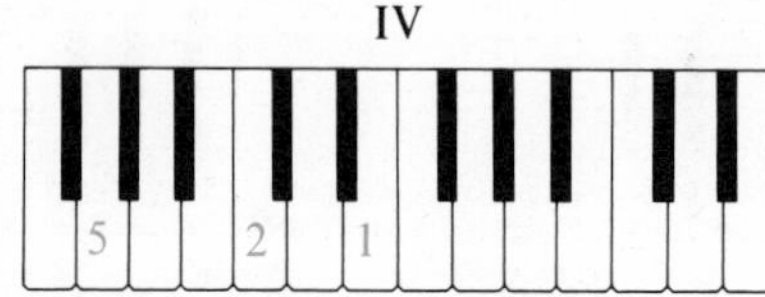

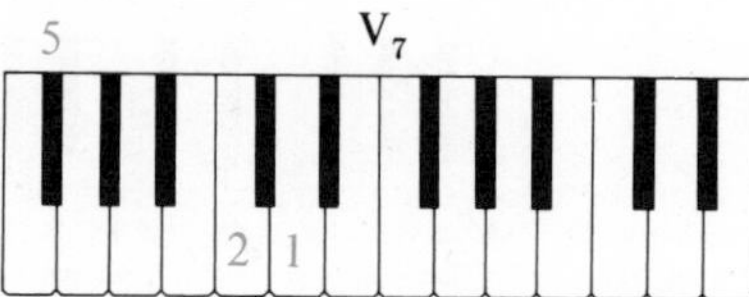

Key: G
Starting Tone: D (5-sol)

Meter: 4 ♩

Record 4, Side B, Band 4

RED RIVER VALLEY

Folk Song

3. Come and sit by my side if you love me,
Do not hasten to bid me a-dieu;
But remember the Red River Valley
And the one that has loved you so true.

TWO CHORD MELODIES IN F MAJOR

Left Hand Pattern:

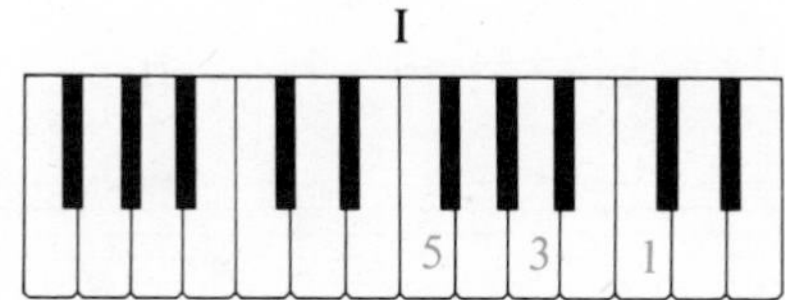

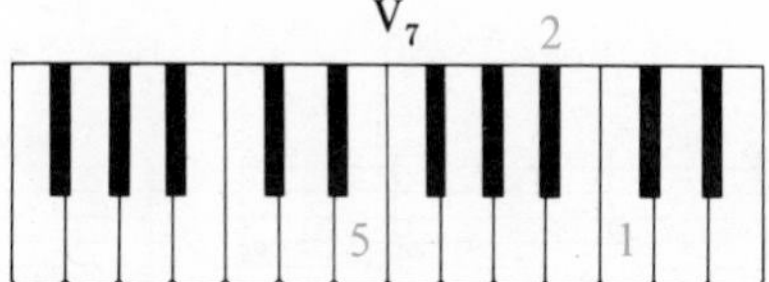

Key: F
Starting Tone: F (1-do)

Meter: 3

Record 4, Side B, Band 5

CLEMENTINE

Folk Song

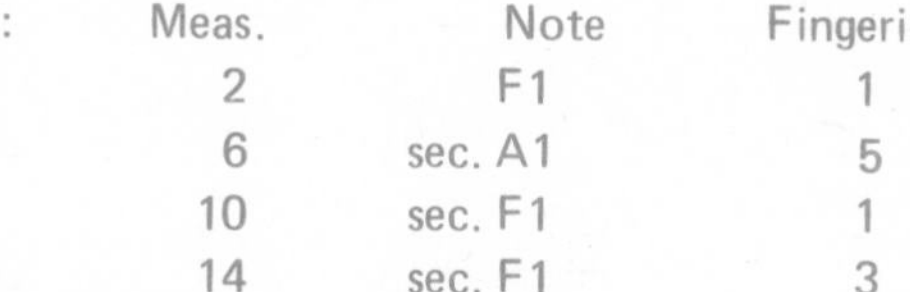

Fingerings:

Meas.	Note	Fingering
2	F1	1
6	sec. A1	5
10	sec. F1	1
14	sec. F1	3

In a cav - ern, in a can - yon ex - ca - va - ting for a mine, ___ Dwelt a

min - er, for - ty nin - er, and his daugh - ter Cle - men - tine. O my

dar - ling, Oh my dar - ling, Oh my dar - ling Cle - men - tine, You are

lost and gone for - ev - er, Dread - ful sor - ry Cle - men - tine.

Key: F
Starting Tone: C (5-sol)   Meter: 2 ♩   Record 4, Side B, Band 6

SIMPLE GIFTS

Shaker Song

Study the melody of this famous Shaker song. Notice that there are no chord markings above the melody. A simple piano accompaniment can be played using the F and C7 chords. Sing the melody and discover where the two chords sound better.

Moderately F
'Tis the gift to be sim - ple, 'tis the gift to be free, 'Tis the
F
gift to come down where you ought to be, And when we find our -
C7
selves in the place just right, 'Twill be in the val - ley of
F F
love and de - light. When true sim - plic - i - ty is gained, To
F C7 F
bow and to bend we shan't be a - shamed, To turn, turn will
C7 F
be our de - light, Till by turn - ing, turn - ing we come round right.

FINGERINGS:

Meas.	Note	Fingering	
2	A F A	4 2 3	
5	G	4	
10	F	1	
11	A	3	
15	G F E	2 1 3	(cross over thumb)
16	F	1	
26	F	1	

Transpose this melody for clarinet.

What key will you need to use? Since the clarinet sounds a major 2nd below the written notation, the key is G Major for the transposition.

Aaron Copland has used this song as an important part of the ballet Appalachian Spring.

RELATED LISTENING: Columbia Recording MS6355.

THREE CHORD MELODIES IN F

Left Hand Pattern:

F Bb C7 F
I IV V7 I
I IV V7
5 3 1 2 5 1 2 5 1
Key: F
Starting Tone: C (5-sol)
Meter: 2
Record 4, Side B, Band 7
FOR HE'S A JOLLY GOOD FELLOW
Folk Song
Meas. Note Fingering
1 sec. A 3
5 first A 2
8 A 2
For he's a jol - ly good fel - low, for he's a jol - ly good
fel - low, For he's a jol - ly good fel - low, Which no - bod - y can de - ny.
Which no - bod - y can de - ny, Which no - bod - y can de - ny, For
he's a jol - ly good fel - low, for he's a jol - ly good
fel - low, For he's a jol - ly good fel - low, Which no - bod - y can de - ny.
D. S. al Fine

UNIT 6

Soviet dutar (top), Bolivian pan flute (above right), Corpus Christi festival, Bolivia (below left), Japanese sendai drum (opposite left), Ghanaian elephant tusk horn (opposite right)

SEE GUIDE FOR UNIT LEARNING OBJECTIVES

Ethnic Worlds

ALL SONGS OF CURRENT LANDS COME SOUNDING ROUND ME

Walt Whitman
American poet (1819-1892)

The group of countries included in Ethnic Worlds is representative, not all-inclusive. The music of some countries reflects the musical sound or idiom of the parent countries, yet the words illustrate the unique language of the settlers. The United States owes its musical heritage to the music of the Native Americans and of various Western European and African countries. It contains a fusion of folk styles.

In contrast, civilizations like those of India, China, and Japan have a totality of sound in musical idiom, language, and instruments.

The word *ethnic* is derived from a Greek word *ethnos* which means "people" or "nation." It pertains to a social group within a cultural and social system. Each group has special characteristics which may be caused by differences of religion, speech, family, or environment.

Certain patterns of sound or rhythm appear so frequently in the music of a particular ethnic group that the sound becomes characteristic of those people. Some combinations of sound are said to be "Russian" or "African" or "Andalusian" or "Oriental." Another ethnic trait in the musical world concerns the instruments that are unique to that particular civilization: the *balalaika* to Russia, the *mbira* to Africa, the *koto* to Japan, the *crwth* to Wales.

This unit will introduce you to the music of some of these ethnic worlds.

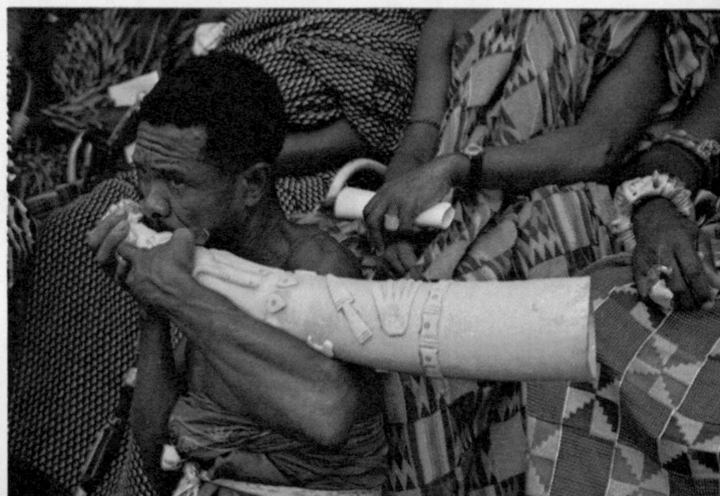

The Welsh have been a singing people for hundreds of years, and the tradition continues in contemporary Wales with an *Eisteddfod,* or music festival, which brings participants from all over the world to the little town of Llangollen. It is stirring to hear "God Save the Queen" followed by the Welsh national anthem, and the strains of continued music as people move from the great tent, in which the festival concerts are held, out to their homes and hotels, still singing as they leave.

Castle in Wales
Courtesy of British Tourist Authority

RELATED ACTIVITIES

1. Read "A Snowy Day" by Dafydd ap Gwilyn in Lyrics of the Middle Ages, New York: Grove Press, 1959. Compare this with the Dylan Thomas excerpt.

2. Show color slides of North Wales. Woodmansterne, Set 98. The Bookstore, Westminster Abbey SWI, London, England.

3. Listen to a recording of this selection. Caedmon Recording TC 10002.

4. Plan a Christmas program using the Dylan Thomas excerpts as a connecting narrative. Decide how it will be read. See T.G. suggestions, p. 26.

A Child's Christmas In Wales (Excerpts)

One Christmas was so much like another,
in those years around the sea-town corner now
and out of all sound except the distant speaking
of the voices I sometimes hear a moment before sleep,
that I can never remember whether it snowed
for six days and six nights when I was twelve
or whether it snowed for twelve days and
twelve nights when I was six . . .

And I remember that we went
singing carols once, when there wasn't the shaving
of a moon to light the flying streets. At the end
of a long road was a drive that led to a large
house, and we stumbled up the darkness of the drive
that night, each one of us afraid, each one holding
a stone in his hand in case, and all of us too brave
to say a word. The wind through the trees
made noises as of old and unpleasant and maybe
webfooted men wheezing in caves. We reached
the black bulk of the house.

"What shall we give them? Hark the Herald?"

"No," Jack said, "Good King Wenceslas.
I'll count three."

One, two, three, and we began to sing . . .

Dylan Thomas
Welsh poet (1914–1953)

RELATED LISTENING "God Bless the Prince of Wales" and other Welsh favorites on The World of Wales in Song. London Recording SW 99525.

Key: Fm
Starting Tone: F (6-1a)

Meter: 4

Form: A A B A

Record 5, Side A, Band 1.

ONCE TO EVERY MAN AND NATION

Welsh Melody (Ton-y-Botel), Arr. by A.B.C.

Words by James Russell Lowell

What tone colors are used in the accompaniment? (Bra
What rhythmic devices give the melody variety?

Majestically
and
1. Once to ev - ery man and na - tion Comes the mo - ment to de - cide,
2. Then to side with truth is no - ble, When we share her wretch-ed crust,
3. Though the cause of e - vil pros-per, Yet 'tis truth a - lone is strong;
In the strife of truth with false - hood, For the good or e - vil side;
Ere her cause bring fame and prof - it And 'tis pros-p'rous to be just;
Though her por - tion be the scaf - fold, And up - on the throne be wrong,

STUDENT INVOLVEMENT Study the voice parts for examples of voice leading and harmonic sound: 1 parallel octaves 2 contrary motion 3 parallel fourths 4 parallel sixths.

Some great cause, God's new Mes - si - ah, Of - f'ring each the bloom or blight,
Then it is the brave man choos - es, While the cow - ard stands a - side,
Yet that scaf - fold sways the fu - ture, And, be - hind the dim un - known,
rit.
And the choice goes by for - ev - er 'Twixt that dark - ness and that light.
Till the mul - ti - tude make vir - tue Of the faith they had de - nied.
Stand - eth God with - in the shad - ow, Keep - ing watch a - bove his own.
rit.
rit.

RELATED ACTIVITIES Have students bring in other examples of Welsh songs. Recommended listening: Roger Wagner Chorale in Folk Songs of the Old World. Capitol Recording P-8387. Vol. 1 includes Welsh songs.

Key: E flat
Starting Tone: B flat

Meter: 3 (quarter note)
Form: A A B B'

Record 5, Side A, Band 2

TURN YE TO ME

Scottish Folk Song
Words by John Wilson

Is this melody tonal or modal? (Tonal, the melody revolves around E flat and the leading tone is present. The Cm chord in measure 1 gives the accompaniment a modal flavor.)

The word Mhairi dhu is pronounced *mah-ree doo.*

Cm
Eb
1. The stars are shin - ing cheer - i - ly, cheer - i - ly, Ho - ro,
Bb7
Eb
Cm
Mhai - ri dhu, Turn ye ___ to me. The sea - mew is moan - ing
Eb
Bb7
drea - ri - ly, drea - ri - ly, Ho - ro, Mhai - ri dhu, Turn ye ___ to
Eb
Eb
Eb
me. Cold is the storm-wind that ruf - fles his breast, But warm are the
Bb
Eb
down - y plumes lin - ing his nest, ___ Cold blows the storm ___ there, soft falls the
Bb7
Eb
Bb7
Eb
snow ___ there, Ho - ro, Mhai - ri dhu, Turn ye ___ to me.

2. The waves are dancing merrily, merrily,
Horo, Mhairidhu, Turn ye to me.
The seabirds are wailing wearily, wearily,
Horo, Mhairidhu, Turn ye to me.
Hushed be thy moaning, lone bird of the sea,
Thy home on the rock is a shelter to thee;
Thy home is the angry wave, mine but the lonely grave,
Horo, Mhairidhu, Turn ye to me.

RELATED ACTIVITIES Listen to Mendelssohn's Symphony No. 3 in A minor, the "Scotch" Symphony. The second movement includes a theme resembling the five-note scale of the Scottish Bagpipe.

STUDENT INVOLVEMENT 1. Find examples of the "Scotch snap" (♬.) in the song. (measures 7, 15, 31) 2. Does the melody suggest a legato or a detached style? (legato). 3. How would you phrase the melody? (see phrasing above) 4. Experiment in composing a simple harmony part or descant for the melody.

LEARNINGS AND SKILLS After listening to the recorded examples, lead the class in a discussion of the sound and flavor of this folk instrument.

THE BAGPIPE

The bagpipe is used in the folk music of many countries—Africa, Spain, Bulgaria, Ireland, and Scotland. It is basically a tube, or pipe with holes, similar to a recorder, with a reed mouthpiece. This pipe, known as the chanter, plays the melody. Two or more other pipes which produce one note each, play a drone accompaniment. These pipes are inserted in an airtight bag of skin which serves as the air supply.

The most highly developed form of the instrument is the great highland pipe of Scotland *(piob mor)*, used for martial music. There are three other kinds of bagpipes: the smaller lowland pipe, the two-drone pipe brought from Ireland, and the small pipe.

The bagpipe displaced the earlier Scottish harp; it was more popular and more suitable for the outdoors. Music for the pipes falls into two divisions:

Ceol Mor: The "classical" music of pipers which was often a theme and variations.

Ceol Beag: The "little" music—dances, marches

Record 9, Side B, Band 4

LISTENING . . .

Mahbri Bhan Og *(Slow March)*
Killworth Hills *(Retreat March)*
The Black Watch

Marches in Scotland may be duple ($\frac{2}{4}$ or $\frac{6}{8}$), triple, or quadruple. What is the meter of the slow march? Of the retreat march?

LISTENING . . . Record 9, Side B, Band 5

O'Carolan's Air
17th century

O'Carolan was a blind Irish harper. The Irish harp is small and used especially by folk singers. Play this tune on flute or recorder. The melody may be accompanied by guitar, autoharp, or harp.

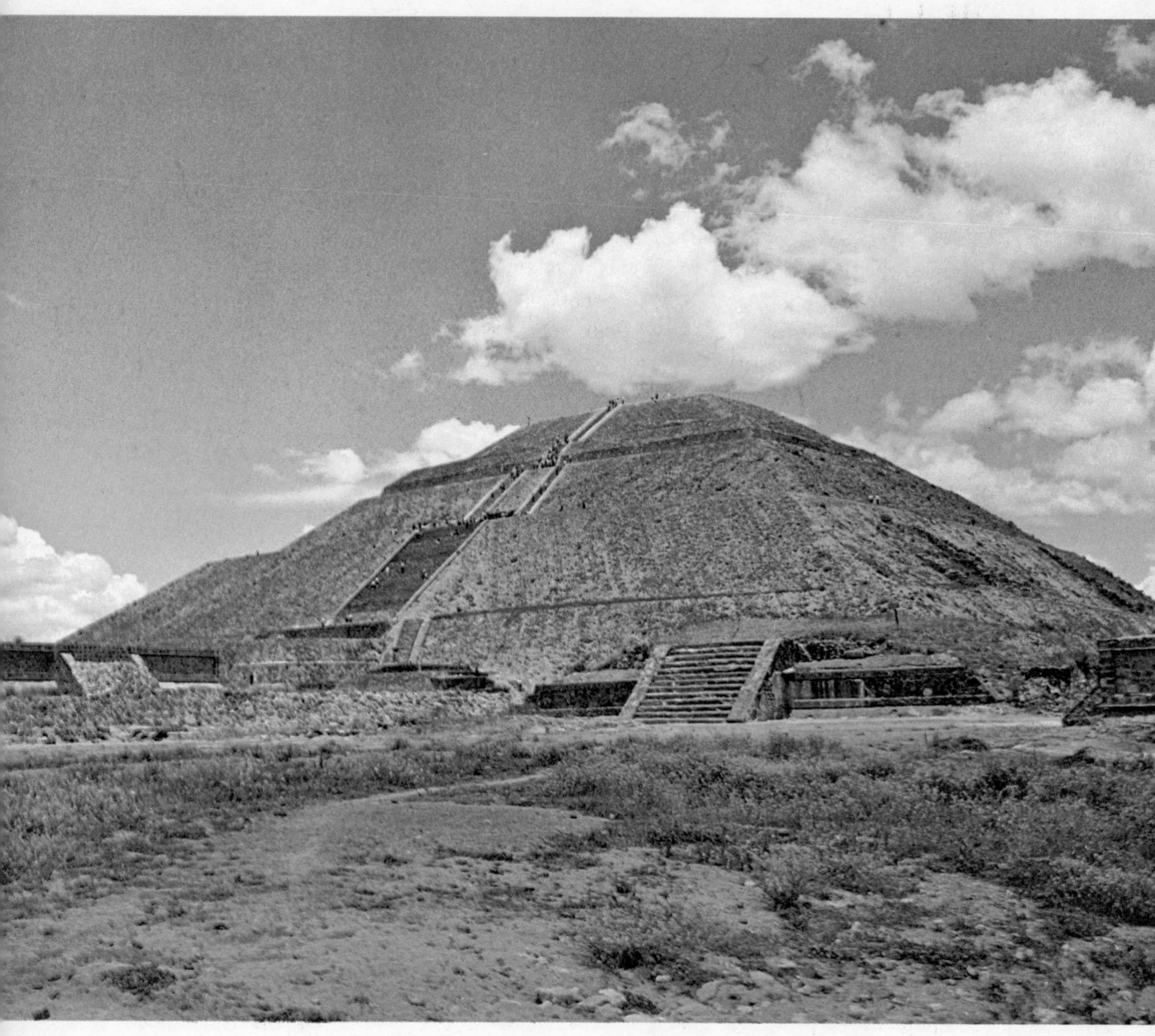

Pyramid of the Sun, Teotihuacan, Mexico

In Mexico, the popular *mariachi* bands perform for birthdays, weddings, and festivities of many kinds. The *mariachi* consists of violins, harps, mandolins, guitars of various sizes, sometimes trumpets, and often a marimba. One of Mexico's important composers, Carlos Chávez, has used both Spanish and Indian themes in his compositions.

Record 9, Side B, Band 5

LISTENING . . .

Zapateado from *La Tempranica*

Geronimo Gimenez

This composition is an example of the Spanish *zarzuela*. The word is derived from *zarza,* the bramble thicket that surrounded the hunting lodge of Philip IV near Madrid. Court musicians and famous playwrights of the seventeenth century like Calderón and Lope de Vega developed a type of musical play called the Fiestas de Zarzuela. Thus the *zarzuela* was the Spanish equivalent of the Viennese operetta and the Italian comic opera.

Record 9, Side B, Band 6

LISTENING . . .

Preludio from *La Revoltosa*

Ruperto Chapi

This introduction to another *zarzuela* has the following characteristics of Spanish music: lively rhythms, minor tonality, and very dramatic themes. The prelude sets the mood for the opening scene that takes place in Madrid in 1897.

Record 10, Side A, Band 1

LISTENING . . .

Danza Moro

Andalusia, the district of Spain where the Arabs left their deepest imprint, is the region where flamenco is most widely practiced today. Although the word "flamenco" is often applied to every gypsy musician or dancer in Spain, the purest type is called *Cante Hondo.* It is a combination of Moorish, Byzantine, Jewish, and Gypsy sounds.

Record 10, Side A, Band 2

LISTENING . . .

Sevillianos

This short flamenco piece in sets of three is typical of the Andalusian music of Seville. What instruments accompany the guitar?

Record 10, Side A, Band 3

LISTENING . . .

Seguidillas Gitanos

Listen for the subtle, but definite rhythm changes. In flamenco singing the Moorish influence is strongest. It is customary for singers and dancers to encourage each other while sitting in a half circle, clapping and shouting "Ole!" There is much freedom of interpretation in the singing, to fit the mood of the moment, and the melodies are richly ornamented.

Key: F
Starting Tone: C (5-sol)

Meter: 3 over a quarter note

Record 5, Side A, Band 3

Form: A B

CAMPANAS VESPERTINAS

EVENING BELLS

Words by Juana Guglielmi
Music by Julio Z. Guerra

Expand experience with Spanish and Spanish-influenced music by singing "North Argentinian Folk Dance" on p. 228.

Listen carefully to the recording to learn the Spanish text. Where do both voice parts sing in unison? (see markings in music)

Andante
mf
unison
Lohs kuhm - pah - nahs deh lay-ee - gleh - syah dahn ehl
Los cam - pa - nas de la i - gle - sia, dan el
Dis - tant bells, now soft - ly ring - ing, toll the
mf
unison
sung in thirds
toh - keh deh-oh-rah - syohn ee lah loos dehl sohl key mweh - reh ah - oh - troh
to - que de-o - ra - ción y la luz del sol que mue - re a o - tro
hour when day is done; And the stars of ear - ly eve - ning Rise a -

RELATED ACTIVITIES 1. Listen to the songs, "El son del viento," "El Perro," "Flor de Canela," and "Kuinchikua" on "The Real Mexico in Music and Song," Nonesuch Records H-72009. 2. Look at ancient art objects and contemporary paintings by Diego Rivera, Rufino Tamayo, David Alfaro Siqueiros, and José Clemente Orozco in Mexican Art, ed., Justine Fernandez, London: Spring Books, 1966.

mf
mp
moon - doh ee-rah - loom - brrahr. Keh dool - seh ah sehn - toh, deeng, deeng,
mun - do i - rá a-lum - brar. ¡Qué dul - ce a cen - to, ding, ding,
bove the set - ting sun. How sweet at five to hear, ding, ding,
dohng! Soo bohs ah - leh - grah mee koh - rah - sohn. Deeng, deeng, deeng,
dong! Su voz a - le - gra mi co - ra - zón. Ding, ding, ding,
dong! The vil - lage bells in their e - ven - song. Ding, ding, ding,
dong! Soo bohs ah leh - grah mee koh - rah - sohn.
dong! Su voz a - le - gra mi co - ra - zón.
dong! The vil - lage bells ring their e - ven - song.
HOLD THREE FULL BEATS.

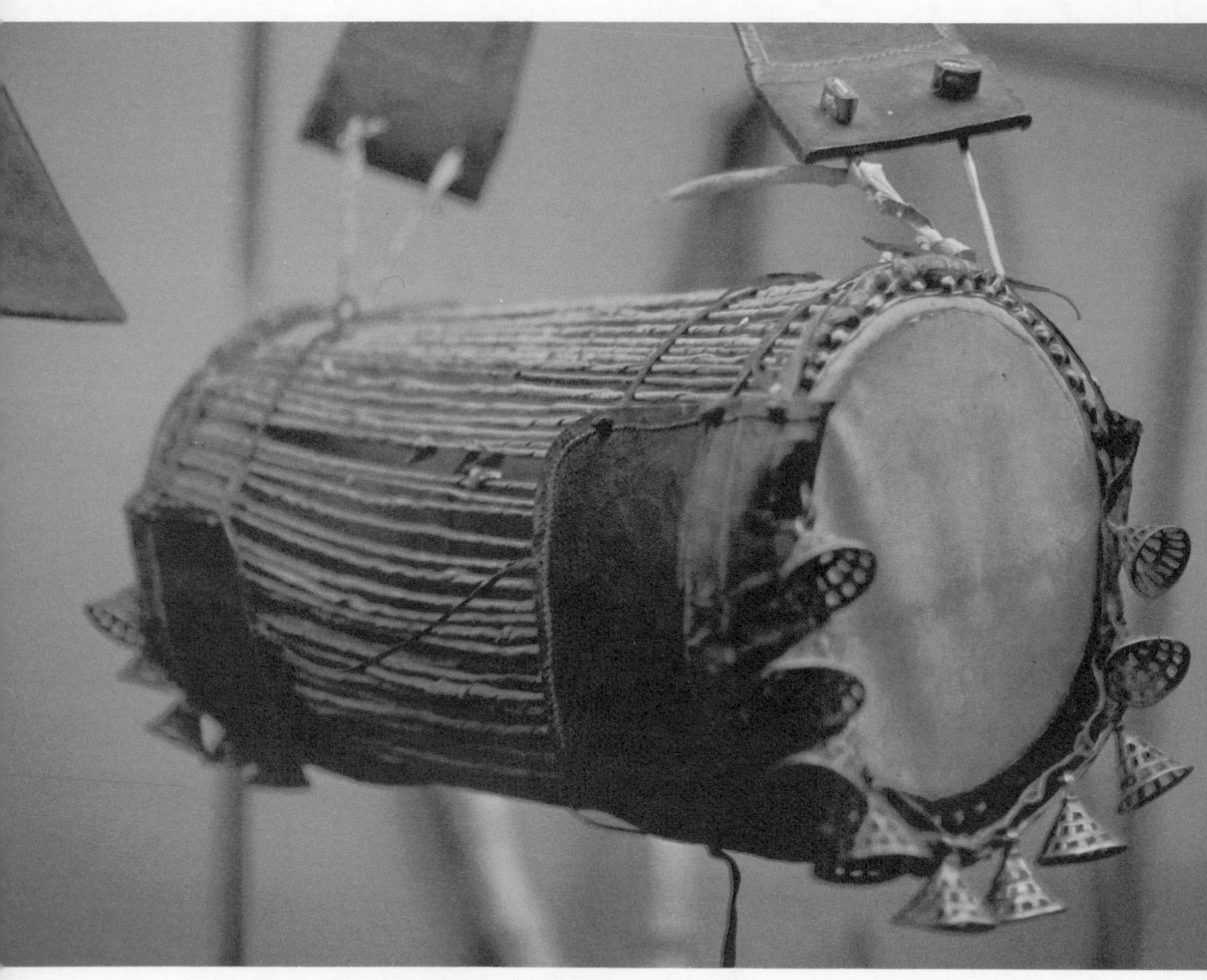

Pressure drum with bells, Yoruba Tribe
The American Museum of Natural History

AFRICAN RHYTHMS

The rhythms of African music have inspired contemporary composers all over the world to experiment with this exciting element. Simple rhythms are combined to create complicated sounds. The following example illustrates the complex patterns created by the combination of eight relatively simple rhythms.

Combine the rhythmic patterns, which are only the primary patterns. The clapping varies with each repetition and is greatly accelerated in tempo as it progresses.

Big Drum: 12/8

1 2 3 4 5 6 7 8 9 10 11 12

Medium Drum: 12/8

1 2 3 4 5 6 7 8 9 10 11 12

Small Drum: 12/8

1 2 3 4 5 6 7 8 9 10 11 12

Woodblock: 12/8

1 2 3 4 5 6 7 8 9 10 11 12

Claves: 12/8

1 2 3 4 5 6 7 8 9 10 11 12

Cowbell: 12/8

1 2 3 4 5 6 7 8 9 10 11 12

Guiro: 12/8

1 2 3 4 5 6 7 8 9 10 11 12

Maracas: 12/8 U D D U D D U D U D U D

1 2 3 4 5 6 7 8 9 10 11 12

STUDENT INVOLVEMENT Detect African and Latin rhythms in the music of Santana, El Chicano, and other contemporary rock artists. Can you distinguish the African from the Latin? If so, how?

Compose and notate your own rhythm pattern for your class. How can you make your rhythm pattern into a composition?

RELATED ACTIVITIES 1. See 16mm. color film, Buma: African Culture Speaks, 9 minutes, Encyclopedia Britannica Films. 2. Look at illustrations of African art and musical instruments and compare with other cultures.

Key: Modal | Meter: 2 (3) | Record 5, Side A, Band 4

Starting Tone: D | Form: A B

MESU MEFRE AGYA, KATAKYIE

Ghanaian Folk Song

This song is called an *asaadua.* Performances are given by *asaadua* bands. The membership of these bands is predominantly young. Often bands choose older men to act as patrons in order to give the music and dancing social status.

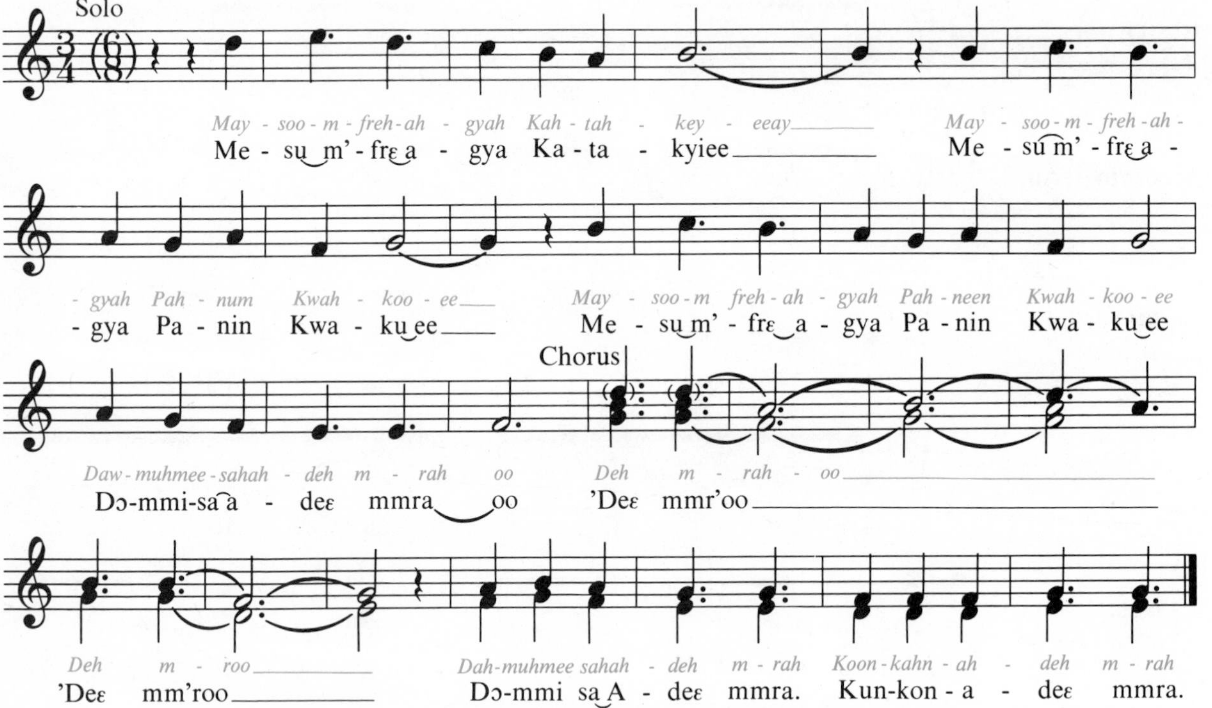

Play the three examples. Have the students compare the sound, beat, and feeling of each selection.

LISTENING . . .

Listen to three examples of African music collected from the rural areas of this huge continent. In what ways do you think the folk music of Africa has influenced music of other cultures?

Mitamba Yalagala Record 10, Side A, Band 4

A Madogoli dance song accompanied by drums and rattles, sung by the Zaramo People.

Shumba Record 10, Side A, Band 5

A hunting song accompanied by a 22-note *mbira.* (thumb piano)

Pi Mcinanga Record 10, Side A, Band 6

A song story accompanied by rattles sung by the Zezuru People.

INSTRUMENTAL ACCOMPANIMENT FOR MESU MEFRE

When you are familiar with the vocal part of this *asaadua,* listen to the recording for the instrumental accompaniment.

Experiment with various rhythm patterns and instruments in order to create a short composition which catches the "flavor" of the asaadua.

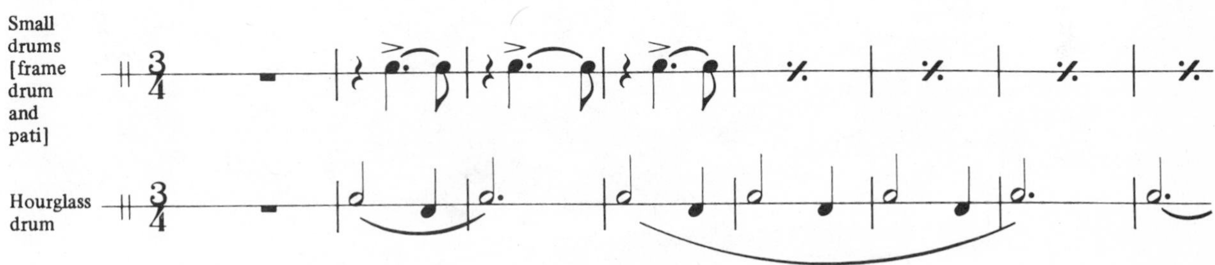

RELATED ACTIVITIES

1. Filmstrip: Africa: Musical Instruments, Textiles, Jewelry, and Architecture (Six Filmstrips), Warren Schloat Productions 316.

2. See 16mm. color film with a master drummer of Ghana, Discovering the Music of Africa, 22 minutes, Bailey-Films Associates.

Key: B flat
Starting Tone: D (3-mi)
Meter: 4 (quarter note)
Form: A B A
Record 5, Side A, Band 5

NE NKANSU

Luba People
The Congo

The solo-chorus of this song is typical of work songs the world over. Ask the class if they feel the rhythm and tempo of the song reflect the activity involved – hoeing and leveling the ground for planting.

Listen to the recording of this solo-chorus work song. Compose and notate an appropriate percussion accompaniment for this song. Use the rhythm patterns on page 173 for an example.

LEARNINGS AND SKILLS
1. Clap, sing, and play instrumentally the melody rhythm pattern.
2. Discover functions of African music (rituals, work songs, boat songs, etc.).

STUDENT INVOLVEMENT
1. Have the class discover the special features of the song: solo-chorus arrangement, repeated patterns, and three-part response.
2. Ask the class to improvise an accompaniment after they have listened to the recording.
3. Report on some aspect of African art.

Baluba Tribe, Chimbundu Mask
The American Museum of Natural History

FOLK SONGS AROUND THE WORLD

Kutnasy, Ghana: Drummers
Susan Baldwin from Monkmeyer

Tamale, Ghana: Man playing squeeze drum in street
Halperin from Monkmeyer

RELATED ACTIVITIES

1. Read Jewels for a Crown: The Story of the Chagall Windows by Miriam Freund, N.Y.: McGraw-Hill, 1963.

STUDENT INVOLVEMENT

1. Discover Jewish Symbols in the design: Menorah, Dove, Inscriptions.
2. How is color often symbolic?

Marc Chagall, *The Twelve Tribes of Israel*—Hadassah-Hebrew University Medical Center Synagogue, Jerusalem

This is a detail of one of the twelve windows depicting the Twelve Tribes of Israel. The windows are located in the Hadassah-Hebrew University Medical Center Synagogue, Jerusalem. The windows are considered by many to represent Chagall's finest work.

RELATED ACTIVITIES 2. View filmstrip "A Stained Glass Artist." Traditional Handcrafts Today series. #326-3 (record or cassette). Educational Development Corp.

Key: Bm
Starting Tone: B (6-la)
Meter: 2/♩.
Form: A B C
Record 5, Side A, Band 6

HALLELUJAH

Israeli Folk Song
Three-Part Round

Israel, a relatively young nation, reflects a rich heritage of both east and west in its music. This round typifies the lyrical melodies of Israeli music.

Hallelujah is from the Hebrew and means *Praise Ye the Lord.* Sing this melody as a song of praise and thanksgiving.

SHOFAR CALLS

The shofar, or ram's horn, has no mouthpiece. To sound the calls of the Jewish Service, one blows across the hole at the narrow end of the horn, tightening the lips for overtones.

Key: Gm
Starting Tone: D (3-mi)

Meter: 4 (quarter note)
Form: AB

Record 5, Side A, Band 7

LEARNINGS AND SKILLS

1. Identify and perform the following rhythm patterns:

HAVAH NAGILAH

Israeli Folk Song
Adapted Words

The hora is the symbol of unity in every kibbutz and settlement of Israel.

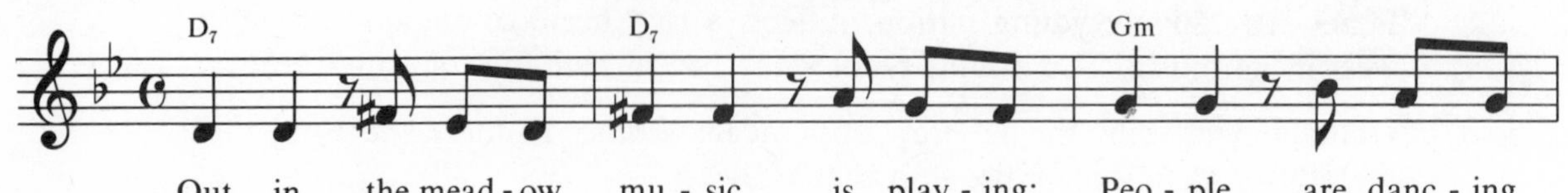
D7 D7 Gm
Out in the mead - ow mu - sic is play - ing; Peo - ple are danc - ing,

D7 3 D7 D7
They cir - cle a - bout. Arms linked with one an - oth - er, They dance the

Gm D7 3 D
ho - ra And while they dance mer - ri - ly shout: "Come, do the ho - ra now,

Cm Cm D 3
Watch, and we'll show you how; Step, hop, and once a - gain. See how it is done.

D Cm Cm
Hear how we keep the beat, Step - ping with live - ly feet; Come, join our cir - cle now;

D 3 Gm Gm
Come, dance with your friends! Now that we're to - geth - er,

Gm 3 Gm 3
Ev - 'ry - one steps a lit - tle fast - er, Ev - 'ry - one hops a lit - tle fast - er;

D
3
D
3
See how the cir - cle's turn - ing fast - er, See how the cir - cle's turn-ing fast - er!

D
3
3
D a tempo
Gm
Now it is done; rest, ev - 'ry - one. We've danced the ho - ra joy - ful - ly!

RELATED ACTIVITIES Listen to Folk Songs and Dances of Israel.
Capitol Record DT-10490

Israeli Hora

The basic step for the hora is the stop-hop described in the words of the song. It may be easier to learn the steps in a line, then move to a circle formation. For variety, try it with right hand on the left shoulder of the person in front of you as you use the line version.

Temple of Sarangapani, India (above left), Ravi Shankar (above right)

This light has come, of all the lights the fairest . . .
Night now has yielded up her place to morning.
Dawn has awakened every living creature.
from the *Rig Veda*

The Rig Veda is a collection of Vedic hymns based on the Upanishads literature. The accurate singing of a vedic hymn is essential to the ritual and to the stability of the universe for the nada (vibrations of musical sound) are intimately related to the spiritual world. The Rig Veda represents one of the oldest vocal traditions in the world, continuously in use from about 2000 B.C.

Ravindranath Tagore, *Portrait*

Tagore was the foremost Indian artist of the 20th century. He was a poet, composer, novelist, playwright, and actor. He wrote the National Anthem of India.

Record 10, Side A, Band 8

LISTENING . . .

Sindhi-Bhairavi

The music of India uses melodies which are based on tone structures called *ragas,* similar to scales. Each *raga* has its unique mood and color appropriate for seasons and hours of day and night. The rhythmic structure of Indian music is called *tala*. The beat of the *tala* is called *matra*. The most common *talas* have 16, 14, 12, 10, 7, or 6 matras.

The *sitar* is the most popular stringed instrument of India. It can be traced back in time for over 700 years. The *sitar* is fashioned from seasoned gourds and teakwood. It has a track of twenty metal frets with six or seven strings above them and thirteen resonating strings below. The *tabla* is the most popular two-piece drum of North India.

The *tamboura* is a long-necked gourd instrument with no frets and four or five strings which produce a hypnotic drone background to all Indian music. Describe the similarities and differences you hear in the various sections of this composition.

Record 10, Side A, Band 9

LISTENING . . .

Kathak Dance

The Kathak dancer of India conveys ideas and emotions rather than a story. Yet, this dance originated in the courts of north India as a story told through mime. Listen for:

- rhythmic syllables spoken by the dancer before he performs the rhythms with his feet.
- the *sarod,* a plucked string instrument.
- the echo of dancer's rhythms by the tabla player at the end.

The that is a classification of Hindustani (North Indian) ragas. The Bhairavi that is one of ten primary thats.

BHAIRAVI THAT

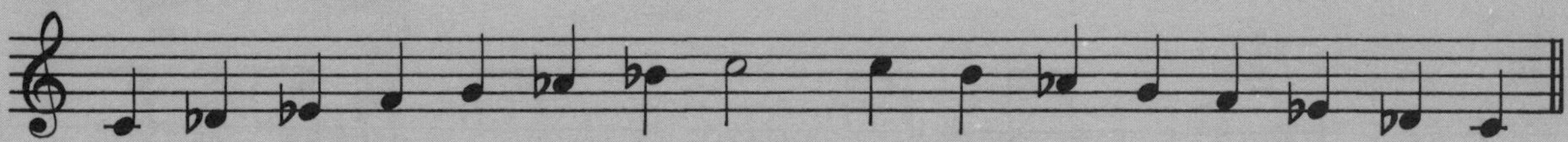

BHAIRAVI RAGA

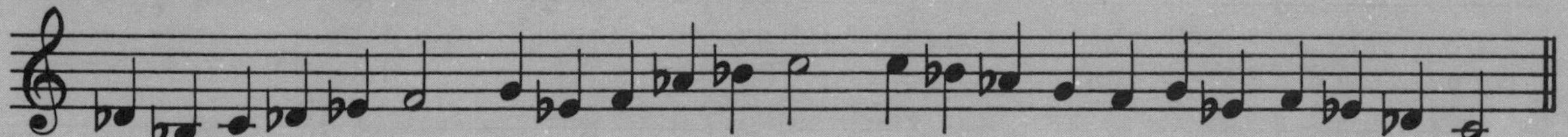

Key: Bhairav that
Starting Tone: C

Meter: 4 ♩

Form: ABA' B (AA)

Record 5, Side A, Band 8

HYMN TO SHIVA

Tāyumānayar
Arr. by Harold Schramm

LEARNINGS AND SKILLS

1. Where does the melody give an indication of Indian ornamentation? (measures 6, 7, 14, 15). 2. The Bhairav that is another primary that of the ten North Indian classifications.

Bhairavi That

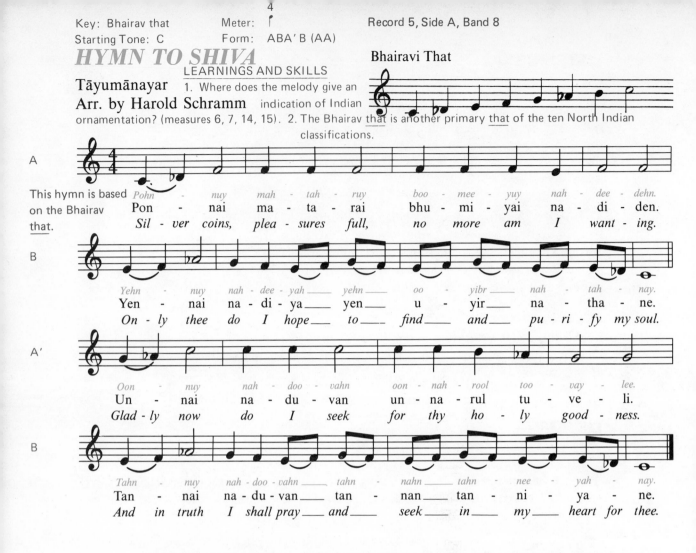

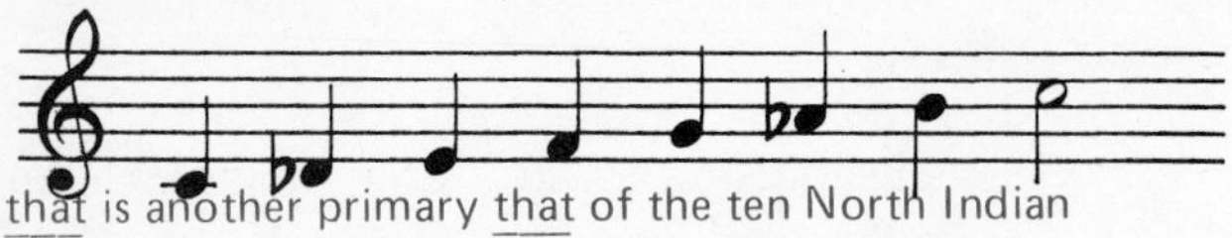

This hymn is based on the Bhairav that.

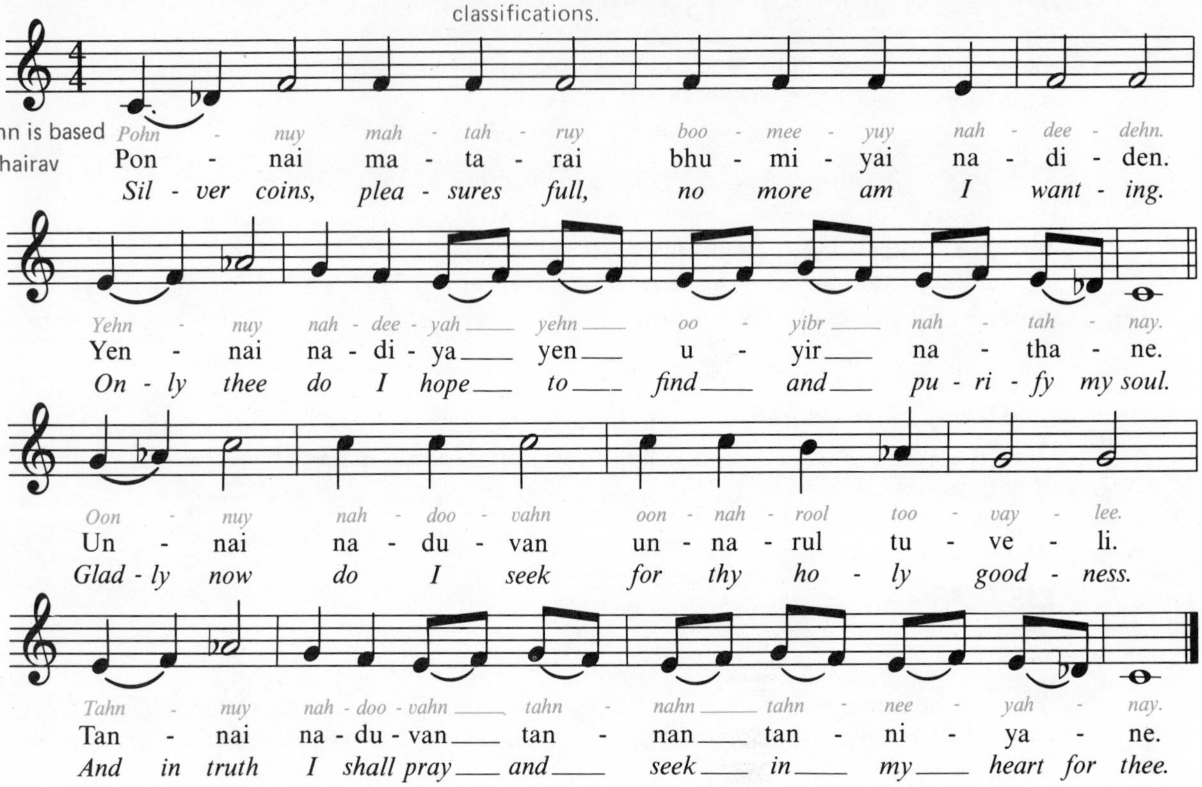

A

Pohn - nuy mah - tah - ruy boo - mee - yuy nah - dee - dehn.
Pon - nai ma - ta - rai bhu - mi - yai na - di - den.
Sil - ver coins, plea - sures full, no more am I want - ing.

B

Yehn - nuy nah - dee - yah yehn oo - yibr nah - tah - nay.
Yen - nai na - di - ya yen u - yir na - tha - ne.
On - ly thee do I hope to find and pu - ri - fy my soul.

A'

Oon - nuy nah - doo - vahn oon - nah - rool too - vay - lee.
Un - nai na - du - van un - na - rul tu - ve - li.
Glad - ly now do I seek for thy ho - ly good - ness.

B

Tahn - nuy nah - doo - vahn tahn - nahn tahn - nee - yah - nay.
Tan - nai na - du - van tan - nan tan - ni - ya - ne.
And in truth I shall pray and seek in my heart for thee.

Half-sing, half-say the syllables for a "drum language" accompaniment to the song. The drum part may be doubled on various percussion instruments.

STUDENT INVOLVEMENT

Clap a teental rhythm. This is the most popular tala, sixteen beats, grouped 4-4-4-4. Clap strong beats (sam), count other beats on fingers (little finger, ring finger, middle finger in succession).

Tune eight porcelain bowls by filling each with enough water to produce one note of the that. Play the that and then the melody of the hymn on this jala taranga.

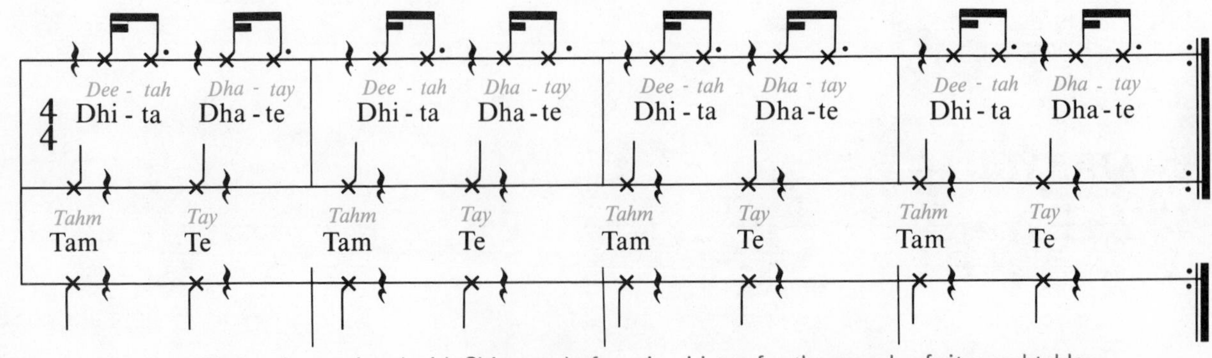

The Raga Bhairav is associated with Shiva, god of music. Listen for the sounds of sitar and tabla.

In Japan, folk song is an important part of life. At one time, the ability to sing, perform a folk dance, or play the *shakuhachi* was as much a part of a businessman's qualifications as his golf score or accounting skills. Japanese art music includes the *gagaku,* or court orchestral music, and *shomyo,* or Buddhist chant. Music also plays an important role in the various theatrical performances.

The koto is sometimes, but not regularly, used in gagaku music.

Record 10, Side B, Band 1

LISTENING...

Lingering Moonlight

Listen to this example of Japanese koto music performed by Shinichi Yuize, an outstanding musician on this instrument. The koto has thirteen strings of starched silk, tuned by movable bridges. What is the sound of the scale which provides the melodic material?

This composition was composed during 1781-1800 by Kohoto Minezaki.

Key: Hexatonal scale (B, C, E, F#, G, A) Meter: 2 ♩ Record 5, Side B, Band 1

Starting Tone: B

KOCHAE-BUSHI

Japanese Folk Song
Arr. by Shuichi Tsugawa

In some parts of the world, Japan, China, and India in particular, the interval of the major third was heard within the fourth of the pentatonic scale to produce a semitonal pentatonic. Semitonal and tonal pentatonics later combined to produce a hexatonal scale.

This song describes the journey of the son of a feudal lord on his way to visit a castle. The melody was used by Puccini in his opera, *Madama Butterfly*.

Accompany the song with a plucked string instrument to simulate the shamisen. The Autoharp or guitar may be used melodically.

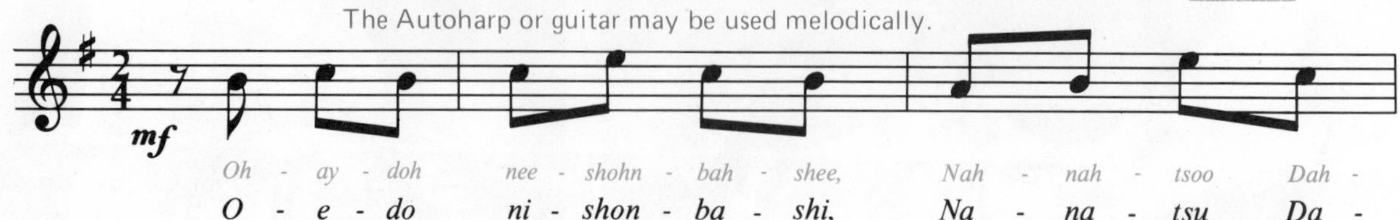

mf
Oh - ay - doh nee - shohn - bah - shee, Nah - nah - tsoo Dah -
O - e - do ni - shon - ba - shi, Na - na - tsu Da -

chee, Hah - tsoo - noh - boh - ree; Geeoh - ray - tsoo
chi, Ha - tsu - no - bo - ri; Gyô - re - tsu

soh - roh - eh - teh Ahreh - wahee - sah - noh - sah. Koh - cha,
so - ro - e - te Are - wai - sa - no - sa! Ko - cha,

Tah - kah - nah - wah yoh - ah - kee noh, Choh
Ta - ka - na - wa yo - a - ke no, Chô -

cheen kay - soo Koh - cha - eh. Koh - cha - eh.
chin ke - su; Ko - cha - é! Ko - cha - é!

Listen for the sound of koto and flute on the recording.

High on a mountain
faintly we heard, far below,
a skylark singing

Basho

Snow fell until dawn
now every twig in the grove
glitters in sunlight

Rokwa

RELATED ACTIVITIES

1. Read May Sarton's reminiscenes of Japan, "Japanese Prints" in A Private Mythology, New York: W. W. Norton, 1966.
2. Listen to the "Humming Chorus" from Madame Butterfly, Angel Recording S-3604.
3. Create an accompaniment for one of the haiku on this page.
4. View filmstrip "Japanese Prints" Arts of Japan series. #330-1 (record or cassette). Educational Development Corporation

Hiroshige's paintings inspired many processional songs, including "Kochae-Bushi."

Utagava Hiroshige, *The Long Bridge* (top), Katsushika Hokusai, *A Gust of Wind at Ejiri*—Metropolitan Museum of Art, New York

Have the students compose an accompaniment for one of the Basho haiku.

An old silent pond . . .
Into the pond
a frog jumps,
Splash! Silence again.

Basho

My eyes following
Until the bird
Was lost at sea
Found a small island.

Basho

Key: Pentatonic
Starting Tone: Bb

Meter: 4 (quarter note)
Form: AB

Record 5, Side B, Band 2

HUA KU KO

THE FLOWER DRUM

Chinese Folk Song

The most famous legend connected with the origin of Chinese music concerns a young poet who was sent by his emperor to the western mountains. While in the mountains, the young man cut bamboo stalks of different lengths and created the first music.

Tsoh___ shohoo___ loh, yoo___ shoo___ goo Shoo nah___ loh goo___
Tso___ shou___ lo, yu___ shou___ gu_ Shou na___ lo gu___
lahee___ chang___ kov Peeeh tee___ koo eyr,___ hoo yeh boo hooee chang;
lai___ chang___ ko, Pieh tí___ ko er,___ who yeh bu hui chang;
Tahn hooee___ chang koo___ fehng___ yhang___ koo, Fehng feng___ yhang___ koo___
Tan hui___ chang ko___ feng___ yang___ ko, Feng feng___ yang___ ko___
fast ♩ = 144
ay___ ahow___ yah Drr ling dahng peeaho ay peeaho Drr ling dahng peeaho ay peeaho
e___ ao___ ya. Drrr ling dang piao e piao, Drrr ling dang piao e piao,
Drr peeaho drr peeaho Drr peeaho drr peeaho peeaho you drr, Ling dahng peeaho ay peeaho.
Drrr piao, drrr piao, Drrr piao, drrr piao piao yu drrr, Ling dang piao e piao.

Record 10, Side B, Band 2

LISTENING . . .

Snow in Sunny Spring

The traditional music of the Chinese was closely related to their ideas of politics, the universe, and philosophy. There were instruments representing the "eight elements"–earth, stone, metal, bamboo, silk, wood, skin, gourd. As you listen to an example of traditional music, which of these types of instruments do you hear?

Youth Record 10, Side B, Band 3

Compare this traditional music with "Youth," a contemporary composition by a group of Chinese composers, influenced strongly by Russian music.

Contrast the traditional music of China with a contemporary Chinese composition.

Key: A
Starting Tone: E (5-sol)

Meter: $\overset{2}{\text{♩}}$

Record 5, Side B, Band 3

JOHN HENRY

Adapted and Arranged by Alan Lomax

American folk music is constantly changing by the addition of new features and loss of old ones. As long as each year brings discoveries of formerly unknown styles and instruments, folk music will remain a living art. The ballad of John Henry illustrates this change in folk music.

Where do the "blues" notes occur? (circled in red)

Vigorous ♩ = 126
A
D7
A
Well, it's hon - ey an' it's dar - lin' when I'm here, An' it's
E7
A
big nas - ty man when I'm gone, An' when you see me
D7
A
D7
com - in' with a twen - ty - dol - lar bill, It's 'Ba - by, where you been so
A
D7
E7
A
long, long, long?' It's 'Ba - by, where you been so long?'

1 Well, it's honey an' it's darlin' when I'm here,
An' it's big nasty man when I'm gone,
An' when you see me comin' with a twenty-dollar bill,
It's 'Baby, where you been so long, long, long?'
It's 'Baby, where you been so long?'

2 'It's where did you get yo' slippers from,
And the dress you are wearin' so fine?'
'I got my slippers from a railroad man, man, man,
And my dress from a driver in the mine'. *etc.*

3 'Who's gonna shoe your little feet,
Who's gonna glove your hand,
Who's gonna kiss your red, ruby lips, lips, lips,
And who's gonna be your man?' *etc.*

4 'My mama gonna shoe my little feet,
My papa gonna glove my hands,
My sister gonna kiss my red, ruby lips, lips, lips,
And John Henry gonna be my man.' *etc.*

RELATED ACTIVITIES

1. Read Louis Simpson, Mississippi, "American Poetry," in Selected Poems, New York: Harcourt, 1965.
2. See 16mm. color film, Discovering Jazz, 21 min. Bailey Films Associates.
3. Compare this song with other versions of the song.

UNIT 7

SEE GUIDE FOR UNIT LEARNING OBJECTIVES

Temporal Worlds

This unit is designed to introduce the students to the musical characteristics of six major historical periods—20th century, Middle Ages, Renaissance, Baroque, Classical, and Romantic—and to relate musical developments with events of the past and of the ever-changing present. Examples of art are included in order for the students to compare the stylistic elements of the visual and the aural expressions of these periods.

THE TIME MACHINE

Terms such as Medieval, Renaissance, Baroque, Classical, Romantic, and Contemporary are time-saving devices to describe the general style of a span in history. A characteristic style prominent in one period sometimes is reflected in other periods as well. Today we speak of some composers, living in the twentieth century, but trained in nineteenth-century techniques, as "Romantic." Although contemporary, their music sounds as if it had been written in the nineteenth-century Romantic style.

In every time period some composers are carry-overs from a previous age. Composers like Palestrina, Handel, Haydn, Brahms, or Bartók represented the spirit of their time. Perhaps some of the most significant composers are those who are ahead of their time. Gabrieli, Mozart, Beethoven, Schubert, Debussy, Ives, Varèse, Stravinsky, and Cage experimented with new techniques and new sounds; some of them incorporated the past; others broke completely with what went before.

You will find some of the characteristics of six musical periods charted on the following pages. As you listen to music, be a time detective and determine its historical period from clues that are given in the charts. You may look down the column and have a sleuth's-eye view of what the whole period was like musically, or you can follow one strand through its development.

COMPARATIVE STYLE CHART

	I. Medieval (c. 500–1450)	II. Renaissance (c. 1450–1600)	III. Baroque (c. 1600–1750)
Rhythm	Early: unmeasured (chant) Development of measured Rhythm c. 1240	Changing groupings (meters)	Driving Rhythms Rigid metrical control
Melody	Modal	Development of some chromaticism	Unity of theme, as in fugue
Harmony and Counterpoint	Organum Based on church modes	Modal Increasing polyphony	Major-Minor tonalities crystallize Chords determine harmonic motion
Forms	Mass Troubadour-Trouvere Songs Cantus firmus	Madrigal Lied Chanson Motet Mass	Ritornello principle Binary principle Chorale, Concerto grosso Oratorio, Suite Cantata, Fugue Opera, Variation forms Overture, Sonata
Dynamics	Responsorial effects	Antiphonal effects; double chorus	"Terraced"
Instruments	Accompanying instruments for vocal music or dance	Growing importance of instruments Consorts	Strings—few winds Continuo Harpsichord, Clavichord Organ
Special Features	Neumatic notation Illuminated manuscripts	Music printing	Equal temperament Mood—"affect" Improvisation Figured bass
Composers and Theorists	Adam de la Halle Guido d'Arezzo Raimbaut de Vaqueiras Bernard de Ventadour Philippe de Vitry Guillaume de Machaut	Guillaume Dufay ↔ Josquin des Pres ↔ Giovanni da Palestrina ↔ Thomas Tallis ↔ Thomas Morley John Dowland	↔ Byrd, Lully ↔ Gabrieli, Purcell ↔ Bull, Vivaldi ↔ Monteverdi, Bach Corelli, Handel

	IV. Classical (c. 1750–1825)	V. Romantic (c. 1825–1900)	VI. Contemporary (c. 1900–)
Rhythm	Regular meters	More complicated rhythm; hemiola used in other periods too, but to great degree here	Dynamic, syncopated, motonic Jazz, ballet influences Irregular meters and polyrhythms
Melody	Structured, balanced, Homophonic style	More extensive chromaticism Extended, developing melodies	Wide leaps Folk and ethnic influences Fragmented
Harmony	Related keys Comparatively simple harmonies	Varieties of 7th chords 9th—11th—chords	Atonal, polytonal, modal, whole tone, pentatonic Twelve tone (tone row; serial technique) Dissonance
Forms and Types	Opera Symphony Sonata Quartet Concerto Symmetrical Forms Ternary Forms	Art Song and piano piece Program Music-Symphonic poem Grand Opera, Music Drama Concert overture Increasing freedom	Experimentation Revival of 18th century procedures in some cases Range from strict to free forms Aleatoric or chance music
Dynamics	Development of gradual effects	Long dynamic curve Building of climaxes	Extreme contrasts, sudden or extended
Instruments	Clarinet added Piano developed Stabilization-Mannheim Orchestra	Increase in size, Percussion brass	Chamber Orchestra renewed Increasing percussion Computer, synthesizer, Tape recorder
Special Features	Writing out parts Moving away from patronage	Importance of interpreter	Electronic music Objectivism, primitivism Nationalism Environmental sound sources
Composers and Theorists	Haydn Hopkinson Billings Mozart	Beethoven Schubert Berlioz Mendelssohn Chopin Schumann Liszt Wagner ←→ Verdi Brahms Mahler Debussy	Strauss Schoenberg Ravel Bartók Stravinsky Berg Varèse Milhaud Orff Hindemith Gershwin Luening Menotti Cage

ABOUT THE ARTIST Georges Rouault (1871-1958) is acknowledged as one of France's leading 20th century artists. Many of his paintings and prints deal with religious and sociological themes.

MUSIC OF THE TWENTIETH CENTURY

The twentieth century saw two world wars, the Russian Revolution, Freud, Gandhi, Churchill, Kennedy, and Martin Luther King, Jr. The telephone, electric light, automobile, television, and computer were invented. The stream of the contemporary arts was forever changed by such leaders as Joyce, Stravinsky, and Picasso.

The music of the seventies is a synthesis of all the musical worlds – both ethnic and temporal – that have preceded it. If you listen to the Beatles in a performance of "Penny Lane" you will hear a baroque trumpet; in "Eleanor Rigby" you hear a classical string quartet.

Georges Rouault, *Joan of Arc*

Pablo Picasso, *Guernica*—Museum of Modern Art, New York

RELATED ACTIVITIES
1. Compare the music of Bartok, Stravinsky, Milhaud, Foss, and other contemporary composers to the selections in the previous unit, 'Ethnic Worlds.' 2. Bring to class examples of contemporary art, poetry, and prose. Compare the stylistic elements with the music studied in this unit. 3. Make a "Jazz Age to Space Age" display of 20th century achievements.

ABOUT THE ARTIST
Pablo Picasso (1881-1973) was born in Spain and lived in France. No artist has had a greater impact on 20th cent. art than Picasso. He has produced works of unquestioned originality and imagination.

The Beatles used the modal sounds of the Renaissance period, as do many other contemporary groups today. Bartók, Stravinsky, and Milhaud at times have turned to jazz and the dynamic rhythms of African music. To the heritage from many places and many times, the twentieth century has added its own distinctions—electronic innovations, an awareness of the musical possibilities of new sound sources, and a wide-spreading involvement in creating, performing, and listening to music.

Henry Moore, *King and Queen*—W.J. Keswick Collection, Shawhead, Dumfries, England

LeCorbusier, Notre-Dame-du-Haut, Ronchamp, France

Joan Miro, *Dutch Interior*—Museum of Modern Art, New York

Joan Miro (b. 1893) a Spanish artist, is known for his humor and designs in art.

Record 5, Side B, Band 4

1. Review the relationship of canon to round and fugue.
2. Compare this canon with other canons in the book on pages 226 and 227.

CANON

George Burt

The above work is to be performed by at least three groups of singers. The first group starts to be joined by the second group at that point where the first group has moved on. Signals for cue changes are to be given by the conductor. A clockwise progression results in a soft to loud dynamics level; a counterclockwise performance results in a loud to soft dynamic progression. Rehearsal time should be spent shaping each cue before attempting the entries.

Record 10, Side B, Band 4

LISTENING . . . LEARNINGS AND SKILLS 1. Identify instrumental timbres. 2. Combine melodies to form a musical composition. 3. Identify American composers and their works.

Geod

Lukas Foss

A "geode" is a stone having a cavity lined with crystals – an "earthlike" form. Buckminster Fuller's geodesic, or "earthlike" dome was developed by a type of mathematics also applied to measuring or determining the shape of the earth.

Lukas Foss has composed a four-section orchestral work, using a 132-note row which consists of:

I overlapping string clusters

II overlapping patterns in woodwinds, harp, piano, and organ

III brass instruments, each sustaining one note of a major chord

This Section on recording.

IV twelve folk tunes (for 11 instruments, 4 percussionists and choir) which vary according to the country in which the work is performed. In the United States, Foss selects melodies such as "OLD FOLKS AT HOME," "RED RIVER VALLEY," "TAPS," "WHEN THE SAINTS GO MARCHING IN." Which do you hear?

What do you hear in the music to convey the "geod" idea? Plan a performance like Part IV in which you are a composer-conductor. Select melodies from Unit 6 and other sources for a country of your choice.

RELATED ACTIVITIES

1. Introduce other American composers – past and present – Listen to: Virgil Thomson. The Plow that Broke the Plains (Van. 2095), or The River (Van. 2095).
2. Sing: "Lines from 'The Ancient Mariner'" by Randall Thompson, page 230.
3. Read: "All Revelation" by Robert Frost, in The Poetry of Robert Frost (New York: Holt, Rinehart and Winston).
4. Find picture examples of buildings using Buckminster Fuller's geodesic dome.
5. See 16mm. film Around Perception, 16:27 minutes, color or Opus 3, 6:56 minutes, color. Both are based on geometric forms. Both films may be obtained from National Film Board of Canada.
6. Listening. Silver Apples of the Moon. Composition for Buchla Synthesizer by Morton Subotnick. Nonesuch Recording H. 71174.

The art present on these pages serves both as reference and background to the listening examples of the Middle Ages. Compare both sound and sight of this age. Are they similar? How?

MUSIC OF THE MIDDLE AGES

The Dark Ages were transformed into a Gothic civilization of cathedrals and crusades. The thirteenth century of Philip Augustus, Marco Polo, and St. Francis of Assisi was followed by the Hundred Years' War and the Black Death. Yet, this era witnessed Guillaume de Machaut's polyphony, Giotto's Arena Chapel, the literary works of Dante and Chaucer, the Magna Carta, and Gutenberg's first printed Bible.

Limbourg Brothers, *Les Très Riches Heures du Duc de Berry*—Musée Condé, France

Château Gaillard, Les Andelys, France

The time-world of peasants, priests, and kings was filled with music that expressed their feelings and ideals. The concepts underlying Medieval music and the tonal results of these ideas are strange to modern ears. It is perhaps the very "strangeness" of the sound that makes Medieval music an intriguing source of techniques for composers of the twentieth century.

Chartres Cathedral

Amiens Cathedral

Reims Cathedral

Record 10, Side B, Band 5

LISTENING . . .

STUDENT INVOLVEMENT

Report to the class on the performances of:

1. jongleurs
2. troubadours
3. trouvères
4. minnesingers
5. mastersingers

during the Middle Ages.

Victimae Paschali

(Sound: Dorian mode: Meter: Free; Form: Sequence)

This hymn-like section of the mass for Easter Sunday is called a sequence. It was sung by choir and cantors or by two choirs alternately.

Have students detect modal quality on first playing.
Have students identify the many notes used on only one syllable.

La Quinte Estampie Real

Record 10, Side B, Band 6

The estampie (or estampida in Provence) is among the earliest known examples of medieval instrumental music for *vielle*. It was meant to be played to the *stamping* of dancers, by the *jongleurs*, entertainers who travelled with troubadours.

Distinguish the recorder in the estampie real from the shawm in the estampie royale. Both are combined with the drum.

La Seconde Estampie Royale

Record 10, Side B, Band 7

Here is another estampie. What instruments are used?

Compose a poem in the estampie form:

$a\,b'\,a\,b^2$ $c\,b'\,c\,b^2$ $d\,b'\,d\,b^2$ $e\,b'\,e\,b^2$

Kalenda Maya

(Sound: Ionian Mode)

Raimbaut de Vaqueiras (1155?-1207)

Record 10, Side B, Band 8

Raimbaut's works show the international character of the troubadour. It is said that "Kalenda Maya," the oldest known estampida, originated from his setting words to an estampida which had been played for him on the vielle by a company of *jongleurs*. (A *vielle* is the medieval ancestor of the string family.)

Troubadour Estampie

Discuss the use of songs and instruments to accompany rhythmic movement: emphasis on melodic line and beat.

The language of the text is Old French. Compare the Old French with French and English.

Maya	Mai	May
Chanz	Chants	Songs
Auzelh	Oiseau	Bird
Flors	fleurs	flowers
Amors	Amour	love
Ans	Ans	year

"Troping" is the addition of words to a melismatic musical passage.

Compare the sound, beat, and feeling of the Recessional with "Kalenda Maya."

LISTENING...

The Play of Daniel

Twelfth Century

Record 11, Side B, Band 1

"The Play of Daniel" was created by the youth of Beauvais. Here in narration and song is one episode from Daniel's life—his reading of the handwriting on the wall at Balshazzar's court. The Queen leaves, entreating Balshazzar to consult Daniel in interpreting the mysterious handwriting. She is accompanied by a group of children and the sound of instruments. Listen for the melody quoted below. This same music is repeated seven times throughout the play.

Sound: Mixolydian

Meter: 3

The English translation of the text reads:

In the book of Solomon is written fitting and becoming praise to women. Let this woman be compared to one who is a support to her king. For her power of speech defeats the wisdom of the learned. With reverence sing her praise. All come along and join in song.

Play the vocal line, substituting a melody instrument.

Lead the class in a discussion of some of the principal accomplishments of this period in fields other than music. See "Happenings," p. 288.

MUSIC OF THE RENAISSANCE

The Renaissance was a gradual revolution in politics with Joan of Arc, Henry VIII, and Machiavelli; in religion with Huss, Luther, and Calvin; in literature with Petrarch, Erasmus, Cervantes, and Shakespeare; in science and technology with Columbus, Copernicus, Paracelsus, and Galileo; in music and art with Josquin des Prez, Palestrina, Thomas Tallis, Jan van Eyck, Masaccio, Leonardo da Vinci, and Bosch.

ABOUT THE ARTIST

Pieter Bruegel (1520–1569) is acknowledged to be the last of the great Antwerp painters of the 16th century. He was well-educated and an outspoken critic of his day. He was nicknamed "Peasant Bruegel" because of his close association with the peasants of the countryside and their festivities. His compositions are classic in their balance and design. His landscapes capture the character of the environment with almost photographic detail.

Pieter Bruegel the Elder, *Peasant Wedding*—Kunsthistorisches Museum, Vienna

ABOUT THE ARTIST

Sandro Botticelli (1445-1510) is especially known for his sacred paintings and his works based upon mythological characters. His strong use of line and form influenced the artists in the following historic period – the Baroque.

Compare the architecture and paintings of the Renaissance with those of the 20th century.

Sandro Botticelli, *Primavera*—Uffizi Gallery, Florence

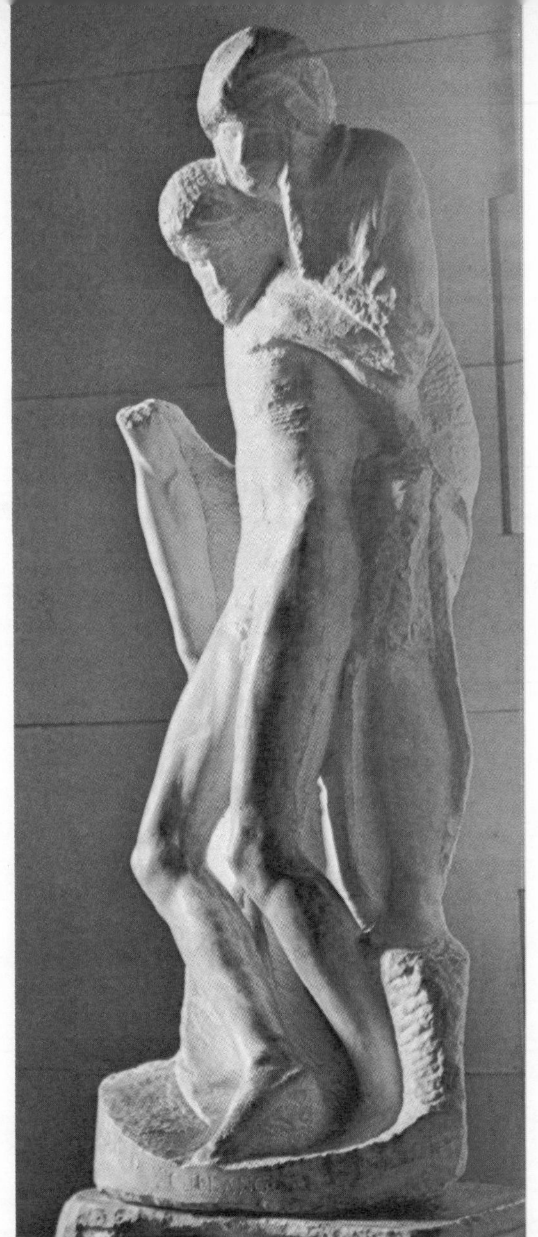

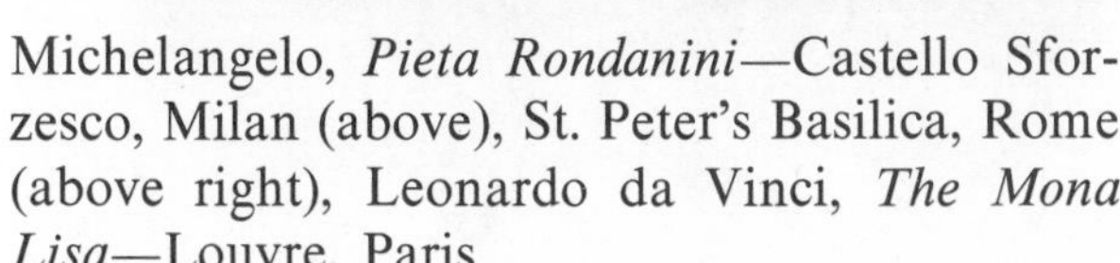

Michelangelo, *Pieta Rondanini*—Castello Sforzesco, Milan (above), St. Peter's Basilica, Rome (above right), Leonardo da Vinci, *The Mona Lisa*—Louvre, Paris

Music in the years 1450–1600 presented a complex picture. As in the twentieth century, there were increasing numbers of professionals and interested amateurs; as more people began to play and sing, there were books telling how to play or sing as well as books on the theory of music. The advent of music printing in 1501 encouraged the growth of interest in music.

Michelangelo Buonarroti (1475-1564) Italian master painter, sculptor, and architect.

Leonardo da Vinci (1452-1519) Italian genius of the Renaissance. Leonardo was recognized as a painter, sculptor, architect, and musician.

Music of the Renaissance included dance pieces, instrumental pieces, and vocal compositions (masses, madrigals, and popular songs).

LISTENING . . .

(Sound: Dorian)

L'Homme Armé

Record 11, Side A, Band 2

Guillaume Dufay (ca. 1400–1474)

The armed man is to be feared;
Everywhere it has been said that
Everyone should arm himself
With a coat of mail. (trans.)

The custom of using a well-known secular song as the basis of a mass was inherited from the Middle Ages. Such a favorite song was "The Armed Man." It was used by almost every composer of the late fifteenth and sixteenth centuries in a mass. It might appear backwards, with a repeated rhythm pattern, or with rhythmic variations.

3/4
Lhom - muh, Lhom - muh, Lhom arr - may; lhom - arr - may,
L'hom - me, L'hom - me, L'homme ar - mé; l'homme ar - mé,
Fine
Lhom arr - may dwah - tohng doo - tay, dwah - tohn doo - tay.
L'homme ar - mé doibt on doub - ter, doibt on doub - ter.
Ohn ah fay pahr too cree - yay, Kuh sha - kung suh
On a fait par - tout cri - er, Que cha - cun se
D.C. al fine
vyeng - gu - arr - may duhn oh - bray - gohn deh fair.
viengue ar - mer D'un hau - bre - gon de fer.

M.638—The Pierpont Morgan Library, New York

STUDENT INVOLVEMENT 1. Make a rhythmic variation of the melody. 2. Sing or play the melody backwards. (Crabwise or "cancrizans")

Palestrina's music represents a culmination of the vocal style of the Renaissance. (flowing vocal line, tonal arch in melodic line, and tonal sound — approaching the Baroque Period.)

LISTENING . . .

Parts of the ordinary of the mass most frequently set to music include: Kyrie Eleison, Gloria, Credo, Sanctus, Agnus Dei.

Gloria

ecord 11, de A, and 3

Giovanni da Palestrina (1525–1594)

The composer took his name from his birthplace, the hill town of Palestrina. He attended choir school in Rome. His famous "Pope Marcellus Mass" is typical, in its clarity, of much Renaissance music. The "Gloria" is one of the main parts of the ordinary of the mass.

E'LATED ACTIVITY Sing Palestrina "Sanctus" in the choral unit on page 230.

Gentile Bellini, *Procession in the Piazza San Marco*—Academy, Venice

Instrumentation of the canzona includes: 3 recorders, 2 oboes, English horn, 2 clarinets, bass clarinet, 3 basoons, contra bassoon, horna, viola, diskant-gamba, bass gamba, 3 positive organs.

LISTENING . . .

Canzona Quarti Toni A 15 Record 11, Side A, Band 4

Giovanni Gabrieli (1557–1612)

An English visitor to Venice in the seventeenth century called the music "so good, so delectable, so rare, so admirable, so super-excellent, that it did even ravish and stupifie all those strangers that never heard the like." Gabrieli's music reflects the pageantry of the Venetian church. His church, St. Mark's, was especially suited to the use of several choirs.

As I Went to Walsingham (Sound: Am) Record 11, Side A, Band 5

Variations for Harpsichord by John Bull (1562–1628)

John Bull belongs to the group of composers who did much to develop harpsichord music. In the Music School Collection at Oxford a portrait of Bull represents him in the gown of a Bachelor of Music.

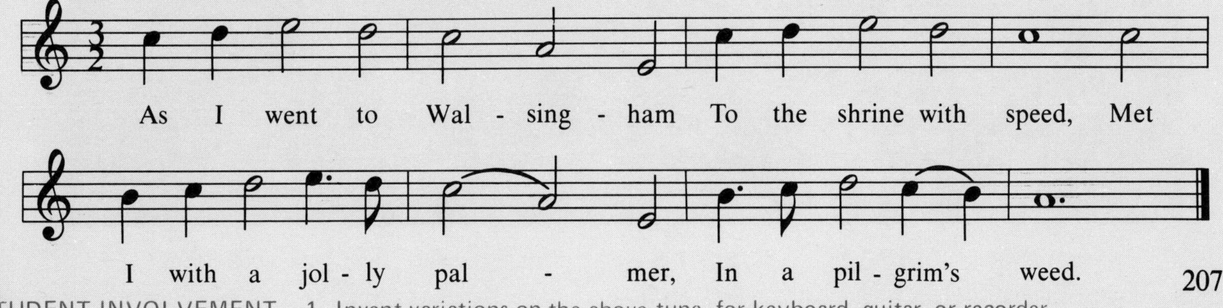
As I went to Wal - sing - ham To the shrine with speed, Met
I with a jol - ly pal - mer, In a pil - grim's weed.

STUDENT INVOLVEMENT
1. Invent variations on the above tune, for keyboard, guitar, or recorder.
2. Compose a ballad which involves the name of an American town.

The common trait uniting the variety of Baroque music was the belief in the power of music to move the "affections." An affection meant the mental reaction to sensations which stimulated the mechanisms of the body.

MUSIC OF THE BAROQUE PERIOD

The Baroque era flourished when Louis XIV was absolute ruler in France, Cromwell governed the English, and Peter the Great opened Russia's window on the West. It was the age of great thinkers: Descartes, Spinoza, Locke, Swift, and Voltaire. Rubens painted at Antwerp in the grand manner and in music giants like Monteverdi, Purcell, Vivaldi, Handel, and Bach signified the spirit of their time. Use selected music to develop aural concepts of terms and definitions. See chart, p. 194.

ABOUT THE ARTIST El Greco (c. 1541-1614) Greek-Spanish painter, architect, and sculptor and one of the major artists of the Baroque style.

Encourage the students to describe how architecture, painting, and sculpture reflected the Baroque spirit.

To seventeenth-century ears Baroque music seemed confused in harmony, dissonant, unnatural in the difficult leaps of the melody, and repetitive in its rhythmic patterns. In the Late Baroque period there arose the delicate, ornamental *Rococo* style of Couperin, Telemann, and Scarlatti.

El Greco, *View of Toledo*—Metropolitan Museum of Art, New York (opposite), Rembrandt van Ryn, *The Prodigal Son*—Hermitage, Leningrad (left), Diego Velazquez, *The Maids of Honor*—Prado, Madrid (bottom left), Palazzo Barberini, Rome (top), Gianlorenzo Bernini, *The Ecstasy of St. Theresa*—Santa Maria della Vittoria, Rome (below)

Record 11, Side A, Band 6

LISTENING . . . (Sound: D, Meter: in fours, Form: Binary – A A B B)

Bois Epais

Have the class determine sound, meter, and form.

Jean Baptiste Lully (1632–1687)

Lully rose from the low position of lute player and singer with a group of travelling Italian players to a high social and professional position as the favorite of France's Louis XIV. An entertainer for the court, he was also a serious musician who reorganized the court orchestra and composed elaborate productions.

Record 11, Side B, Band 1 (First Movement, First Section)

Sonata for Violin and Continuo, Opus 5, No. 5

The complete sonata is in five movements: Adagio, Vivace, Adagio cantabile, Vivace, and Giga (Allegro).

Arcangelo Corelli (1653–1713)

Both the first and last movements of this sonata illustrate the tendency of some Baroque composers to use binary or two-part form.

Record 11, Side B, Band 2

Trumpet Tune (King Arthur)

Henry Purcell (1658–1695)

Listen to this stirring theme which reflects the fine sense of drama Purcell displayed as the greatest English composer of his time.

Record 11, Side B, Band 3

Concerto in D Major, Opus 10, No. 3 ("Il Gardellino")

Review the general form of the concerto.

Contrast concerto with concerto grosso.

Antonio Vivaldi (c. 1675–1743)

The balancing of solo groups or solo instruments against the orchestra was a hallmark of Baroque music. What other kinds of contrast do you find in Vivaldi's music?

This concerto is nicknamed "Il Gardellino," for Vivaldi was presenting a sound portrait of the goldfinch. What is the musical device near the end which is particularly effective for this purpose? (Cadenza)

Record 11, Side B, Band 4

V'Adoro Pupille (Giulio Cesare)

(Sound: F, Dm; Meter: in threes; Form: A B A)

Have students identify the sound, meter, and form.

George Frederic Handel (1685–1759)

This opera, based on episodes in the life of Julius Caesar, was composed in 1724 at the height of Handel's London success. Here, Cleopatra appears on a terrace and sings to the stars without knowing that Caesar is watching from the garden; this is his first glimpse of the Egyptian princess, soon to be crowned queen with his help.

Listen first to the aria as representative of a part of the story.
Accompaniment: orchestra, divided in concerto grosso style.
Concertino group: oboes, muted violins, viola.
Continuo: viola da gamba, theorbo, harp, bassoons, celli.

Record 11, Side B, Band 5

(Sound: D, Meter: in twos, Form: Ritornello)

LISTENING . . .

Brandenburg Concerto No. 5 in D Major

Johann Sebastian Bach (1685–1750)

Johann Sebastian Bach's music exerted more influence on composers of later centuries than on the composers who immediately followed him in the same century. It has been said that the compositions of Bach's mature years were like a postscript to the Baroque period in general.

Explain the ritornello principle; compare with a rondo. Each is a kind of recurring refrain.

IMPORTANT TERMS:
- concertino — solo group
- ripieno — larger instrumental group
- tutti — combination of the above

Call Number		
1	Ritornello Theme in D Strings	Ripieno
2	Flute solo: solo theme in D	Concertino
3	Triplets	
4	Ritornello Theme in A	
5	Tutti	
6	Tutti: smooth syncopation in flute and violin	
7	Solo Theme in B minor	Concertino
8	Tutti	
9	Transition	
10	𝄾 ♪ ♪ ♪ pattern	
11	Extended trills	
12	Ritornello Theme in A	
13	Soloists Theme in D	Ripieno
14	Ritornello Theme in D	
15		Concertino
16	Dialogue in Concertino Runs in harpsichord Repeated notes in ripieno	
17	Harpsichord alone	
18	Cadenza-like passage	
19	Theme in D	

[Initiate discussion of characteristics of the Classical Period – balance, order, and design.

MUSIC OF THE CLASSICAL PERIOD

The Classical Age erupted in the American and French Revolutions. Rousseau's *Social Contract,* Kant's *Critique of Pure Reason,* Paine's *The Rights of Man,* and Adam Smith's *Wealth of Nations*—these were hallmarks of the Enlightenment. David and Ingres proclaimed the taste in art for Greece and Rome, and Napoleon dominated Europe when Haydn, Mozart, and Beethoven composed music unrivalled in design and formal beauty.

ABOUT THE ARTIST Jean-August Ingres (1780-1867) was a French painter and draftsman associated with the Classical Style. His style was greatly influenced by the simplicity of line and form of the art of Ancient Greece.

Ingres, *Portrait of Madame Riviere*—Louvre, Paris (left), Jean Antoine Houdon, *George Washington*—State Capitol, Richmond, Virginia (below right)

ABOUT THE ARTIST Jean Antoine Houdon (1741-1828) French sculptor and teacher. Houdon's works include busts and statues of Gluck, Benjamin Franklin, Jefferson, Washington, and John Paul Jones.

Benedictine Abbey, Ottobeuren, Germany (top left), the Pantheon (Ste-Geneviève), Paris (top right), Jacques Louis David, *The Horatii*—Louvre, Paris (below)

The qualities usually associated with classicism are truth, wholeness, and universality of meaning. Eighteenth-century composers felt that these qualities could best be achieved musically through balance and order. The public became an important patron of music as well as princes, dukes, and archbishops in the past. Music making at home became as vital in the middle class as among the aristocracy, bringing about the need for a tremendous musical output.

STUDENT INVOLVEMENT Have students locate and identify examples of architectural forms which exemplify classicism.

Record 12, Side A, Band 1

Mozarts' First Symphony (K. 16) was written at the age of nine. His symphonic compositions culminate in the "Jupiter" written in 1788 when Mozart was 32. His earlier symphonies seem to give greatest importance to the first movement. In the "Jupiter" Mozart builds toward the finale with passages in a fugal style as the grand climax after the minuet (3rd movement).

PROGRAMMED TAPE

LISTENING...

Symphony No. 41 in C Major "Jupiter," K. 551 (Third Movement)

Wolfgang Amadeus Mozart (1756–1791)

Third Movement of Symphony — Key: C
Meter: In threes
Form: A B A (Minuet and Trio)

LISTENING...

Adagio and Rondo in C Minor, K.617

Record 12, Side A, Band 2

Wolfgang Amadeus Mozart

Meter: In twos
Form: ABACADA Coda

Mozart used the existing musical resources of his day in form and in timbre, but he was also quick to recognize the possibilities of new instruments. What instrument does the sound suggest to you? It is one that became a fascinating attraction at court in the 1750's, invented by Benjamin Franklin and played by Mesmer, the renowned hypnotist. The rondo theme is below:

The key of the rondo is C Major.

The familiar timbres heard in K. 617 are the flute, oboe, viola, and violoncello. The unfamiliar sound is the glass harmonica.

RELATED ACTIVITIES View 16mm film Music of Williamsburg to hear baroque, classical and folk music in early Virginia. A glass harmonica is played during the film.

Record 12, Side A, Band 3
(Key: A, Meter: In threes, Form: A B A B A)

LISTENING...

Sonata in A Major for Violoncello and Piano, Opus 69 (Second Movement)

Ludwig van Beethoven (1770–1827)

The Sonata in A Major is dated 1808.
Compare musical works of Beethoven in light of the "Heiligenstadt Testament."
RELATED LISTENING Piano Sonata #1 in F Minor, (Opus 2 No. 1) First movement, Vanguard 10084
Piano Sonata #23 in F Minor (Opus 57—"Appassionata") First Movement RCA LSC-4001. Compare the complexity of the second work to the simplicity of the first in terms of harmony, melody, mood.

In 1802 Ludwig van Beethoven, knowing his future life of total deafness, went to live in the village of Heiligenstadt, near Vienna. He addressed to his brothers the now-famous "Heiligenstadt Testament" in which he wrote:

> *How could I proclaim the defect of a sense that I once possessed in the highest perfection—in a perfection which few of my colleagues possess? . . . Forgive me, then, if you see me draw back when I would gladly mingle with you . . . what a humiliation, when any one standing beside me could hear at a distance a flute that I could not hear, or anyone heard a shepherd singing, and I could not distinguish a sound!*

It is generally known that, from this time, Beethoven developed new powers as a composer, although the change is not easily expressed in words. Listen to an example of how Beethoven's compositions moved into new dimensions of technique and drama.

Compare this listening example with the Mozart "Adagio and Rondo."
Theme I

Theme 1

What kinds of contrasts are there in the two themes?
1. Major-minor, 2. staccato-legato, 3. syncopation – no syncopation,
4. theme introduced by piano – theme introduced by cello.

Composers of the 19th century experimented with every possible musical component. Melodies became more chromatic and more extensive; harmonies became richer; the size of the orchestra doubled; forms became free; performers became public idols.

MUSIC OF THE ROMANTIC PERIOD

Romanticism exalted the ideal of mystery and imagination in literature with Byron, Keats, Scott, and Hugo; in painting with Gericault, Delacroix, and Friedrich; in music with Schubert, Mendelssohn, Chopin, Berlioz, Liszt, Wagner, Verdi, and Brahms. Darwin revealed nature's marvels in his *Origin of Species;* Stephenson's locomotive, Morse's telegraph, and Daguerre's photography accelerated the tempo of modern life.

Caspar David Friedrich (1774-1840)

Much music became intertwined with non-musical subject matter, or program music. Glorification of emotion, depiction of nature, expression of nationalism — all helped set the scene of the Romantic Period.

Eugene Delacroix (1798-1863)

Have the students compare the representative art on pages 216-217 with that of the Classical Period on pages 212-213.

The essence of the word "Romantic" is a spirit of adventure that was a keynote of the period—a new freedom of thinking and communication that had brilliant expression in the music of the nineteenth century. In any period a "romantic" is a person not ashamed to express himself freely, a person with the desire to invent, to innovate.

Theodore Gericault (1791-1824)

Caspar David Friedrich, *Gazing at the Moon*—Staatliche Gemaldegalerie, Dresden (opposite top), Eugene Delacroix, *St. George and the Dragon*—Louvre, Paris (opposite bottom), Theodore Gericault, *The Raft of the Medusa*—Louvre, Paris (top right)

Joseph Turner, *Rain, Steam, and Speed*—National Gallery, London (left), The Opera, Paris (above)

Record 12, Side A, Band 4

LISTENING...

Overture: Benvenuto Cellini

Hector Berlioz (1803–1869)

Berlioz' opera, which is based on the life of Benvenuto Cellini, opens with this overture. The first lively theme was intended as a portrayal of the spirited character of the Italian goldsmith, who lived from 1500 to 1571 and became one of the best-known craftsmen of the Renaissance, in sculpture as well as in the goldsmith's art.

The small Baroque orchestra consisted of strings, harpsichord, and winds (oboe, flute, trumpet and reeds as the occasion demanded). The strings carried over into the Classical Period, which added horns, a bassoon, and oboes. By the beginning of the 19th century, the strings were doubled; more bassoons, two flutes, two clarinets, two trumpets and kettledrums were added. By the end of the 19th century there were approximately a hundred instrumentalists.

Attributed to Jacopo Bilivert, Rospigliosi Cup—Metropolitan Museum of Art, New York

STUDENT INVOLVEMENT

Follow the sonata form of the first movement. Identify dramatic and lyric themes.

Record 12, Side B, Band 1

LISTENING...

Piano Concerto No. 1 in D Minor, Opus 15 (First Movement)

Brahms' concerto was originally planned as a symphony, then as a sonata for two pianos. First Movement – Maestoso, Second Movement – Adagio. Third Movement – Rondo: Allegro ma non troppo.

Johannes Brahms (1833–1897)

The D Minor Concerto was composed by Johannes Brahms when he was a young man. Even before settling in Vienna, his Romantic music showed a deep concern for human nature and the musical traits of his native Hamburg in North Germany.

LEARNINGS AND SKILLS

1. Brahms' style
   - –Broken chord figures
   - –Doubling of melodic line in octaves, thirds, sixths.
   - –Cross rhythms
   - –Rich harmonies
   - –Importance of form
   - –Avoidance of "program"

Un Ballo in Maschera

Giuseppe Verdi (1813–1901)

Record 13, Side A, Band 1

During rehearsals of "The Masked Ball" Felice Orsini made his attempt to kill Napoleon III, and Verdi was ordered to change the words of the opera because it contained a conspiracy scene. He refused, the manager brought suit, and the disappointment of the people almost caused a riot in Naples. Crowds gathered, shouting:

Viva **V** ittorio **E** mmanuele **R** e **D** i **I** talia

This implied a royalist political connection as well. The ball scene follows the "conspiracy scene" and includes orchestra, military band, and a string quartet behind the dance music.

Listen to the three examples and make a comparison of the musical elements and how they are used. Compare Brahms with his models, Schumann and Beethoven. Contrast his style with that of Chopin and Liszt (see p. 220).

Key: Dm

Meter: In fours

STUDENT INVOLVEMENT

Listen to the 2nd movement of the Dm String Quartet (1824). This consists of 5 variations on the melody. Which variation is in a major key? (4th). The movement from minor to major or vice versa is a familiar characteristic of Schubert's style.

DER TOD UND DAS MADCHEN

Franz Schubert (1797–1828)

Franz Schubert's six hundred songs cover an immense range of emotions. The melody, Death's theme from the song below, is also heard in Schubert's String Quartet.

Record 13, Side A, Band 2

pp
Geep digh-nuh hahnt doo shayn unt tsahrt guh-bilt! bin froynt, unt
Gieb dei - ne Hand du schön und zart Ge - bild! bin Freund, und
Give me thy hand my fair and ten - der child. As friend I
Kawm'-muh nikht tsoo shtrah - ten. Zigh goo- tes Moots! Ikh
kom - me nicht, zu stra - - ten. Sei gu - tes Muths! Ich
come, and not to chas - - ten. Be of good cheer! I
bin nikht vilt, zawlst zahnft in mighn-en ahr-men shlah' - fun!
bin nicht wild, sollst sanft in mei - nen Ar - men schla - fen!
am not wild; To sleep with - in these fond arms has - ten.

Movements of the entire quartet are: Allegro, Andante con moto, Scherzo, Finale: Presto, Allegro molto.

Record 13, Side A, Band 3

Chopin's four ballades are in 6/4 or 6/8 meter; however, the title has been applied to pieces with romantic feeling which do not have a precisely different form.

STUDENT INVOLVEMENT

1. Assign a "role" (Chopin or one of his friends) to members of the class. Have each study the character, then stage an improvised cafe or salon scene. Let students base the spontaneous dialogue on their research. Tape.
2. Discover beat and background patterns by tapping each in successive hearings of the Chopin ballade.

LISTENING...

Ballade in G Minor, Opus 23

PROGRAMMED TAPE

Frédéric Chopin (1810–1849)

Chopin became a notable musical personality in the life of Paris, numbering among his friends and admirers Liszt, Berlioz, Meyerbeer, Musset, Balzac, Heine, Delacroix, and George Sand. The Rothschilds were among his patrons. His early compositions for piano, like the "ballade," reveal the same characteristics as his later works:

- ▶ a lyric style, influenced by Italian opera
- ▶ harmonic and rhythmic traits from the national music of Poland
- ▶ a continual study of Bach
- ▶ sensitivity to form

Help the students discover characteristics of Chopin's style:

* rich texture
* careful workmanship
* emotional impact
* chromaticism
* lyric quality

Record 13, Side A, Band 4

LISTENING...

Mazeppa

Franz Liszt (1811–1886)

Liszt reached the final form of each of his twelve symphonic poems only after many sketches and changes. "Mazeppa" was inspired by a Victor Hugo poem about a knight whose pride and ambition cause conflicts while he lives at the court of the Polish king. He is bound to his horse which gallops into the desert. A group of Cossacks rescue Mazeppa, who soon becomes their leader. Compare "Mazeppa" with another symphonic poem, "Orpheus." What is the story of Orpheus? How do the differences in the music emphasize the differences in the programmatic content?

LEARNINGS AND SKILLS

1. Identify examples of characteristics of Liszt's style.
   * chromatic
   * theme transformation
   * dramatic changes
   * highly emotional
   * emphasis on long melodic lines
   * thick texture
2. Compare the sound, beat, and feeling of the Liszt listening example with a composer from the 20th century, the Middle Ages, the Renaissance, the Baroque Period, or the Classical Period.

Record 13, Side A, Band 5

Blondel's Lied

Robert Schumann (1810–1856)

The year 1840 was rich in song composition for Schumann. The cycles *Myrthen, Frauenliebe und Leben,* and *Dichterliebe* were soon followed by several volumes of *Romances and Ballads.* One included this song recalling Blondel's loyalty to Richard Coeur de Lion. Afterward Schumann continued to write songs, but for the first time he became interested in symphonic writing.

For a library project, listen to part of Schumann's First Symphony in B♭ Major ("Spring"). Do you hear similarities in the style of the song and of the symphony? In your own words, describe how they reflect "Romantic" characteristics.

Record 13, Side B, Band 1

Violin Concerto in D Major,
Opus 35 (First Movement)

PROGRAMMED TAPE

Peter Ilyich Tchaikovsky (1840–1893)

Part of every concert violinist's repertoire, this concerto was originally rejected as being too "radical." Tchaikovsky wrote to Madame von Meck, his patroness, ". . . The first movement of the concerto . . . contains, as does every piece that serves virtuoso purposes, much that appears chiefly to the mind; nevertheless, the themes are not painfully evolved: the plan of this movement sprang suddenly into my head and quickly ran into its mold."

LISTEN FOR: Unison passages
A B A form
Martial rhythm (in fours)
The recurring refrain — Suche treu, so findest du!
(Search faithfully and you will find!)

First theme — Moderato assai

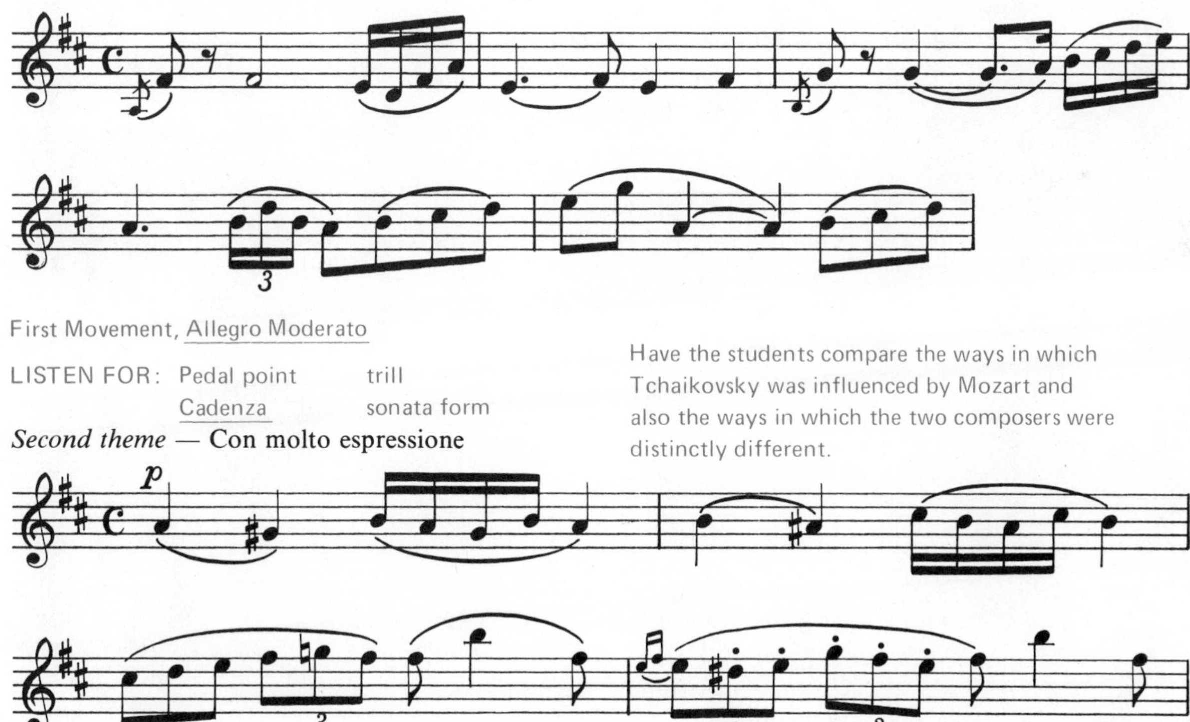

First Movement, Allegro Moderato

LISTEN FOR: Pedal point, Cadenza, trill, sonata form

Have the students compare the ways in which Tchaikovsky was influenced by Mozart and also the ways in which the two composers were distinctly different.

Second theme — Con molto espressione

Record 12, Side A, Band 5

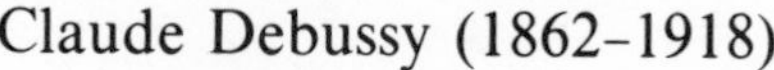

LISTENING...

La Fille Aux Cheveux De Lin (Girl With the Flaxen Hair)

Claude Debussy (1862–1918)

One of the musical transitions from the romantic century to the twentieth century was the period known as Impressionism, best typified by the work of Debussy. Debussy felt that the purpose of music was to please the senses; as the impressionist painters experimented with the reflection of light, the composer equipped himself with a palette of sounds that would reflect aural images. Many of Debussy's musical experiments opened the way to more extreme experimentation in the early twentieth century.

Listen for musical devices that were used by Debussy and became typical of his "impressionist" style:

- whole-tone melodies
- wide-spaced chords
- chords that do not resolve in the customary manner
- free-moving rhythms
- new emphasis on color

Auguste Renoir, *Girl with Basket of Fish* and *Girl with Basket of Oranges*—National Gallery of Art, Washington

Pierre-Auguste Renoir (1841–1919) French impressionist painter and sculptor.

RELATED ACTIVITIES View filmstrip "Debussy's Afternoon of a Faun" #976-R (record), #976-C (cassette). Educational Development Corporation.

Temporal Thoughts in Verse and Prose

Now sinks the sun beneath the wood
(Mary, I pity your lovely face):
Now sinks the sun beneath the Rood
(Mary, I pity your son and you).
Medieval English Verse

Encourage the class to collect and exhibit their favorite poetry, art reproductions, music examples of various historical periods. This can be accomplished by individual reports or as a bulletin board project.

To be, or not to be: that is the question
Whether 'tis nobler in the mind to suffer
The slings and arrows of outrageous fortune,
Or to take arms against a sea of troubles,
And by opposing end them? To die: to sleep
No more; and by a sleep to say we end
The heart-ache and the thousand natural shocks
That flesh is heir to. 'Tis a consummation
Devoutly to be wished.

Have the students refer to "Happenings," on page 277 for specific ideas for special projects.

William Shakespeare — English playwright and poet (1564–1616)
Hamlet, Act III, Scene I

No man is an Iland, intire of itselfe; every man is a peece of the Continent, a part of the maine . . . any man's death diminishes me, because I am involved in Mankinde; and therefore never send to know for whom the bell tolls; it tolls for thee.

John Donne — English poet and preacher (1591–1631)

If a man does not keep pace with his companions, perhaps it is because he hears a different drummer. Let him step to the music he hears, however measured or far away.

Henry David Thoreau — American writer (1817–1862)

I'm nobody! Who are you?
Are you nobody, too?
Then there's a pair of us—don't tell!
They'd banish us, you know.

How dreary to be somebody!
How public, like a frog
'To tell your name the livelong day
To an admiring bog!

Emily Dickinson — American poet (1830–1886)

UNIT

8

SEE GUIDE FOR UNIT LEARNING OBJECTIVES

Music for Chorus

Use the recordings of the music from this unit to:

1. Give the students a concept of the whole musical work rather than only the parts they are singing.

2. Listen for the correct pronunciation of the texts.

3. Develop awareness of interpretative nuances.

4. Stimulate individual practice sessions—students may take the recordings to a practice room to work on their own parts.

The compositions in this unit offer an opportunity for the study and performance of works especially suited for choral programs. Various historical styles of composition are included as well as a variety of voice combinations.

Principles of Choral Singing

- ► Practice good posture . . . stand or sit correctly.
- ► Keep your throat open and your jaw relaxed.
- ► Hear the intervals as you sing them.
- ► Listen to the other voices in your chorus.
- ► Enunciate words clearly.
- ► Watch for the conductor's attacks and releases.
- ► Sing with the appropriate tone and dynamics.
- ► Express the text and music through your singing.
- ► Listen to the total sound.

Key: C Meter: 4 (quarter note) Record 5, Side B, Band 5

Starting Tone: E (3-mi) Form: A B C

THE 3-WAY CANON BLUES

Words and Music by Henry Brant

STUDENT INVOLVEMENT 1. Read text through in unison for continuity. 2. Read and clap basic rhythm patterns. 3. Identify "blue" notes (Bb and Eb). 4. Sing in unison before attempting canon.

Moderately slow, but rhythmic
(Keep time with foot)
Here's an 8 - bar sit - u - a - tion
2.
In this can - on tone re - la - tions
3.
Pol - y - phon - ic com - bi - na - tions
With the u - su - al syn - co - pa - tion, and Scored for voic - es,
Are not ab - stract for - mu - la - tions; There's no room for
Are the can - on's best sen - sa - tions. Mixed with bar - ber -
un - ac - com - p'- nied. On the 3 - way Can - on Blues.
2.
12 - tone sys - tems On the 3 - way Can - on Blues.
3.
shop pro - gres - sions On the 3 - way Can - on Blues.

From Modern Canons as edited by Herman Reichenbach.

Key: F

Starting Tone: F (1-do)

Meter: 3 ♩

Form: A B C

Record 5, Side B, Band 6

Canon

DONA NOBIS PACEM (GIVE US PEACE)

Traditional Round

STUDENT INVOLVEMENT 1. Observe legato movement as indicated by slurs. 2. Sustain half notes for two full beats.

(1.)

Doh - nah no - bees pah - chem, pah - chem, Doh - nah

Do - na no - bis pa - cem, pa - cem, Do - na

no - bees pah - chem.

no - bis pa - cem.

(2.)

Doh - nah no - bees

Do - na no - bis

pah - chem, Doh - nah no - bees pah chem.

pa - cem, Do - na no - bis pa - cem.

(3.)

Doh - nah

Do - na

no - bees pah - chem, Doh - nah - no - bees pah chem.

no - bis pa - cem, Do - na no - bis pa - cem.

Key: Bb
Starting Tone: F (5-sol)

Meter: 2 (half note)
Form: AB

Record 5, Side B, Band 7

ALLELUIA

Words and Music by W. A. Mozart

STUDENT INVOLVEMENT Before reading, or immediately after a trial reading, examine the two approaches to F# alteration. Sing the half-step approach and departure G-F#-G).

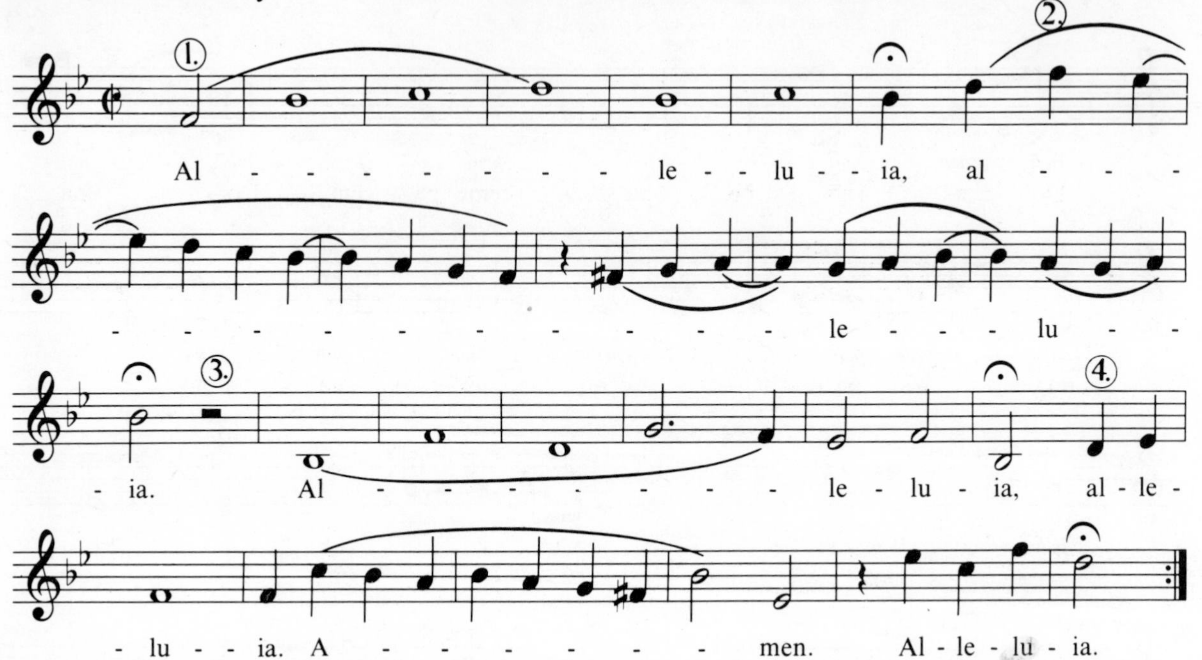

1.
2.
Al - - - - - - - - le - - lu - - ia, al - - - -
- - - - - - - - - - - - - le - - - - lu - - -
3.
4.
- ia. Al - - - - - - - - - le - lu - ia, al - le -
- lu - - ia. A - - - - - - - - men. Al - le - lu - ia.

Key: G
Starting Tone: A (2-re)

Meter: 3 (quarter note) = 2 (dotted quarter note)

STUDENT INVOLVEMENT 1. Sing verses in unison, then as a canon. The first voice thus sings the entire two verses, the second voice goes to the coda at (3.); the third voice goes to the coda at (2.). 2. In the coda, make the most of the chromatic line in the middle voice part.

NORTH ARGENTINIAN FOLK DANCE

Arr. by Alberto Ginastera

Vivace
f
Pah - lah pah - lah pul - péh - ro ___ *pah - lah pah - lah pul - pér-roh* ___
1. Pa - la, pa - la pul - pe - ro, ___ pa - la, pa - la pul - pe - ro, ___
Ahm-páh - tu - keh - whoh-néh-roh ___ *Ahm-páh-tu keh-whoh-néh-roh* ___
2. Am - pa - tu ca - jo - ne - ro, ___ am - pa - tu ca - jo - ne - ro, ___

From Modern Canons as edited by Herman Reichenbach.

páh - lah páh - lah pul - péh - roh chú nyah sohl - téh roh chú nyah sohl - téh - roh
pa - la, pa - la pul - pe - ro, chu ña sol - te - ro chu ña sol - te - ro,
ahm - páh - tu keh - whoh - néh - roh u tu gué - tah - rréh roh tu gué - tah - rréh - roh
am - pa - tu ca - jo - ne - ro u tu gui - ta - rre - ro u - tu gui - ta - rre - ro,
2.IIªvolta: Terza voce alla CODA
mf
p sub.
Páh - lah páh - lah Tra lah lah lah lah Páh - lah páh - lah Tra lah lah lah lah
Pa - la, pa - la Tra la la la la Pa - la, pa - la Tra la la la la
cresc.
f
lah lah lah lah lah lah lah lah lah lah lah lah lah Tra lah lah lah lah
la la la la la la la la la la la la la, Tra la la la la,
Observe the cresc. and decresc.
IIªvolta:
3.IIªvolta: Seconda voce alla CODA
Prima voce alla CODA
A, A, Pa - la, Pa - la, Pa - la, pa - la.
CODA
f cresc.
ff
Páh - lah pah - lah pul - péh - roh páh - lah pul - péh - roh Tra lah lah lah
Pa - la, pa - la pul - pe - ro, pa - la pul - pe - ro, Tra la la la
Páh - lah Tra lah lah Tra lah lah Tra lah lah lah lah
Pa - la, Tra la la, Tra la la, Tra la la la la.
Páh - lah páh - lah Tra lah lah lah lah Tra lah lah lah
Pa - la, pa - la, Tra la la la la, Tra la la la.

Alberto Ginastera (b. 1916), is considered to be one of the most exciting contemporary South American composers. Much of his material and inspiration are drawn from South American folklore.

Key: C
Starting Tone: G (5-sol)

Meter: 4 (quarter note)

Form: canon

Record 5, Side B, Band 9

Sing in 4-measure phrases. Stress primary accents. (1 and 3)

LINES FROM "THE ANCIENT MARINER"

Words by Samuel Taylor Coleridge
Music by Randall Thompson

Randall Thompson (b. 1899) is recognized for his many contributions to American choral literature. Among his compositions are The Peaceable Kingdom, Testament of Freedom, and Alleluia.

Moderato
He pray - eth well, who lov - eth well Both man and bird and beast.
2.
He pray - eth best, who lov - eth best All things both great and small, For the
3.
dear God who lov - eth us, He made and lov - eth all.

From Modern Canons as edited by Herman Reichenbach.

Key: G
Starting Tone: G (1-do)

Meter: 4 (quarter note) (2 (half note))

Record 6, Side A, Band 1

STYLISTIC CHARACTERISTICS Melody — few repeated notes, step-wise intervals, relatively small range (interval of a 9th), and few skips greater than a 3rd; Harmony — tonic-dominant feeling, anticipating the century to follow, little chromaticism; Rhythm — regularity of rhythm, each voice following its natural rhythm, suspensions on strong beats, measures derived from harmony changes; Texture — equally important voice parts.

Palestrina's style was the first to be consciously imitated as a model by later choral composers.

SANCTUS

Music by Giovanni Palestrina (1525-1594)

Holy, Holy, Holy, Lord God of Sabaoth.

mp
Girls
Sang - tuhs Sang - tuhs Sang -
Sanc - tus Sanc - tus Sanc -
mp
Boys
Sanc -

In early choral music of the church, the polyphonic style tended to be so involved that the words were often difficult to understand. Palestrina's Pope Marcellus Mass was designated as a model for choral music by leaders of the church in Rome.

Key: D
Starting Tone: D (1-do)

Meter: $\frac{4}{\text{quarter note}}$
Form: Canon

Record 6, Side A, Band 2

NON NOBIS, DOMINE

Words from Psalm 115
Music by William Byrd

The music of William Byrd (1543-1623) often contains examples of beautifully conceived dissonances which were quite unconventional for his time. Observe the dissonances in measures 6, 7, 9, 10, and 11.

This is a famous setting of a Latin text by the English composer, William Byrd. The text is from Psalm 115—*Not unto us, O Lord, not unto us, but unto thy name give glory.*

STUDENT INVOLVEMENT 1. Work for effective performance of the dissonances and of the diatonic-chromatic juxtapositions (C# and C). 2. Use the frequent "n" consonant as a vocalise. Intone the "n" and let the "o" grow out of resonant "n." Extend this to the word "Domine" to secure a more musically voiced consonant in the "D" sound. 3. Use the first three measures of part 1 as a vocalise. Sing on syllable "ah," then on "oo," then "ee," then return to "ah" and there will be added warmth and richness in the sound. ("Ah" helps relax jaw and frees the throat. "Oo" rounds the tone. "Ee" establishes resonance.)

Key: G
Starting Tone: G (1-do)

Meter: 2

Record 6, Side A, Band 3

Form: canon

STUDENT INVOLVEMENT Have the class analyze the melody of this Praetorius round. Help the students discover the number of phrases (three) and the number of fermatas (five).

PSALM 66

Text Setting by H. R.
Music by Michael Praetorius

Michael Praetorius (1571-1621) is remembered for both choral and instrumental works. He was the author of the important document Musical Treatise which has been the source of much information about the music of his time.

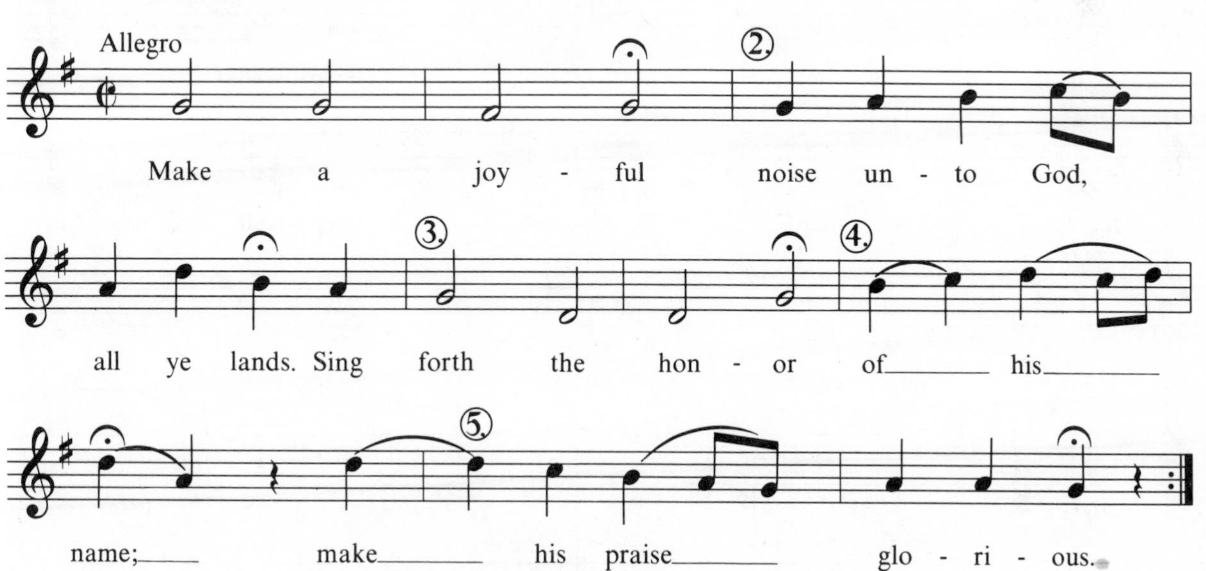

Key: Gm
Starting Tone: G (6-la)

Meter: $\frac{3}{\text{♩}}$
Form: Theme and Variations

Record 6, Side A, Band 4

ISRAELI LULLABY

Words by John Murray
Music by Harold Solomon
Arranged by Frank Metis

There are primarily two types of Jewish folk songs: semi-religious, or ceremonial, songs and social-domestic songs. This composed lullaby has many of the characteristics of the latter type of folk song. Jewish folk songs in the minor mode use a harmonic movement which resembles the harmonic minor.

Point out the importance of the F# in each part for the sound of a harmonic minor, and of the B♮ in measures 13-14, 29-30, 45-46 to effect a modulation to the subdominant (IV).

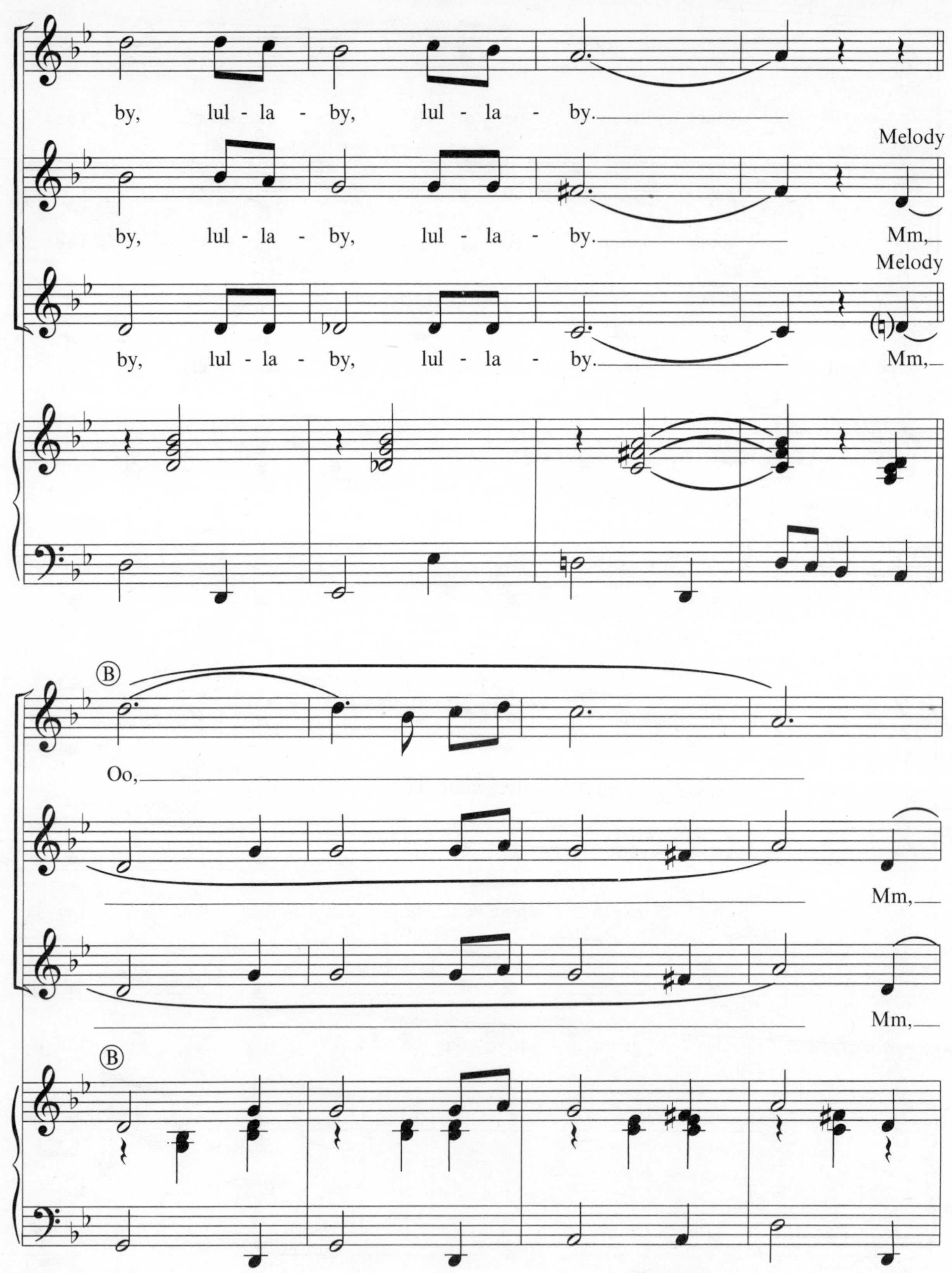
by, lul - la - by, lul - la - by.
Melody
by, lul - la - by, lul - la - by. Mm,
Melody
by, lul - la - by, lul - la - by. Mm,
B
Oo,
Mm,
Mm,
B

Oo,
Oo
Oo
Oo
Lul - la -
Lul - la -
Lul - la -

by, lul - la - by, lul - la - by. Good
by, lul - la - by, lul - la - by. Good
by, lul - la - by, lul - la - by. Good
C
mf
night, sleep well, may the crops in - crease, Some -
mf
night, sleep well, may the crops in - crease, Some -
mf
night, sleep well, may the crops in - crease, Some -
C
mf

day, my child, may-be wars will cease; And
day, my child, may-be wars will cease; And
day, my child, may-be wars will cease; And
we will live in a world at peace, With an
we will live in a world at peace, With an
we will live in a world at peace, With an

a tempo
poco a poco cresc.
Is - rae - li lul - la - by,
With an
Is - rae - li lul - la - by,
With an
Is - rae - li lul - la - by,
With an
a tempo
poco a poco cresc.
Freely
ritard.
mf
p
f
Is - rae - li lul - la - by.
Is - rae - li lul - la - by.
Is - rae - li lul - la - by.
G

STUDENT INVOLVEMENT

1. A flowing vocal line should characterize the choral style of this composition. Breath marks are provisional and should be eliminated by staggered breathing when performed by a fairly large group. Particularly avoid a breath after the second "holy."

2. Emphasize the bell-like character of the two main accents in each measure.

For the beauty of the earth,
For the glory of the skies,
For the love which from our birth
Over and around us lies:
Lord of all, to thee we raise
This our hymn of grateful praise.

For the beauty of each hour
Of the day and of the night,
Hill and vale, and tree and flower,
Sun and moon, and stars of light:
Lord of all, to thee we raise
This our hymn of grateful praise.

F. S. Pierpoint

Key: Gm
Starting Tone: G (6-la)

Meter: 2 over half note
Form: Theme and Variations

Record 6, Side A, Band 5

DAWN (MATINS)

Words and Music by Houston Bright

Matins is one of the hours of the day set for worship as the Offices of the Roman Catholic Church. Houston Bright has used "Dawn," with "Evensong" (Vespers), "Nightfall" (Compline), and "Sunrise" (Lauds) as the basis for a choral suite.

Houston Bright has used this composition with three other works as the basis for a choral suite dedicated to young people of a Texas school.

Make certain that the dynamic markings are carefully observed.

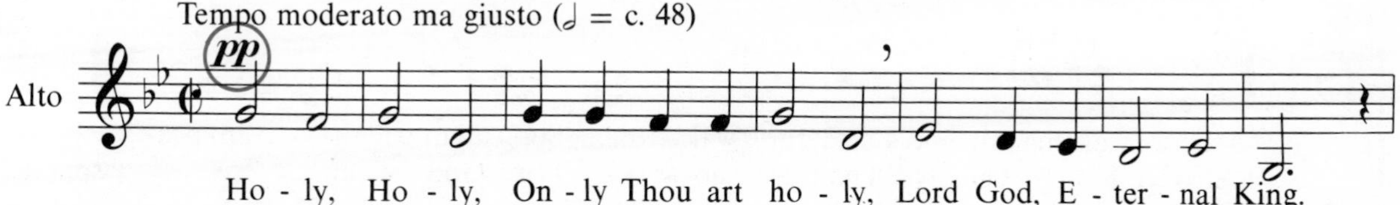
Tempo moderato ma giusto (𝅗𝅥 = c. 48)
Alto
pp
Ho - ly, Ho - ly, On - ly Thou art ho - ly, Lord God, E - ter - nal King.

A Soprano II
pp
Ho - ly, Ho - ly, On - ly Thou art ho - ly, Lord God, E - ter - nal King.
Alto
pp
E - ter - nal King.

B
Soprano I
1.
2.
p Dawn comes faint-ly, Morn-ing blush-es_ faint - ly,_ Far_ in the East-ern sky.
mf Ho - ly, ho-ly, On - ly Thou art_ ho - ly,_ Al - might-y Lord most high.
Soprano II
p Dawn comes faint-ly, Morn-ing blush-es_ faint - ly,_ Far_ in the East - ern sky.
mf Ho - ly, ho-ly, On - ly Thou art_ ho - ly,_ Al - might-y Lord_ most high.
Alto
East - ern sky.
Lord most high.
B
1.
2.
p-mf
C
f
1.
2.
Earth is wak - ing, All God's crea-tures wak - ing, Soon night will dis - ap - pear.
Ho-ly, ho - ly, On-ly Thou art ho - ly, Lord God of ev - 'ry sphere.
f
Earth is wak-ing, All God's crea-tures wak - ing,_ Soon night will dis - ap-pear.
Ho-ly, ho - ly, On - ly Thou art ho - ly,_ Lord God of ev - 'ry sphere.
f
dis - ap - pear. sphere.
ev - 'ry
C
1.
2.
f

D
ff-f
2nd time: poco dim.
Morn-ing bright-ens, Now the new day bright - ens, Gild - ing the sweet sea - side.
Ho - ly, ho - ly, On - ly Thou art ho - ly, Lord God of time and tide.
ff-f
2nd time: poco dim.
Morn-ing bright-ens, Now the new day bright - ens, Gild - ing the sweet sea - side.
Ho - ly, ho - ly, On - ly Thou art ho - ly, Lord God of time and tide.
ff-f
2nd time: poco dim.
D
ff-f
2nd time: poco dim.
E
mf Sop. II
Ho - ly, ho - ly, On - ly Thou art ho - ly, Lord God, E - ter - nal King.
mf Alto
E - ter - nal King.
F
p Alto
dim.
pp
morendo
Ho - ly, ho - ly, On - ly Thou art ho - ly, Lord God, E - ter - nal King.

Key: Modal
Starting Tone: E

Meter: 3 (quarter note)
Form: Strophic

Record 6, Side A, Band 6

WATERFALL AT BAC-YON

Words by Thulia Snow
Korean Folk Song arranged by Livingston Gearhart

Much Korean folk music uses triple rhythms and syncopated effects. What general mood is created by this folk song?

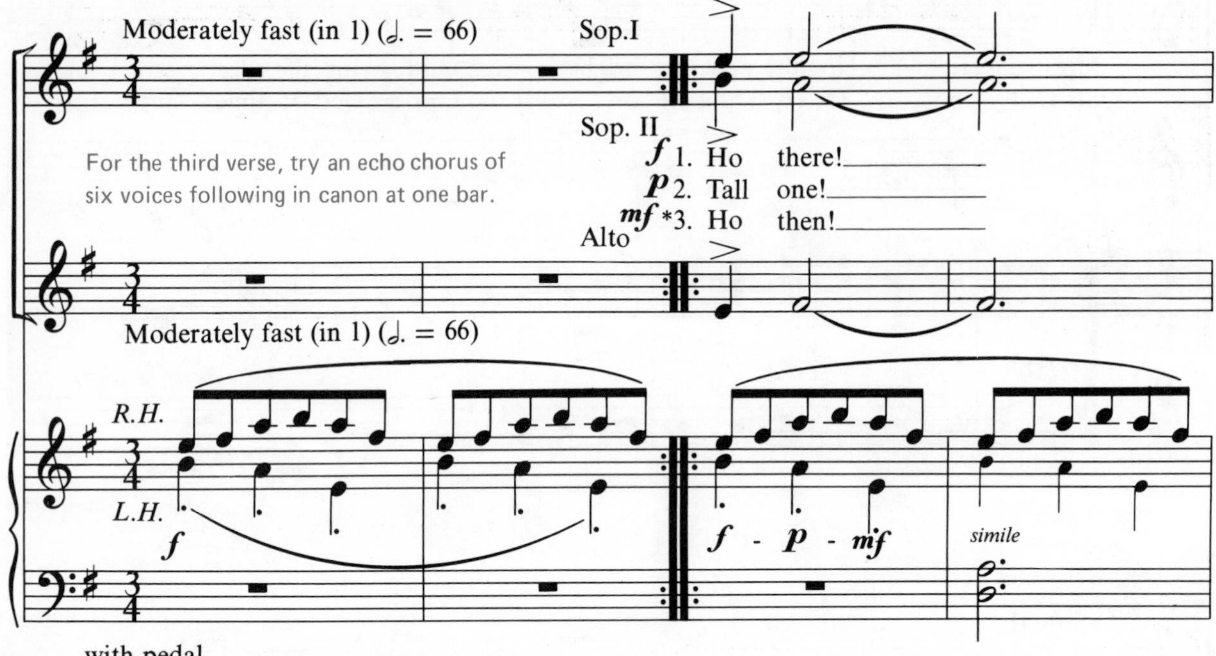

Moderately fast (in 1) (♩. = 66)
Sop.I
Sop. II
For the third verse, try an echo chorus of six voices following in canon at one bar.
f 1. Ho there!
p 2. Tall one!
mf *3. Ho then!
Alto
Moderately fast (in 1) (♩. = 66)
R.H.
L.H.
f
f - p - mf
simile
with pedal

First verse: Pianist play treble staff throughout.
Second and third verse: both staves, leaving out cue-size notes.

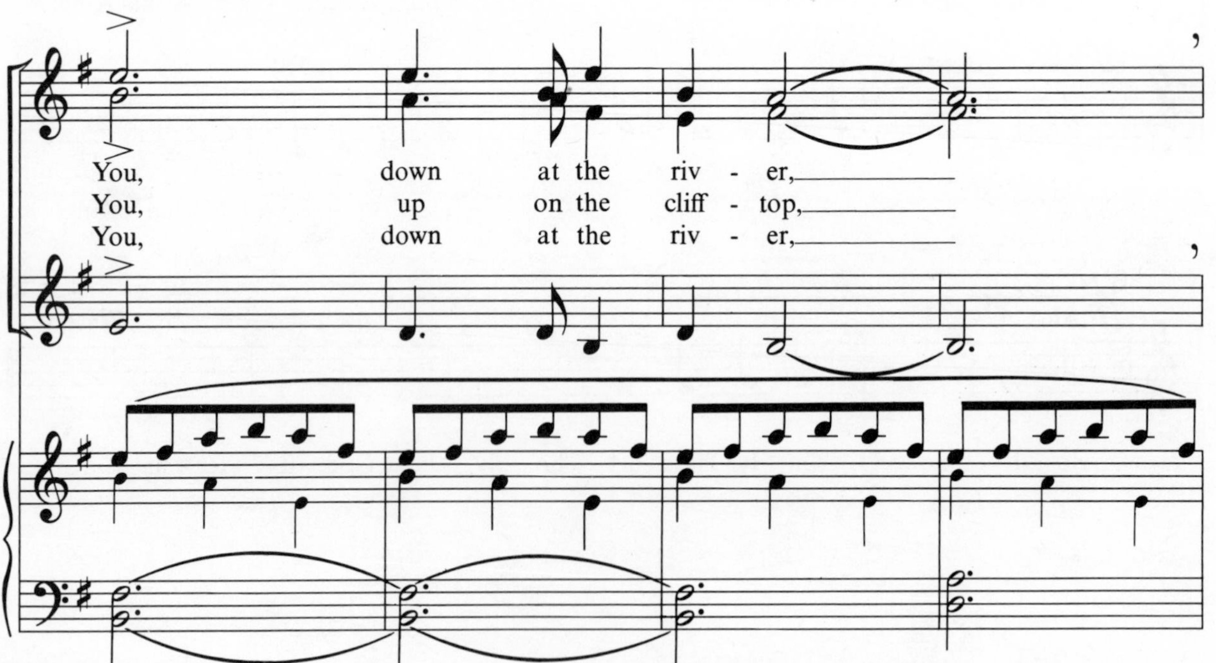

You, down at the riv - er,
You, up on the cliff - top,
You, down at the riv - er,

Have you seen my bird - ling?
I have heard your bird - ling,
I will stay on cliff - top,
met me here,
with her song,
danc - ing spray,
Ear - ly each morn - ing she has met me here,
Fall - ing of wa - ter blend - ing with her song,
For she will see me thro' the danc - ing spray,

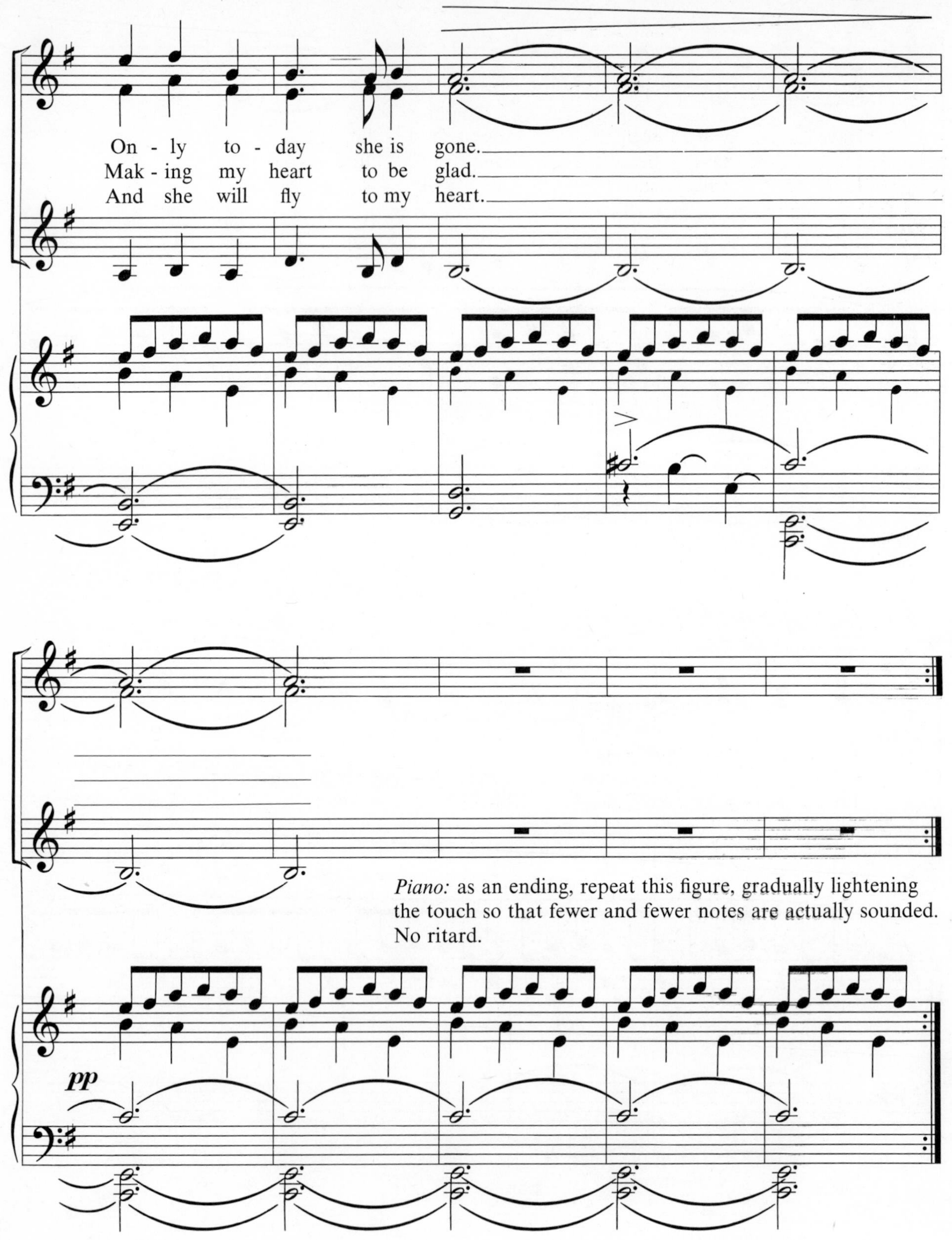
On - ly to - day she is gone.
Mak - ing my heart to be glad.
And she will fly to my heart.
pp
Piano: as an ending, repeat this figure, gradually lightening the touch so that fewer and fewer notes are actually sounded. No ritard.

Key: G
Starting Tone: B (3-mi)

Meter: 4 (quarter note)
Form: Strophic

Record 6, Side B, Band 1

COME, YE THANKFUL PEOPLE, COME

Words by Henry Alford
Music by George J. Elvey

Moderately
to Em
f
1. Come, ye thank-ful peo - ple, come, Raise the song of har - vest home;
2. All the world is God's own field, Fruit un - to His praise to yield;
to D
All is safe - ly gath - ered in, Ere the win - ter storms be - gin;
Wheat and tares to - geth - er sown, Un - to joy or sor - row grown;
mf
to C
God, our Mak - er, doth pro - vide For our wants to be sup - plied;
First the blade and then the ear, Then the full corn shall ap - pear;
to A
Come to God's own tem - ple, come, Raise the song of har - vest home.
Grant, O har - vest Lord, that we Whole-some grain and pure may be.

Analyze for brief modulations.

Key: Eb
Starting Tone: Eb (1-do)

Meter: 4 over a quarter note
Form: Strophic

Record 6, Side B, Band 2

GOD OF OUR FATHERS

Words by Daniel C. Roberts
Music by George William Warren, Arr. by A.B.C.

Concept: Phrase

When singing, observe the four-measure phrases. Sustain full note values for the dotted-half and whole notes.

Have the students compare the homophonic texture of this composition with the polyphonic textures in the Byrd and Palestrina works on pp. 230 and 232.

Soprano, Alto

f

1. God of our fa - thers, whose al - might - y
2. Thy love di - vine hath led us in the

Tenor

(Trumpets)

hand
past,
Leads forth in beau - ty all the star - ry
In this free land by Thee our lot is

The trumpet parts are found on page 250.

Soprano
band Of shin - ing worlds in splen - dor through the
cast; Be Thou our rul - er, guard - ian, guide, and
Alto
band Of shin - ing worlds in splen - dor through the
cast; Be Thou our rul - er, guard - ian, guide, and
Tenor
band Of shin - ing worlds in splen - dor through the
cast; Be Thou our rul - er, guard - ian, guide, and
3
skies, Our grate - ful songs be - fore Thy throne a - rise.
stay, Thy word our law, Thy paths our cho - sen way.
skies, Our grate - ful songs be - fore Thy throne a - rise.
stay, Thy word our law, Thy paths our cho - sen way.
skies, Our grate - ful songs be - fore Thy throne a - rise.
stay, Thy word our law, Thy paths our cho - sen way.
3

GOD OF OUR FATHERS

Trumpets in B♭

Key: Eb
Starting Tone: Bb (5-sol)

Meter: 4/♩
Form: Strophic

Record 6, Side B, Band 3

NOW THANK WE ALL OUR GOD

Words Tr. by Catherine Winkworth
Melody by Johann Crueger, Arr. by A.B.C.

Majestically
1. Now thank we all our God, With heart, and hands, and voic - es,
2. O may this boun-teous God Thro' all our life be near us!
1. Now thank we all our God, With heart, and hands, and voic - es,
2. O may this boun-teous God Thro' all our life be near us!
1. Now thank we all our God, With heart, and hands, and voic - es,
2. O may this boun-teous God Thro' all our life be near us!

Who won-drous things hath done, In whom his world re-joic-es;
With ev-er-joy-ful hearts And bless-ed peace to cheer us;
Who won-drous things hath done, In whom his world re-joic-es;
With ev-er-joy-ful hearts And bless-ed peace to cheer us;
Who won-drous things hath done, In whom his world re-joic-es;
With ev-er-joy-ful hearts And bless-ed peace to cheer us:
Who from our moth-er's arms Hath blessed us on our way
And keep us in his grace, And guide us when per-plexed,
Who from our moth-er's arms Hath blessed us on our way
And keep us in his grace, And guide us when per-plexed,
Who from our moth-er's arms Hath blessed us on our way
And keep us in his grace, And guide us when per-plexed,
With count-less gifts of love, And still is ours to-day.
And free us from all ills In this world and the next.
With count-less gifts of love, And still is ours to-day.
And free us from all ills In this world and the next.
With count-less gifts of love, And still is ours to-day.
And free us from all ills In this world and the next.

Key: Modal | Meter: 3 | Record: 6, Side B, Band 4

Starting Tone: C | Form: Strophic

CHRISTMAS EVE

Words by Laurence Lo Presti
Music by Ronald Lo Presti

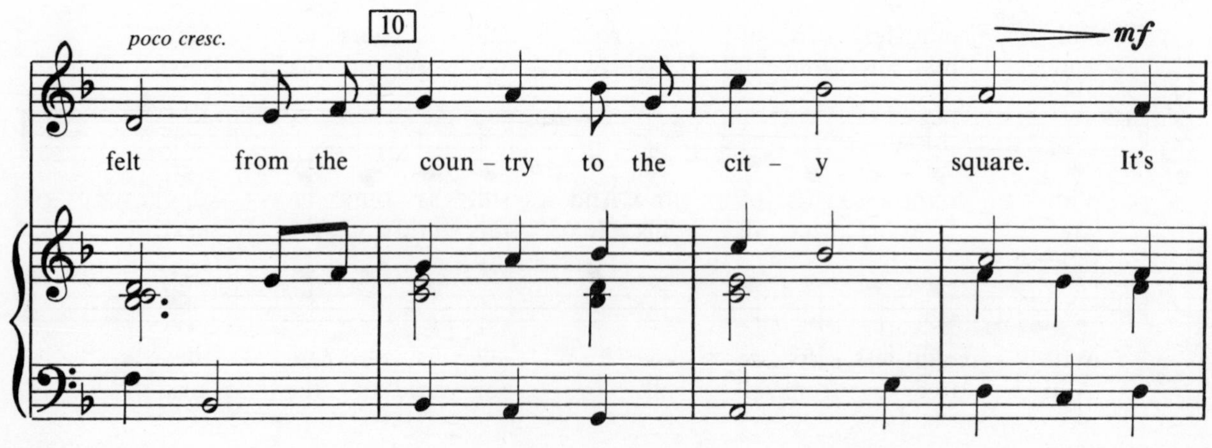

15
not some–thing you smell or hear, it's 'cause
rit.
dim.
40
Christ – mas is near, Christ – mas is near. It's a
rit.
p
a tempo
time to re – joice, a time to be gay, a
a tempo

25

time to give thanks, and a good time to pray.

30

Peo – ple are hap – py and all hearts are light on this the

Key: Modal
Starting Tones: A–A

Meter: 2 / 𝅗𝅥

Form: Strophic

Record 6, Side B, Band 5

A LITTLE SONG OF LIFE

Words by Lizette Woodworth Reese
Music by Emma Lou Diemer

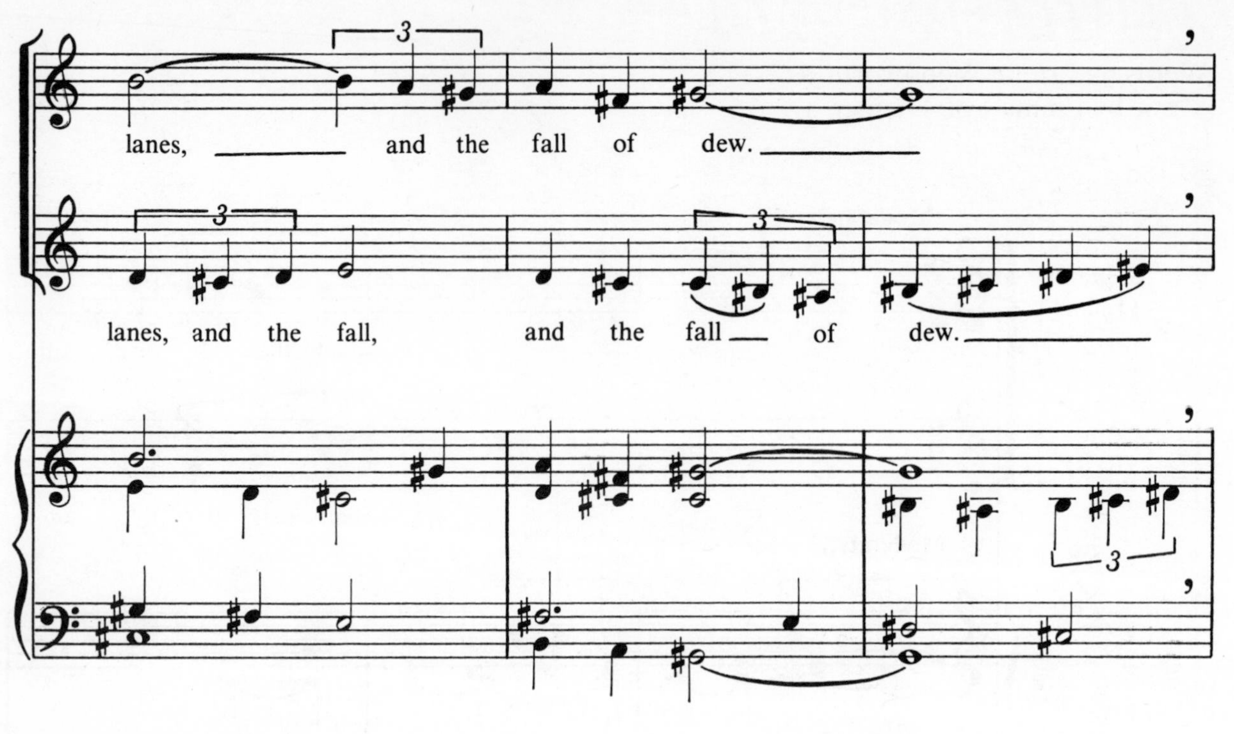
lanes, and the fall of dew.
lanes, and the fall, and the fall of dew.

10
After the sun the rain, After the rain the
After the sun the rain, After the rain the
10

15
cresc.
mf
sun; This is the way of life, Till the work be done.
cresc.
mf
sun; This is the way of life, Till the work be done.
15
cresc.
mf
mp
All that we need to do, Be we
mp
All that we need, All that we need to do, Be we
mp

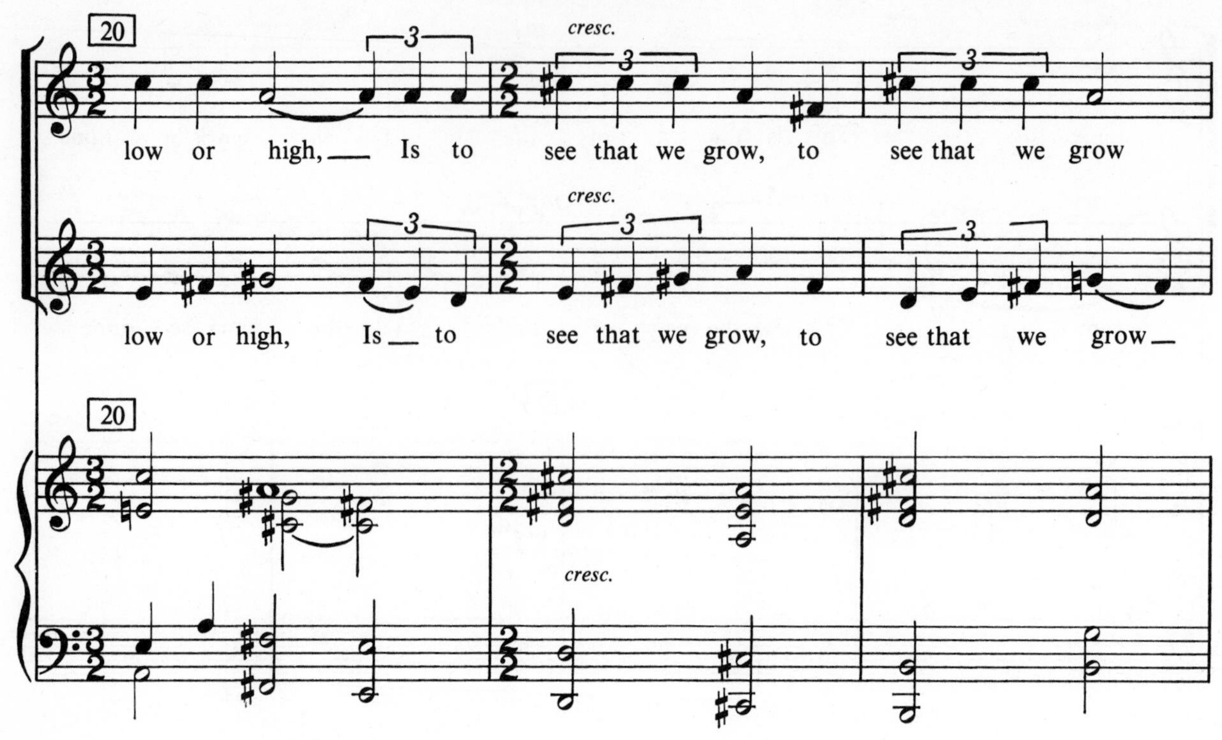
20
cresc.
low or high, Is to see that we grow, to see that we grow
cresc.
low or high, Is to see that we grow, to see that we grow
20
cresc.

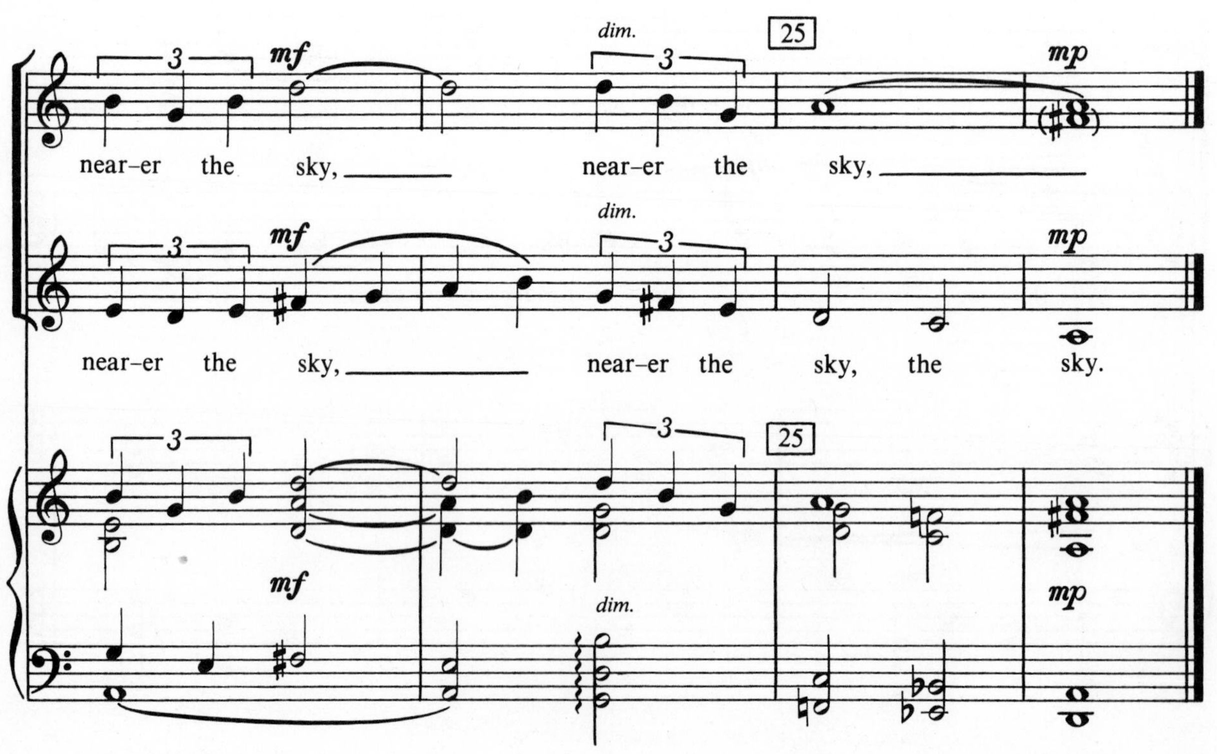
mf
dim.
25
mp
near-er the sky, near-er the sky,
mf
dim.
mp
near-er the sky, near-er the sky, the sky.
25
mf
dim.
mp

Key: Modal
Meter: 4/♩
Starting Tones: C, Eb, G
Form: Strophic

THE NIGHT

Record 6, Side B, Band 7

Words by Laurence Lo Presti
Music by Ronald Lo Presti

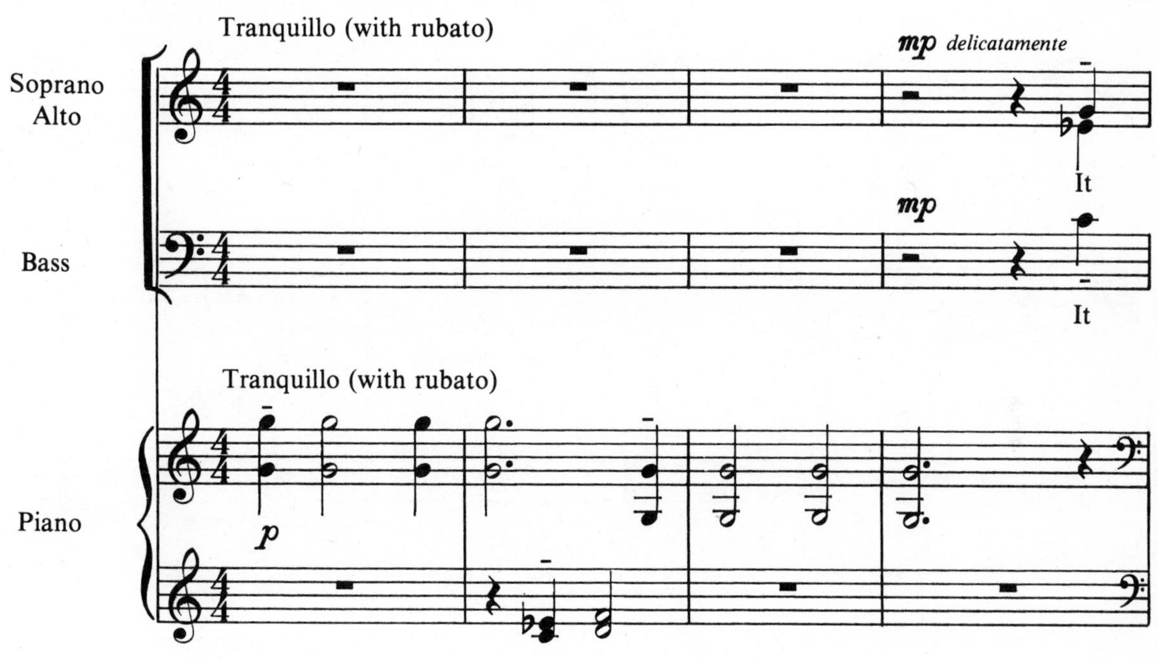

10
ten.
It starts at dusk and does-n't go till dawn.
ten.
It starts at dusk and does-n't go till dawn.
10
R. H.
mp dolce
p
15
p
To chil - dren it is a
p
To chil - dren it is a
15
pp

20
time to stop their play, But, it seems to me
p
time to stop their play, me
20
p
25
niente
a time in space, that can - cels out the day.
niente
a time in space, that can - cels out the day.
25
pp

Key: Bb
Starting Tone: F (5-sol)
Meter: 3 (quarter note)
Form: Strophic
Record 6, Side B, Band 7

THE STAR-SPANGLED BANNER

Words by Francis Scott Key
Music by John Stafford Smith

Francis Scott Key (1779–1843), a Washington lawyer and amateur poet, wrote the words to our national anthem while watching the British fleet's bombardment of Fort McHenry in Baltimore harbor. The words were printed in Baltimore in 1814. The tune "To Anacreon in Heaven" was combined with Key's words and was adopted as the national anthem by the United States Congress in 1931.

f
1. Oh,___ say! can you see, by the dawn's ear - ly light, What so proud - ly we
2. On the shore, dim - ly seen through the mists of the deep, Where the foe's haugh - ty
3. Oh,___ thus be it ever when___ free men shall stand Be - tween their loved
hailed at the twi - light's last gleam - ing, Whose broad stripes and bright stars, through the
host in dread si - lence re - pos - es, What is that which the breeze, o'er the
homes and the war's des - o - la - tion! Blest with vic - t'ry and peace, may the
per - il - ous fight, O'er the ram - parts we watched were so gal - lant - ly
tow - er - ing steep, As it fit - ful - ly blows, half con - ceals, half dis -
heav'n - res - cued land Praise the Pow'r that hath made and pre - served us a

mf
stream - ing? And the rock - ets' red glare, the bombs burst - ing in air, Gave
clos - es? Now it catch - es the gleam of the morn - ing's first beam, In full
na - tion! Then __ con - quer we must, when our cause it is just, And
f
proof through the night that our flag was still there. Oh, say, does that _ Star - Span-gled
glo - ry re-flected now __ shines on the stream; 'Tis the Star - Span - gled _ Ban - ner, oh,
this be our motto: "In __ God is our trust!" And the Star - Span - gled _ Ban - ner in
Ban - ner _ yet _ wave _ O'er the land _ of the free and the home of the brave?
long may _ it __ wave _ O'er the land _ of the free and the home of the brave!
tri-- umph _ shall wave _ O'er the land _ of the free and the home of the brave!

TABLE OF THE ELEMENTS OF MUSIC

RHYTHM—DURATION

Rhythm in music is recognized through:
- beat and meter: its organization and its movement.
- accented and unaccented beats in sets of 2, 3, 4, 5, 6, 7, 8, 9, etc.
- patterns: using dotted rhythms, syncopated rhythms and tied notes.

Characteristics:
- tempo—slow, fast, gradations
- measure—constant or shifting
- accent—regular or irregular; strong or weak
- beat—regular or irregular; measured or unmeasured
- patterns of duration—long or short; *legato* or *staccato*
- rhythmic combinations–polyrhythms; hemiola (2 beats against 3)

Rhythm and its relation to the other arts is recognized through the use of:
- polyrhythms • hemiola • repeated patterns

PITCH—MELODY

Line in music is recognized through the use of:
- stepwise progression
- intervals
- sequences
- triads

Line in music is based on:
- tonality
- atonality—tone row
- length—long or short
- shape—jagged or smooth
- register—high or low
- pitch range—narrow or wide
- direction—up or down
- development—fragmentary or complete

Line and its relationship to the other arts is recognized through the use of:
- length • shape • direction • repeated patterns

HARMONY—TEXTURE

Texture in music is described as:
- monophonic—a single melody
- homophonic—a primary melody with a chordal accompaniment
- polyphonic—two or more melodies sung or played together

Harmony is achieved through the use of:
- dialogue songs
- descants
- rounds
- ostinatos
- canons
- part songs

Characteristics:
- tonality—consonance or dissonance; major or minor; modal; atonal
- density—thick or thin
- cadences—strong or weak; anticipated or deceptive
- modulation—gradual or abrupt; expected or unexpected

FORM—DESIGN

Form in music is identified by:
- unity and variety
- repetition and contrast
- variation and alteration
- development—sectional, imitative, or free

Forms based on repetition and contrast
- binary
- ternary
- sonata allegro
- rondo
- ritornello

Forms based on repetition and variation
- theme and variations
- fugue

Free forms:
- toccata
- prelude
- fantasia
- etude
- impromptu
- rhapsody

Combinations of forms:
- sonata
- symphony
- concerto
- suite
- opera, musical theater
- oratorio, cantata, mass

COLOR—TIMBRE

Color in music is recognized by the use of different:
- voices—soprano, alto, tenor, bass
- instruments—strings, winds, percussion, brass
- sounds—altered

Color is recognized by:
- mood—combining words and melody
- tonal and non-tonal sounds
- ethnic music
- solo performance
- group performance
- texture—thick or thin
- register—high or low
- dynamics—soft or loud, gradations

GLOSSARY

A-B A design in music or art consisting of two contrasting parts. (binary)

A-B-A A design in music or art consisting of a main section, a contrasting section, and a repetition of the main section. (also called ternary)

absolute music Music which does not depend on literary associations, but on essentially musical considerations.

abstract In art, a term denoting non-representational styles of the twentieth century.

a cappella Music written for unaccompanied singing.

accelerando Gradually becoming faster.

accent A stress or emphasis

accidental A chromatic sign not found in the key signature but introduced during a composition.

accompaniment A part added to the main melody or part to support or enrich it.

acoustics The science of sound.

acoustic suspension speaker A speaker or speakers sealed in an airtight chamber.

adagio Slow.

air A self-contained solo movement from a larger work.

allargando Slowing down.

allegretto Moderately fast.

allegro Quick, fast, lively.

alphanumeric notation Music notation made up of letters and numerals for use in computer programing.

amplifier An electrical instrument that increases the voltage of a signal.

andante At a walking tempo; moderately.

antiphonal Music in which groups of performers answer each other, often applied to choral music.

architecture The art and technique of building.

aria A composition for solo voice and instrumental accompaniment, often, but not always, part of a larger work.

arpeggio A chord in which the notes are sounded one after the other instead of simultaneously.

articulation Clear and precise production of consonants.

art song A composed song that combines text, a vocal part, and an accompaniment.

a tempo Return to previous tempo after change.

atonal Having no fixed tonal center.

augmentation Expanding of note values in a given theme proportionately.

ballad A song that tells a story.

ballet A dance composition that tells a story in movement.

baritone Male singing voice between tenor and bass in range and quality.

bar line A vertical line on the staff that marks off a measure.

Baroque Generally used to signify the ornate style of art and music of the seventeenth and part of the eighteenth centuries, e.g., the music of Bach and Handel.

bass The lowest register in a voice or an instrument; the lowest part of a musical composition.

bass drum A percussion instrument consisting of a hollow cylinder covered at each end with skin heads.

bassoon A woodwind instrument which uses a double reed.

beat The basic rhythmic unit.

binary A two-part design. (A-B)

biwa A Japanese lute.

brass Wind instruments; the principal instruments are the trumpet, French horn, trombone, and tuba.

bridge passage A musical passage which connects two themes or sections.

cadence A melodic or harmonic pattern which indicates varying degrees of finality during a composition.

cadenza An extended ornamental section in a free, improvisatory style.

calando Decrease in speed and volume.

canon A composition in which one melody is imitated by another voice on any pitch level.

cantabile Smooth, singing style.

cantata Originally a sung work, it now means a secular or sacred work for soloist and chorus generally with an instrumental accompaniment.

cartoon In art, a preliminary drawing used as a guide in completing a finished work.

cassette A miniature, reel-to-reel magnetic tape system.

castanet A rhythm instrument made of wood or plastic used by Spanish dancers.

celesta A keyboard instrument with steel plates which are struck by hammers, producing clear tones similar to a glockenspiel.

cello A member of the string family which is tuned one octave below the viola. (familiar form of violoncello)

chaconne A continuous variation in slow triple meter, often but not always with the theme in the bass.

chamber music Compositions written for a concert room; music generally performed by small musical groups.

chimes A musically tuned set of bells in the percussion family.

Chinese temple block A small, hollow block of wood which is played with a small mallet.

chorale A hymn tune of the German Protestant Church. The hymn tune is usually slow and dignified.

chord Tones sounded simultaneously.

chromatic Moving by half tones in contrast to diatonic.

clarinet A single-reed woodwind instrument.

classicism The style of composition in which the emphasis is on formal symmetry. The term is particularly applied to the music of Haydn, Mozart, and Beethoven.

clavichord A precursor of the piano; a keyboard instrument in which the strings are struck by small brass tangents operated by the keys.

coda A phrase or section ending a composition.

collage In art, a composition created by pasting together various textured materials to form a work of art.

color The use of musical timbres or chromatic alterations. In art, the choice and treatment of the hues in a painting.

composition The arrangement of form, color, and line in a work.

con Italian word used in music, meaning with.

concerto A sonata for one or more instrumental soloists and orchestra.

concerto overture An orchestral composition which is either in sonata or free form and frequently programatic.

concertino A small ensemble of the soloists in a *concerto grosso.*

con moto With movement.

consonant A restful sound in music, varying in meaning with stylistic periods.

continuo Bass part which was used in Baroque music as basis for the accompaniment.

contrabassoon A double reed woodwind instrument which is pitched an octave below the bassoon.

contralto The lowest female singing voice.

contrapuntal Musical term referring to a composition written in counterpoint.

cornet A brass family member similar to the trumpet.

countermelody A melody sounding simultaneously with the main melody.

counterpoint A type of composition in which various musical lines are sounded simultaneously. It is also known as polyphony.

countersubject A second musical theme in a fugue.

crescendo Gradually getting louder.

cymbal An untunable member of the percussion family made of a shaped brass plate.

da capo Repeat from the beginning.

dal segno Repeat from the sign (:𝄋:).

damper pedal A piano pedal which, when used, allows the piano strings to vibrate freely.

damping factor The element in an amplifier that reduces vibrations of sound waves.

decrescendo Gradually getting softer.

depressed mid-range A term denoting certain middle range frequencies that do not receive proper amplification in a speaker system.

design In art, a controlled, rhythmic arrangement of line, color, and form.

development The building up of the thematic material in a work after the theme has been presented.

diatonic Pertaining to the major and minor scale system.

diminuendo Gradually getting softer.

diminution Decreasing the note values in music.

dissonance A term used to describe the combination of certain sounds such as intervals of the 2nd, the 7th, and the tritone.

distortion The untrue reproduction of sound created by changes occuring as signals pass through an electronic system.

dolce Sweetly.

dominant seventh chord The dominant triad with the addition of a seventh from the fifth degree of the scale.

double bar Indicates the end of a piece.

double bass The lowest-pitched member of the string family.

double flat (♭♭) Lowers a flatted note another half step.

double sharp (𝄪) Raises a sharped note another half step.

double stops The playing of two or more tones at the same time on stringed instruments.

drawing In art, a sketch or design created by means of line.

drone A low constant tone also called pedal point.

duple meter Beats which are grouped in twos.

dynamics Specific degrees of loudness and softness or the signs by which these are indicated in the score.

eight-track cartridge A unit that contains a magnetic tape with sound tracks.

eighth note; eighth rest (♪; 𝄾) Musical signs used to show time value equal to one eighth that of a whole note or whole rest.

embellishments Ornamental notes in a melody.

English horn A double-reed woodwind instrument, similar to the oboe.

ensemble A term applied to a group of musicians and to their performance together.

episode A section in a composition which provides a contrast to the main themes.

étude A "study", often designed for developing technical skills.

exposition The first section of a composition in which themes or statements, are exposed or stated for the first time.

fantasia A composition in free form.

F clef or bass clef (𝄢) A sign used to show the pitch of the notes; the fourth line is the F of the staff on which it appears.

fermata Hold, pause (𝄐).

figure An easily recognizable short pattern of notes. Sometimes synonymous with motive.

figured bass A bass part which uses numerals to show chords.

finale The last movement of an extended work; sometimes given the title of a separate piece; also the concluding portion of an operatic act.

fine End, close.

flat (♭) Sign which lowers a note one-half step.

flute Member of the woodwind family.

folk music Music which comes from the people and becomes traditional with them.

form The element which is concerned with the scheme or design of a work of art.

forte Loud.

fortissimo Very loud.

four-track A tape recording in which four separate sound tracks are used in pairs for recording and playback.

fragmentation A method of writing which uses small parts of the melody.

French horn A member of the brass family used for either melody or harmony parts.

fundamental tone The lowest or bass note of a chord.

fugue A contrapuntal composition in which a subject is stated and developed by several voices in succession.

G clef or treble clef (𝄞) A sign used to show the pitch of notes; the second line is the G above middle C.

glissando The effect produced by rapid movement through an extended sequence of notes.

Glockenspiel A pitched percussion instrument with strong bell-like tones.

gong A disk-shaped metal percussion instrument of oriental origin which is struck with a drum beater.

grace note (♪) An ornamental musical note, not included in the note value of the measure.

graphic arts The arts of drawing and printmaking.

grave Very slow, solemn.

Gregorian chant The form of liturgical chanting codified during the time of Pope Gregory the Great (590–604).

guiro A primitive instrument of Latin American origin made of a rough gourd which is rubbed by a stick.

half-step The tonal distance of one half step.

harmonic series A basic tone with its overtones.

harmonics Overtones; e.g., those which are heard on stringed instruments when light pressure is used along with light bowing.

harmonizing A form of singing which supports a melody.

harmony The simultaneous combination of two or more tones.

harp A large stringed instrument which is played by plucking the strings.

harpsichord A keyboard instrument with strings that are mechanically plucked by a plectrum.

hemiola A rhythmic term denoting two against three.

Hertz (Hz) The term used to identify cycles per second.

home tone The letter, number, syllable name or sound of the main tone of the scale.

homophony Music in which one main melody stands out against a chordal or harmonic accompaniment.

illumination In art, a term used for manuscript paintings and illustrations.

illustration In art, the representation of a scene, text or idea.

imitation The repetition of a musical idea in other voices.

improvisation The art of spontaneously composing and performing music, making variations on a theme or embellishing a given melody.

incidental music Music played during the intervals of a dramatic work.

instrumentation The choice of instruments for a composition.

interval The pitch distance between two tones.

invention A short keyboard piece using contrapuntal style.

key The system of tones and half-tones creating a scale and built on a specific tone, the tonic. The home tone or tonic becomes the first note of the scale and the name of the key.

koto A thirteen-string Japanese instrument.

ledger lines Extra lines which are added above or below the staff.

legato Smooth, connected.

largo Slow, broad.

lento Slow.

libretto The book of words of an extended choral composition such as an opera, cantata or oratorio.

Lied Generally used for the great number of art songs by German composers.

Lieder Plural form of *lied.*

light double bar Indicates the end of a musical section such as an introduction.

line In art, a real or imagined outline or contour.

listening station A unit designed for listening, using tape recorders or record players.

madrigal A contrapuntal vocal composition originating during the Renaissance.

major A term used to identify a basic music scale, key or chord.

manual A keyboard (piano or organ) played by the hands.

maestoso Majestic.

marcato Accent, marked (<).

mass A musical setting of the Roman Catholic liturgy. In art, the expanse of color that defines a painted shape.

mazurka A Polish national dance in triple meter and moderate tempo. Frequently it has strong accents on the second beat.

measure The area on a staff which is marked off by bar lines.

mbira A metal or bamboo African thumb piano.

medium In art, the material with which an artist works.

melody A succession of single musical sounds.

meter A specific scheme of rhythm.

metronome A mechanical device which shows the exact tempo to be used in terms of beats per minute.

metronome mark The number shown at the beginning of a piece to indicate the speed of the music, e.g., Mm = 84.

mezzo forte Medium loud.

mezzo piano Medium soft.

Minnesinger The German counterpart of the troubadour—an aristocratic poet-musician of the Middle Ages.

minor A term used to identify a basic music scale, chord, or key.

minuet An old French dance in dignified $\frac{3}{4}$ rhythm. It is conventionally found as the third movement of the classical symphony.

mobile A sculpture made of movable parts. The various parts are set in motion by air currents.

mode Generally, any mode or manner of arranging tones and semitones to form a scale. Especially refers to the Medieval scales used for both religious and folk music, and to the ancient Greek scales.

moderato Moderate.

modular The term that denotes a synthesizer made up of modules.

module A unit of circuity that produces a specific effect in a synthesizer.

monophonic Music consisting of a single melodic line.

motet An unaccompanied polyphonic choral work with a Latin text.

motive A brief musical idea, theme or figure.

movement A division complete in itself, forming part of an extended work.

mridanga A two headed South Indian drum.

multimedia A combination of several media—tapes, lights, slides, etc.

mural A wall painting.

music drama Wagner's name for his operas.

natural (♮) A sign which cancels a flat or sharp, formerly shown by the key signature or by an accidental.

nocturne Usually a composition with subdued or poetic feeling.

note A musical symbol that shows duration of tone by its shape, pitch, and location on the staff.

nuance A shade of difference in tone color, tempo or degree of force.

obbligato Optional part written for a particular instrument—for example, a violin part added to the piano accompaniment of a song.

oboe A woodwind instrument with a double reed mouthpiece.

opera A musical drama accompanied by an orchestra.

opus A word used to indicate the chronological position of a composition in relation to all of the works of the composer.

oratorio The sacred counterpart of an opera.

orchestra A group of instruments consisting of strings, woodwinds, brass, and percussion.

orchestration The arrangement of music for an orchestra.

organum The earliest attempts at harmony in music in which two or more parts progressed in parallel motion (fifths, fourths, and octaves).

ornamentation Any extra embellishment added to the melodic line.

oscillator A device that produces alternating current; an audio-frequency generator.

ostinato A melodic phrase that is persistently repeated.

overtones Higher tones that blend with the basic tone to create a complex musical tone.

overture Instrumental music written as an introduction to an opera or oratorio.

parallel minor A minor scale which begins on the same keynote as a major scale.

passacaglia An early Italian dance in triple time and stately movement with a ground bass; also describes an instrumental composition in this form.

passing tones Non-harmonic notes which occur melodically between chord tones.

pedal point A long-held note, usually in the bass, which sounds against changing harmonies.

pedals Levers or keys used by the feet on instruments such as the piano, organ or harp.

percussion Pitched and non-pitched instruments that are played by being struck, i.e., kettledrum, cymbals, bells, celesta, etc.

phrase A musical entity related to movement, melodic contour, and cadence.

pianissimo Very soft.

piano Soft.

pianoforte Soft-loud. Also the full name for piano.

piccolo A small, shrill flute which sounds an octave higher than the flute.

pitch The highness or lowness of notes.

più More.

più mosso Faster.

più vivo With more spirit.

pizzicato A term used to show that strings are to be plucked with the fingers instead of using the bow.

plainsong The music of the early Christian church based on modal scales. Rhythm and tempo were governed by word accent and the chants were sung in unison.

plan In art, the schematic representation of a three-dimensional structure on a two-dimensional plane.

plectrum A small thin piece of ivory, plastic or metal used to pluck a stringed instrument.

poco A little.

poco a poco Little by little.

polka A fast and lively Bohemian dance.

polonaise A dance of Polish origin in $\frac{3}{4}$ meter and moderate, animated tempo.

polyphonic A style of music in which two or more melodies sound simultaneously.

polyrhythm Two or more different rhythms played at the same time.

prelude An introductory section or movement.

prestissimo Very fast.

presto Very fast.

program music Music based on a literary or extramusical idea.

proportion In art, the relation of the size of any part of a subject to the size of the whole.

quadruple meter The placement of beats into groups of four.

quarter note; quarter rest (♩; 𝄽) Signs used to show time value equal to one quarter that of a whole note or whole rest.

raga A basic scale-melody system of India.

rallentando Slowing down.

range The difference in pitch between the highest and lowest notes of a melody.

recitative A vocal style designed to imitate and accent the natural voice inflections.

repeat Repeat complete section (:‖).

repetition Repeated use of a rhythm or melody.

representational In art, a term denoting recognizable form.

requiem Mass or service for the dead; a memorial choral work.

rest A musical symbol which indicates silence.

rhapsody A declamatory piece in free form.

rhythm The organization of music in time. In art, the regular repetition of a particular form; also, the suggestion of motion by recurrent forms.

ripieno Full orchestra in the *concerto grosso.*

ritardando Slowing down.

ritornello Recurrences of the *tutti* theme in main movements of a Baroque *concerto grosso.*

Rococo The florid, ornamental style which characterized music and art of the early eighteenth century.

romanticism A style of composition emphasizing personal expression, particularly applied to music of the nineteenth century.

rondo A musical form often used in the final movement of classical sonatas and symphonies. (ABACA)

round A short unaccompanied vocal canon.

roundelay A composition in rondo form.

rubato A musical term which allows changes in tempo.

samba A Brazilian dance which originated in Africa.

sarabande A stately dance of Spanish or Oriental origin which has two sections, slow tempo, and triple meter. It is the slowest movement of the suite.

scale A succession of tones used for writing a composition.

scherzo A lively type of third-movement form in triple meter (literally, "joke").

score The parts of the various voices or instruments, organized in printed notation from woodwinds at the top, brasses next, then percussion, finally strings. In vocal scores, the voice line is at the top with the accompaniment below.

sculpture A three-dimensional art form.

semitone A half-tone.

sentence A melodic division, usually composed of two phrases.

sequence The successive repetition of a melodic figure at different pitch levels.

serenade Music suitable for performance in the open air.

sforzando Forced, loud. (Sf or Sfz)

sforzato Strong accent (^).

shakuhachi A Japanese bamboo flute.

shamisen A Japanese three-string lute.

sharp (♯) A sign which raises the tone one-half step.

sho A Japanese mouth organ.

sitar A north Indian lute. The *sitar* has five melodic strings and two drones with a set of thirteen sympathetic vibrators.

sketch In art, a preliminary drawing.

slur A curved line found above notes of different pitch levels which indicates that two or more notes are to be sung on the same word or syllable.

snare drum A small drum with one or more snares stretched across the bottom head.

sonata A complete work for one or more soloists in several contrasting movements.

sonata form The form often used for single movements of the sonata and other musical forms.

song form A name for simple ABA form used in lyrical music.

soprano The high female voice.

sostenuto A term indicating the sustaining of a note.

sousaphone An instrument similar to the tuba in the brass family.

spiccato A term used to show a bowing technique; the bouncing of the bow on the strings.

staccato Shortened value of note with a rest substituted for the value omitted.

staff A series of five horizontal lines on which and between which are written musical notes.

still life A painting or drawing of an arrangement of inanimate objects.

stops Handles or knobs on the organ which can be used to regulate timbre and register.

stretto In a fugue, the subject imitation comes quickly with the answer sounding before the subject is ended.

string bass The lowest pitched member of the string family; also called the double bass or bass viol.

string instruments Violin, viola, cello, and bass.

string quartet A combination of two violins, viola, and cello or the music for these four instruments.

strings A term used in reference to the stringed instruments.

strophic song A song which uses identical music in every stanza.

style A characteristic manner of expressing ideas.

stylus The term denoting the needle of a cartridge that traces the grooves of a recording.

subject A tune or theme.

suite A set of pieces either centering on some general subject or made up of contrasting or associated ideas.

symphony A sonata for orchestra.

symphony orchestra A group of instruments consisting of strings, woodwinds, brass, and percussion.

syncopation The deliberate upsetting of the normal rhythm pattern.

synthesizer An instrument which generates sound electronically for musical composition.

tala A system of rhythm patterns in the music of India.

tambourine A small percussion instrument which is struck by hand.

tambura A drone instrument of India.

tapedeck The tape mechanism of a component recording system.

tempo Time; commonly used to mean pace.

tenor The high male singing voice.

tenuto Give full value to note (♩̄).

ternary See three-part form.

texture The structure of vertical and horizontal music elements.

theme A tune or subject.

theme with variations A composition with each section modifying original musical idea.

three-part form A musical form with a main theme, a contrasting theme, and a return to the original idea. (A-B-A)

through-composed song A song which has continually developing music.

tie (♩⁀♩) A curved line which joins two notes of the same pitch and which unites the notes into one sound equal to the combined durations.

timbre Characteristic tone color.

timpani A set of two or three drums which are tuned to definite pitches (kettledrum).

toccata A piece designed to display brilliance of execution.

tonal center The keynote upon which a composition is based.

tonality The relationship of notes within a given system of keys.

tone color The quality of sound (timbre).

tonic Home tone of a scale.

tonic chord A chord with the tonic note as its root.

tone poem Symphonic music based on a poetic or descriptive idea.

transpose To write or play music in a different key.

transposing instrument One which plays music in a key other than that which is written as the concert key.

trap set A set of drums made up of a snare drum, cymbals, and bass drum.

tremolo The quick repeating of a tone which produces a pulsating sound.

triangle A percussion instrument made of steel which is held in the air and struck by a short steel rod.

triad Chord built on a root, third, and fifth.

triple meter The organization of beats into groups of three.

triplet A group of three notes which are played in the place of two of the same kind of notes.

trombone A member of the brass family which uses a sliding mechanism to change its pitches.

troubadour Aristocratic minstrel in Medieval France, circa 1100–1300.

trouvère The northern French counterpart of the troubadour.

trumpet A brass family instrument, considered to be the soprano of brasses.

tuba The bass of the brass family.

tuner The component of a high fidelity system that receives radio signals.

turntable The section of a phonograph on which the record rests.

tutti Whole orchestra.

unison A tone of the same pitch as a given tone; a higher or lower octave.

variations A new presentation of a musical idea.

vibrato A slight variation of pitch.

vina A South Indian lute. The *vina* has four melodic strings and three drones.

viola The alto member of the string family which is tuned a fifth lower than the violin.

violin The soprano member of the string family.

violoncello The bass member of the violin family.

virtuoso A superlative performer.

vivace Very fast, lively.

voice Term which refers to a separate tonal line.

waltz A dance in triple time with a strong accent on the first beat.

whole-tone scale A scale moving by full tones, e.g., C, D, E, F♯, G♯, A♯, C.

woodwind instruments The flute, oboe, clarinet, and bassoon.

woodwind quintet An ensemble composed of a flute, oboe, clarinet, bassoon, and French horn.

xylophone A percussion instrument made of tuned wooden bars which are struck by two small wooden hammers.

HAPPENINGS

476 A.D. to 1453

476 Fall of Western Roman Empire

527–565 "Golden Age" of Justinian, Byzantium

732 Battle of Tours, France

800 Charlemagne crowned Emperor of Romans by pope

822 Earliest documented church organ at Aachen, Germany

962 Otto I (the Great) crowned emperor by pope

1002 Leif Ericson sails to North America

1066 William the Conqueror wins at Battle of Hastings; becomes king of England

1095–96 First Crusade

1155–90 Frederick Barbarossa rules the Holy Roman Empire

1202–4 Fourth Crusade conquers Constantinople

1215 Magna Carta limits the power of English kings

1226–70 Louis IX, King of France, famous for leading two crusades

1237 Mongol invasion of Russia

1291 Moslems conquer Acre, last Christian stronghold in Holy Land

1309–76 Exile of papacy at Avignon

1326 First use of cannon

1337 Beginning of the Hundred Years' War between England and France

1415 Jan Huss burned at stake for heresy

Henry V defeats French at Agincourt

1417 Council of Constance ends Great Papal Schism

1431 Joan of Arc burned at the stake

1446–50 Gutenberg invents the printing press

1453 Constantinople conquered by Ottoman Turks

End of the Hundred Years' War

WRITERS

Peter Abelard (*1079–1142*)
Geoffrey of Monmouth (*d. 1154*)
St. Thomas Aquinas (*d. 1274*)
Dante Alighieri (*1265–1321*)
Jacobus de Voragine (*active 1266–83*)
Master Eckhart (*d. 1327*)
Geoffrey Chaucer (*c. 1340–1400*)

ARTISTS

Nicholas of Verdun (*12th cent.*)
Cimabue (*c. 1240–after 1302*)
Duccio (*1255/60–1319*)
Nicola Pisano (*active c. 1260–78*)
Giotto di Bondone (*c. 1276–c. 1337*)
Master Honoré (*13th cent.*)
Jean Pucelle (*active c. 1300–1330*)
Ambrogio Lorenzetti (*1319–47*)
Lorenzo Ghiberti (*1378–1455*)
Pol de Limbourg (*active c. 1400*)

MUSICIANS

Leonin (*12th cent.*)
Perotin le Grand (*12th cent.*)
Walter von der Vogelweide (*c. 1170–c. 1230*)
Adam de la Halle (*c. 1238–1288*)
Philippe de Vitry (*c. 1291–1361*)
Guillaume de Machaut (*c. 1300–1377*)
John Dunstable (*c. 1370–1453*)

1469 to 1598

1469 Spain united under Ferdinand and Isabella

1486 Diaz rounds Cape of Good Hope

1492 Christopher Columbus discovers America

1494–99 Invasion of Italy by Charles VIII, King of France

1498 Savonarola burned at Florence for heresy

1506 St. Peter's Basilica begun by Pope Julius II

1513 Balboa sights Pacific Ocean; Ponce de Leon discovers Florida

1517 Martin Luther posts 95 theses at Wittenberg

1519 Cortes wins Aztec empire for Spain

1520–22 First circumnavigation of the globe, by Magellan

1524–25 Peasants' rebellion in Germany

1530–43 Copernicus proposes heliocentric view of the universe

1534 Henry VIII founds Anglican Church

1545–63 The Council of Trent, restates the doctrines of the Roman Catholic Church

1547–84 Rule of Ivan the Terrible in Russia

1555 The Peace of Augsburg

1558–1603 Reign of Elizabeth I of England

1568 Netherlands revolt against Spain

1572 St. Bartholomew's Day Massacre in France

1588 Drake defeats Spanish Armada

1598 Edict of Nantes establishes religious toleration

WRITERS

Francois Villon (*1431–c. 1465*)
Erasmus of Rotterdam (*1466–1536*)
Niccolo Machiavelli (*1469–1527*)
Thomas More (*1478–1535*)
Francois Rabelais (*1490–1553*)
Pierre de Ronsard (*1524–1585*)
Michel de Montaigne (*1533–1592*)
Miguel de Cervantes (*1547–1616*)
Edmund Spenser (*1552–1599*)
William Shakespeare (*1564–1616*)

ARTISTS

Jan van Eyck (*c. 1380–1441*)
Donatello (*1382–1466*)
Masaccio (*1401–1428*)
Piero della Francesca (*1410–1492*)
Giovanni Bellini (*1430–1516*)
Andrea Mantegna (*1431–1506*)
Hugo Van der Goes (*c. 1435–1482*)
Sandro Botticelli (*1447–1510*)
Leonardo da Vinci (*1452–1519*)
Albrecht Dürer (*1471–1528*)
Michelangelo (*1475–1564*)
Raphael (*1438–1520*)
Hieronymus Bosch (*active 1488–1515*)
Titian (*1490–1576*)
Benvenuto Cellini (*1500–1571*)
Pieter Brueghel (*c. 1525–1569*)
Jacopo Tintoretto (*1518–1594*)

MUSICIANS

Guillaume Dufay (*c. 1400–1474*)
Gilles Binchois (*c. 1400–1460*)
Jacob Obrecht (*1430–1505*)
Josquin des Prez (*c. 1450–1521*)
Heinrich Isaac (*c. 1450–1517*)
Thomas Tallis (*c. 1515–1585*)
Giovanni da Palestrina (*1525–1594*)
Orlando de Lassus (*c. 1532–1594*)
William Byrd (*1543–1623*)
Tomas Luis de Victoria (*c. 1549–1611*)
Giovanni Gabrieli (*1557–1612*)
Thomas Morley (*1557–c. 1603*)
Michael Praetorius (*1571–1621*)
John Wilbye (*1574–1638*)
Thomas Weelkes (*c. 1575–1623*)
Orlando Gibbons (*1583–1625*)

1607 to 1740

1607 Jamestown, Virginia settled: first permanent English settlement in America

1618–48 Thirty Years' War: last of the great religious wars of Europe

1620 Plymouth Colony founded by the Pilgrims

1624 Cardinal Richelieu consolidates power of Louis XIII in France

1628 Harvey describes circulation of blood

1649 Charles I of England beheaded for treason

1649–53 Cromwell's Commonwealth in England

1660 Charles II restores monarchy in England

1661–1715 Louis XIV, King of France

1666 Isaac Newton discovers the Law of Gravity

1679 Habeas Corpus Act passed by English Parliament; cornerstone of English and American law

1682–1725 Reign of Peter the Great, who "westernized" Russia

1688 Glorious Revolution in England against King James II

1701–14 War of the Spanish Succession

1714 George I, Handel's patron, succeeds Queen Anne as ruler of England

1715 Founding of first Opéra Comique, Paris

1719 Herculaneum and Pompeii rediscovered, Italy

1737 San Carlo Opera opened at Naples

1740–48 Frederick the Great of Prussia defeats Austria

1740–96 Age of Enlightened Despots

WRITERS

John Donne (*1572–1631*)
René Descartes (*1596–1650*)
Pierre Corneille (*1606–1684*)
John Milton (*1608–1674*)
Molière (*1622–1673*)
Pascal (*1623–1662*)
John Bunyan (*1628–1688*)
Spinoza (*1632–1677*)
John Locke (*1632–1704*)
Jean Baptiste Racine (*1639–1699*)
Daniel Defoe (*1660–1731*)
Jonathan Swift (*1667–1745*)
Alexander Pope (*1688–1744*)
Montesquieu (*1689–1755*)
Voltaire (*1694–1778*)
Henry Fielding (*1707–1754*)
Samuel Johnson (*1709–1784*)

ARTISTS

Peter Paul Rubens (*1577–1640*)
Frans Hals (*1580?–1666*)
Giovanni Lorenzo Bernini (*1598–1680*)
Anthony Van Dyck (*1599–1641*)
Diego Velazquez (*1599–1660*)
Rembrandt van Rijn (*1606–1669*)
Jan Vermeer (*1632–1675*)
Sir Christopher Wren (*1632–1723*)
Jean Antoine Watteau (*1684–1721*)
Giovanni Battista Tiepolo (*1696–1770*)
William Hogarth (*1697–1764*)
François Boucher (*1703–1770*)

MUSICIANS

Claudio Monteverdi (*1567–1643*)
Jean Baptiste Lully (*1632–1687*)
Dietrich Buxtehude (*1637–1707*)
Arcangelo Corelli (*1653–1713*)
Henry Purcell (*1658–1695*)
François Couperin (*1668–1733*)
Antonio Vivaldi (*c. 1675–1743*)
Georg Telemann (*1681–1767*)
Jean-Philippe Rameau (*1683–1764*)
Johann Sebastian Bach (*1685–1750*)
Domenico Scarlatti (*1685–1757*)
George Frederic Handel (*1685–1759*)
Giovanni Battista Pergolesi (*1710–1736*)

1756 to 1812

1756–63 Seven Years' War, also called the French and Indian War

1759 Wolfe captures Quebec in French and Indian War

1762–96 Catherine the Great rules Russia

1765–76 Watt develops the steam engine

c. 1770 Beginning of the factory system

1774 Priestley discovers oxygen

1775–85 The American Revolution

1776 Declaration of Independence

1778 La Scala Opera opened in Milan

1785 First aerial crossing of the English Channel

1787 Constitutional Convention in the United States

1789–97 The French Revolution

1791 Second Opéra Comique opened, Paris

1792 Eli Whitney invents the cotton gin

1793 Louis XVI beheaded; Reign of Terror under Robespierre

1796 Laplace advances nebular hypothesis of the origin of the Solar System

c. 1798 Jenner develops smallpox vaccine

1799 Consulate of Napoleon established after he seized control of France

1803 The Louisiana Purchase

1804 Napoleon crowns himself emperor

1812 Napoleon's Russian Campaign

WRITERS

Jean-Jacques Rousseau (*1712–1778*)
Denis Diderot (*1713–1784*)
Thomas Gray (*1716–1771*)
Immanuel Kant (*1724–1804*)
Edmund Burke (*1729–1797*)
Thomas Paine (*1737–1809*)
Edward Gibbon (*1737–1794*)
Johann Wolfgang von Goethe (*1749–1832*)
William Blake (*1757–1827*)
Robert Burns (*1759–1796*)
Johann Christoph Friedrich von Schiller (*1759–1805*)

ARTISTS

Jean Baptiste Simeon Chardin (*1699–1779*)
Sir Joshua Reynolds (*1723–1792*)
Thomas Gainsborough (*1727–1788*)
Jean-Honoré Fragonard (*1732–1806*)
Jean Antoine Houdon (*1741–1828*)
Francisco Jose de Goya (*1746–1828*)
Jacques Louis David (*1748–1825*)
Antonio Canova (*1757–1822*)
Charles Bulfinch (*1763–1844*)
Jean Auguste Dominique Ingres (*1780–1867*)

MUSICIANS

Christoph Willibald Gluck (*1714–1787*)
Carl Philip Emanuel Bach (*1714–1788*)
Johann Stamitz (*1717–1757*)
Joseph Haydn (*1732–1809*)
Johann Christian Bach (*1735–1782*)
Domenico Cimarosa (*1749–1801*)
Wolfgang Amadeus Mozart (*1756–1791*)
Maria Luigi Cherubini (*1760–1842*)
Ludwig van Beethoven (*1770–1827*)
Gasparo Spontini (*1774–1851*)

1814 to 1870

1814 Stephenson's first locomotive

Napoleon exiled to Elba

1815 The Battle of Waterloo, Napoleon's final defeat

1821 Faraday invents electric dynamo

1822 Greeks declare independence from Ottoman Turks

1824 Bolívar liberates South America from Spanish rule

1825 Opening of the Erie Canal in New York State

1829–37 Andrew Jackson U.S. President

1831 McCormick introduces reaper

1837 Coronation of Queen Victoria

1839 Vienna Philharmonic, N.Y. Philharmonic Society founded

Daguerre invents photographic process

1841 British win Hong Kong from China

1843 Foundation of the Leipzig Conservatory

1844 Telegraph perfected by Morse

1845 Famine and mass emigration from Ireland

1847 First Law of Thermodynamics formulated

1848 France sets up Second Empire under Louis Napoleon

Gold Rush in California

1853 The Crimean War

1855 Charge of the Light Brigade (the Battle of Balaklava, Crimean War)

1858 Opening of Covent Garden as opera house, London

1861–65 Civil War in America

1863 Emancipation Proclamation

1865 Abraham Lincoln assassinated

1870 The Franco-Prussian War

WRITERS

Percy Bysshe Shelley (*1792–1822*)
John Keats (*1795–1821*)
Alexander Dumas (*1802–1870*)
Victor Hugo (*1802–1885*)
Ralph Waldo Emerson (*1803–1882*)
Nathaniel Hawthorne (*1804–1864*)
Edgar Allan Poe (*1809–1849*)
Alfred Tennyson (*1809–1892*)
William Thackeray (*1811–1863*)
Charles Dickens (*1812–1870*)
Robert Browning (*1812–1889*)
Charlotte Brontë (*1816–1855*)
Emily Brontë (*1818–1848*)
Herman Melville (*1819–1891*)
Fëdor Dostoyevsky (*1821–1881*)

ARTISTS

George Stubbs (*1724–1806*)
Caspar David Friedrich (*1774–1840*)
Joseph Turner (*1775–1851*)
Theodore Gericault (*1791–1824*)
Eugene Delacroix (*1799–1863*)
Honoré Daumier (*1808–1879*)
Dante Gabriel Rossetti (*1828–1882*)

MUSICIANS

Carl Maria von Weber (*1786–1826*)
Franz Schubert (*1797–1828*)
Felix Mendelssohn (*1809–1847*)
Frédéric Chopin (*1810–1849*)
Hector Berlioz (*1803–1869*)
Franz Liszt (*1811–1886*)
Richard Wagner (*1813–1883*)
Giuseppe Verdi (*1813–1901*)
César Franck (*1822–1890*)
Edouard Lalo (*1823–1892*)
Johannes Brahms (*1833–1897*)
Peter Ilyich Tchaikovsky (*1840–1893*)
Anton Dvořak (*1841–1904*)
Nicholas Rimsky-Korsakov (*1844–1908*)

1903 to 1969

1903 Wright brothers' first flight with power-driven airplane

1905 Einstein's theory of relativity

Sigmund Freud founds psychoanalysis

1908 Model T Ford produced

1911 Rutherford's theory of positively charged atomic nucleus

1914–18 First World War

1917 Bolshevik Revolution, Russia

1920 U.S. grants women suffrage in 19th Amendment

1927 Lindbergh flies across the Atlantic

1929 Stock market crash in the United States; beginning of the Great Depression

1933 Roosevelt proclaims New Deal

1936–39 Spanish Civil War

1939–45 Second World War

1944 Computer technology developed

1945 Atomic bomb dropped on Hiroshima

United Nations Charter signed

1947 U.S. starts Marshall Plan

1949 Communists under Mao win in China

1950–53 Korean War

1954 U.S. Supreme Court outlaws racial segregation in public schools

1956 Hungarian revolt against Communist regime crushed by Russia

1957 Sputnik, first satellite, launched by Russia

1963 John F. Kennedy assassinated

1969 First manned landing on moon

WRITERS

Marcel Proust (*1871–1922*)
Theodore Dreiser (*1871–1945*)
Gertrude Stein (*1874–1946*)
Robert Frost (*1874–1963*)
James Joyce (*1882–1941*)
Franz Kafka (*1883–1924*)
T. S. Eliot (*1888–1964*)
e. e. cummings (*1894–1962*)
Aldous Huxley (*1894–1963*)
William Faulkner (*1897–1962*)
Ernest Hemingway (*1898–1961*)
Thomas Wolfe (*1900–1938*)
George Orwell (*1903–1950*)
Samuel Beckett (*1906*—)
Albert Camus (*1913–1960*)
Dylan Thomas (*1914–1953*)

ARTISTS

Henri Matisse (*1869–1954*)
Frank Lloyd Wright (*1869–1959*)
Georges Rouault (*1871–1958*)
Piet Mondrian (*1872–1946*)
Constantine Brancusi (*1876–1958*)
Paul Klee (*1879–1940*)
Pablo Picasso (*1881–1973*)
Marc Chagall (*1887*—)
Joan Miró (*1893*—)
Alexander Calder (*1898*—)
Mark Rothko (*1903–1970*)
Salvador Dali (*1904*—)
Jackson Pollock (*1912–1956*)

MUSICIANS

Claude Debussy (*1862–1918*)
Alexander Scriabin (*1871–1915*)
Sergei Rachmaninov (*1873–1943*)
Charles Ives (*1874–1954*)
Béla Bartók (*1881–1945*)
Sergei Prokofiev (*1891–1952*)
Igor Stravinsky (*1882–1971*)
Zoltan Kodaly (*1882–1967*)
Robert Nathaniel Dett (*1882–1943*)
Anton von Webern (*1883–1945*)
Darius Milhaud (*1892*—)
Paul Hindemith (*1895–1963*)
William Grant Still (*1895*—)
Henry Cowell (*1897–1965*)
George Gershwin (*1898–1937*)
Kurt Weill (*1900–1950*)
William Schuman (*1910*—)
Gian Carlo Menotti (*1911*—)
John Cage (*1912*—)
Benjamin Britten (*1913*—)
Leonard Bernstein (*1918*—)
Karlheinz Stockhausen (*1928*—)

ALPHABETICAL INDEX

CLASSIFIED INDEX

CALL CHARTS

COMPOSED SONGS

FINE ARTS

FOLK SONGS

Africa

Argentina

Brazil

Canada

China

England

France

Germany

Israel

Japan

Korea

Polynesia

Scotland

Spain

Trinidad

United States

Wales

West Indies

Yemen

FOREIGN LANGUAGE SONGS

Africa

China

France

Germany

Israel

India

Japan

Latin

Polynesia

Spain

Yemen

INSTRUMENTAL ACCOMPANIMENT

Brass

Three Part

Four or More Parts

PATRIOTIC SONGS AND SONGS OF INSPIRATION

POETRY AND PROSE

ROUNDS AND CANONS

SONGS FOR SPECIAL DAYS

UNISON SONGS

POETRY ACKNOWLEDGMENTS

A Child's Christmas in Wales (Dylan Thomas), *163*
Dylan Thomas, A CHILD'S CHRISTMAS IN WALES. Copyright 1954 by New Directions Publishing Corporation. Reprinted by permission of New Directions Publishing Corporation.

Christus Apollo (Ray Bradbury), *94*
Copyright 1969 by Ray Bradbury, reprinted by permission of the Harold Matson Company, Inc.

Color (Langston Hughes), *24*
From THE PANTHER AND THE LASH by Langston Hughes. Copyright 1967 by Arna Bontemps and George Houston Bass. Reprinted by permission of Alfred A. Knopf, Inc.

Fog (Carl Sandburg), *95*
From CHICAGO POEMS by Carl Sandburg. Copyright 1916 by Holt, Rinehart and Winston, Inc. Copyright 1944 by Carl Sandburg. Reprinted by permission of Holt, Rinehart and Winston, Inc.

The Grasshopper's Song (H. N. Bialik), *107*
Copyright © 1939 by the Union of Hebrew Congregations.

High on a Mountain (Basho), *188*
From CRICKET SONGS: JAPANESE HAIKU, translated and © 1964, by Harry Behn. Reprinted by permission of Harcourt, Brace & World, Inc.

i thank You God (e. e. cummings), *70*
"i thank You God for most this amazing"—Copyright, 1950 by e. e. cummings. Reprinted from his volume POEMS 1923–1954 by permission of Harcourt Brace Jovanovich, Inc.

Moonlight (Thomas Wolfe), *51*
"Moonlight" from A STONE, A LEAF, A DOOR. Poems by Thomas Wolfe, selected and arranged in verse by John S. Barnes, is reprinted by permission of Charles Scribner's Sons. First appearance was in OF TIME AND THE RIVER, page 72, by Thomas Wolfe. Copyright 1935 Charles Scribner's Sons; renewal copyright © 1963 Paul Gitlin.

My Eyes Following (Basho), *189*
Reprinted with permission of Peter Pauper Press, Inc.

Now Sinks the Sun (Medieval English Verse), *223*
"Now sinks the sun beneath the wood" (No. 10, p. 36) from MEDIEVAL ENGLISH VERSE tr. Brian Stone. Copyright Brian Stone, 1964.

An Old Silent Pond (Basho), *189*
Reprinted with permission of Peter Pauper Press, Inc.

Piano and Drums (G. Okara), *90*
From ROSE, WHERE DID YOU GET THAT RED edited by Kenneth Koch. Copyright © 1973 by Kenneth Koch. Reprinted by permission of Random House, Inc.

Snow Fell until Dawn (Rokwa), *188*
From CRICKET SONGS: JAPANESE HAIKU, translated and © 1964, by Harry Behn. Reprinted by permission of Harcourt, Brace & World, Inc.

Stopping by Woods on a Snowy Evening (Robert Frost), *94*
From THE POETRY OF ROBERT FROST edited by Edward Connery Lathem. Copyright 1923 by Holt, Rinehart and Winston, Inc. Copyright 1951 by Robert Frost. Reprinted by permission of Holt, Rinehart and Winston, Inc.

Sun (M. B.), *26*
From THE ME NOBODY KNOWS; CHILDREN'S VOICES FROM THE GHETTO edited by Stephen M. Joseph. Copyrighted 1969 by Stephen M. Joseph. By permission of Avon Books, New York.

FINE ART ACKNOWLEDGMENTS

Alpha—*68* (Lozi), *178* (Gerald Clyde), *206* (Kauffman)

American Federation of Art, *26*

American Museum of Natural History, *104* (C. Valentine), *172, 176*

Apple Records, *30*

Art Reference Bureau, *65* (Bulloz), *92, 93* (Scala), *105, 201, 209, 216* (Agraci), *217* (Reproduced by Courtesy of the Trustees of the National Gallery, London)

Brooklyn Museum, *91*

Capitol, *30*

Collections (Private) *27, 29, 96*

Columbia Records, *30, 31, 49, 52, 127*

Cooper Ltd., A. C., *32* (Gordon H. Robertson)

Cristi, Richard, *227*

Cushing, George M. Jr., *145*

Dementi Studios, Richmond, Va., *212*

Editorial Photo Color Archives, *52, 104, 179, 201, 213* (Maurice E. Mujica)

Electra Corp., *128*

European Art Color, *200, 201, 204, 205, 207, 209, 212, 213, 216, 217* (Peter Adelberg)

Fehl, Fred, *38*

Fisk University, *57*

Fort Worth Art Center, *32* (William E. Scott)

Fowler, Charles B., *17*

FPG, *213* (Dana Brown)

French Reproduction Rights, Inc., *196* (Permission S.P.A.D.S.M. 1971, Photo—Claude Basnier)

Guillumette, Rapho, *13* (Dr. George Gerster), *176* (Marc & Evelyn Bernheim), *201* (Sabine Weiss)

Hadassah, *180* (Detail of one of the 12 stained glass windows, depicting the Twelve Tribes of Israel, at Hadassah-Hebrew University Medical Center Synagogue, Jerusalem). Photograph copyrighted © 1961 by Hadassah Medical Relief Association, Inc.

Hoffman, J. K., *184*

Hurok Attractions, *128*

Israeli Consulate, The (Courtesy of), *178*

Jangoux Jacques, *160, 161, 172, 184*

Japan National Tourist Organization, *187*

Kazuko Hillyer International Inc., *126*

Keystone Press Agency, *162, 197*

Los Angeles Times Photo, *3*

Macmillan Co., *24* (Donald & Ann Crews)

Mahon, Dynecourt *52, 63, 82, 83, 84, 85, 129, 131, 144, 224*

Metropolitan Museum of Art, *93, 104, 189* (Joseph Pulitzer Bequest); (Rogers Fund), *208* (Bequest of H. O. Havemeyer Collection), *218* (Bequest of Benjamin Altman)

Metropolitan Opera Guilde, *57* (Frank Dunand), *126*

Mexican National Tourist Council, *77*

Monkmeyer Press, *53* (Hugh Rogers), *160, 161* (Fujihira), *168* (Herbert Lanks), *178* (Linares), *179, 183* (Pinney), *197* (Leon Weller), *217* (Lehmann)

Morgan, Barbara, *3*

Morgan Library, J. Pierpont, *206*

Museum of Modern Art, N.Y. *28, 29, 51, 93, 192, 196, 197* (on extended loan from artist), *28* (Acquired through the Lillie P. Bliss Bequest), *197* (Mrs. Simon Guggenheim Fund)

National Gallery of Art, Wash., D.C., *222* (Gift of Wm. Robertson Coe)

Pennsylvania Academy of Fine Art, *179*

RCA Records, *86, 128*

Roberts Armstrong H., *131*

Seattle Art Museum, *27* (Gift of Mrs. Thomas D. Stimson)

Seifer, M., *205*

Solomon R. Guggenheim Museum, *92*

Sovfoto (The Hermitage), *209*

Steinway & Sons, *144–145* (Courtesy of)

Time, Inc., *184* (Larry Burrows, Life Magazine)

University of Arizona, *105* (Gallagher Memorial Collection)

UPI, *39*

Warner Records, *128*